Women In
Ochre
Robes

SUNY series in Hindu Studies
Wendy Doniger, editor

Women In Ochre Robes

Gendering Hindu Renunciation

Meena Khandelwal

STATE UNIVERSITY OF NEW YORK PRESS

Published by
State University of New York Press, Albany

For information, address State University of New York Press,
90 State Street, Suite 700, Albany, NY 12207

Production by Marilyn P. Semerad
Marketing by Anne M. Valentine

Library of Congress Cataloging-in-Publication Data

Khandelwal, Meena.
    Women in ochre robes : gendering Hindu renunciation / Meena Khandelwal.
       p. cm. — (Suny series in Hindu studies)
    Includes bibliographical references.
    ISBN 0-7914-5921-7 (alk. paper) — ISBN 0-7914-5922-5 (pbk. : alk. paper)
    1. Sannyasi—India—Haridwār. 2. Asceticism—Hinduism. I. Title. II. Series.

BL1241.54.K43 2003
294.5'657'08209542—dc21

                                    2002045254

For Uma and Jaya Rani

It has been said that the fact that I was listening to, and writing about, saints
while you were in the womb and through your infancies
will affect you positively.

Contents

Acknowledgments

This book is a product of all those teachers, informants, friends—and scholars whom I do not know personally—who have shaped my own thinking about India, gender, and asceticism. I would, however, like to single out the following persons for their support.

Those women renouncers (*sannyasinis*) who welcomed me into their ashrams and lives and sought to teach me something about themselves remain unnamed here. Their generosity of spirit made this research possible. Their wit and eccentricities made it unpredictable and much more fun than I ever imagined living with sadhus could be! I hope that those *sannyasinis* and lay Hindus who read this account will find the results comprehensible, fair, and perhaps even insightful. I would also like to express my sincere gratitude to Prem Bhandari; without his help this project would have not been possible. My research was also facilitated in many ways by my extended family in India. No matter how eccentric they thought my passion for renouncers and ashrams, my relatives always made me feel that India was also my home and supported my research in many ways. In particular, Indu and Satti Punj, Niru and Bijjan Gupta, Gita and Nilander Punj, Ajai Lakhanpal, and Nutan Pandit fed me, housed me, introduced me to people, and helped me get to places I needed to go.

On this side of the globe, the influence of my dissertation committee members has been strong, although this book is significantly revised since its incarnation as a dissertation. Ravindra S. Khare's breadth of knowledge, imaginative insights, and general enthusiasm for this project sustained my own excitement at every stage. He kept me focused on the ethnography, on the *sannyasinis* themselves, and generously reread the manuscript after revisions. Susan McKinnon provided unfailing support of many sorts. Her keen analytic sensibilities always seemed able to see the forest for the trees, the larger point of it all, when I was lost in the patterns of leaves. H. L. Seneviratne's affectionate criticism forced me to rethink certain assumptions and to defend others even more vociferously. David White of Religious Studies offered valuable comments and corrections from the perspective of textual sources, rendering my own lack of training in religious studies a little less obvious. Colleagues who read the manuscript and

offered invaluable comments are Ann Gold, Kirin Narayan, John Cort, Wendy
Singer, Jael Silliman, and three anonymous reviewers for the State University of
New York Press. Other friends and colleagues whose contributions I would like
to acknowledge include Edith Turner, Fred Damon, Roy Wagner, Abigail Adams,
Rafael Alvarado, Sam Bamford, Becky Popenoe, Margo Smith, Gregory Barz,
Patricia Uberoi, Pamila Gupta, Ruhi Grover, Lawrence Cohen, Suchitra
Samanta, Antonia Mills, Edward Abse, Padmini Mongia, Karuna Krishna,
Anish Kumar, Fred Smith, Philip Lutgendorf, Priya Kumar, Paul Greenough,
Kathleen Erndl, Dave Suggs, Vernon Schubel, Ginny Van Dyke, Tryna Lyons,
Cindi Sturtz Sreetharan, Laura Graham, Ellen Lewin, Florence Babb, and,
finally, my late, dear friend Tessa Bartholomeusz. Conversations I had with J. S.
Uberoi, Veena Das, and Punum Zutshi years ago in India influenced me tremen-
dously, although they probably have no recollection of it. The final responsibility
for inaccuracies or misinterpretations, of course, remains my own.

My family has borne the primary cost of this project. My young daughters
Uma and Jaya sacrificed my presence, though not without loud complaint. My
husband Peter's computer savvy averted several potential disasters, his unswerv-
ing faith encouraged me to finish the book when I wanted to abandon it, and his
humor prevented me from taking it too seriously. Most importantly, he followed
me to India with an open mind and heart and came to share my love for our life
there and my respect for the people we know. I wish to thank my mother, Nita
Lakhanpal Khandelwal, for her support throughout, and crucially, for child care
and yummy lunches during the final weeks of writing. I am grateful too for the
supportive lifetime friendships of Lenard Shields, Nisha Agrawal, Mona Barz,
and Mark and Barbara Fried.

Piyusha Mehta assisted with some transcriptions and translations, and Kats
Mendoza and Jill Moffett provided expert research assistance at the University
of Iowa. I would like to extend special thanks to Tom Baer for the cover photo.
It has been a pleasure to work with Nancy Ellegate and Marilyn Semerad at the
State University of New York Press. The research on which this book is based
was funded by an American Institute of Indian Studies junior research fellow-
ship and a United States Department of Education Fulbright-Hays grant. The
Department of Women's Studies and the Department of Anthropology at the
University of Iowa also provided institutional support.

Note on Transliteration

The linguistic context in which I conducted research was complex. Most of my interviews with sannyasinis took place in Hindi, with a few in English. Depending on the mother tongue of a particular person, though, Punjabi or even English words occasionally punctuated their speech. For example, Anand Mata spoke to me in Hindi but used many English phrases, like "total surrender" and "extrovert." As initiates into an elite ascetic tradition and residents of a pilgrimage town, their everyday language included many Sanskrit terms as well. The people I interacted with would, for example, often use *vairagya* rather than *virag*, *bhojan* rather than *khana*. They may have used the Sanskrit or Hindi form or alternated between them.

In an attempt to remain close to the language of those I interviewed, I use some words in Hindi (*sannyasi* rather than *sannyasin*) and others in Sanskrit (*vairagya* rather than *virag*). Depending on popular pronunciations, I have dropped the final Sanskrit "a" for many words (*jap, dan, anand, marg, asan*) and retained it for others (*karma, dharma*). In an attempt to strike a balance between the goals of ethnographic accuracy and textual readability, I have generally chosen one form of a particular word. However, if the reference to another work or an ethnographic context specifically demanded an alternative spelling, I have sacrificed consistency for accuracy.

In my efforts to make this work accessible to nonspecialists and to a wider general audience, I have more often compromised technical accuracy for readability. To this end, I have omitted diacritics in the text (but included some in the glossary) and avoided italicizing foreign words that can now be found in English dictionaries and are in widespread usage: ashram, guru, mantra, swami, sadhu, yoga, and so on. I do, however, include some of these core terms in the glossary. I use the English convention for plurals by simply adding an italicized "s" to Hindi words (*sannyasinis* for *sannyasini*). Although I generally use "k" rather than "c" to signify the unaspirated "k" in Devanagari, I have made an exception for the adjectival noun ending, as in Vedic and karmic. I have sometimes rendered the "v" sound in Hindi as a "w" (even though the latter does not exist in the Devanagari alphabet) when I feel it better approximates popular pronunciation or conventional spelling, as in swami.

Introduction

Sannyasinis as Persons

This is an ethnography of *sannyasinis* in Haridwar, North India. Sannyasinis are Hindu women who have renounced an ordinary life of marriage, family, domestic responsibilities, and worldly pleasures in order to pursue spiritual liberation (*moksha*) full-time. A woman who wishes to enter this path must find a guru willing to initiate her as a disciple and perform an initiation signifying rebirth.[1] During the ceremony, initiates receive from their guru new ochre-colored clothes, a secret mantra, and a title that ends with the name of the guru's monastic order. They also perform their own death rites and thereby sacrifice themselves into a "funeral pyre." Having already undergone this symbolic cremation, renouncers' bodies are not cremated at the time of literal death as are the bodies of ordinary Hindus; instead they are buried in a seated, meditative posture or are submerged in a river. If, along with formal initiation, they abandon all secular property, withdraw from society, and cease to cohabit with their spouse, they are legally recognized as renouncers and can no longer inherit property from natural relatives (Narayanan 1993). Thus, initiation renders them "dead" to their previous social and civil identity. But the people I write about here are very much alive. They struggle with, and joke about, the tensions and ironies of living in the world while trying not to be *of* it. In doing so, as we will see, they constantly shuttle between various levels of reality.

Renouncers are easily distinguishable from lay Hindus, conventionally referred to as "householders," by place of residence and appearance. Most either live itinerantly for much of the year or take up residence in pilgrimage towns such as Haridwar. Haridwar's significance for Hindus lies in its sacred geography;

1

it is the place where the sacred Ganges River descends from the Himalayas and meets the North Indian plains. The precise point of this transition is marked by Haridwar's main bathing *ghat* (steps or landing), and the Ganges' power to wash away sins is held to be greatest at this location. Lay Hindus are drawn to Haridwar from surrounding regions for a variety of reasons. They come to bathe in the holy river on auspicious occasions, to visit personal gurus who reside in the city's many monastic centers, or to immerse the ashes of a relative's cremated body in the river. They pass through, as pilgrims, tourists, and trekkers on their way to sites and mountain passes higher up in the spectacular and holy Himalayas. Just north of the city's main shopping bazaar and bathing area is Sadhubela, a suburb of sorts, built along the banks of the Ganges; here both sides of the main thoroughfare are lined with ashrams. Although the term "ashram" is usually glossed as "hermitage," it refers to both large monastic communities and small, loosely organized places where a handful of people (both ascetic and nonascetic) live and where pilgrims may stay for short visits. In Sadhubela, older ashrams and temples are interspersed with spanking new ones that attract tourists and electronically broadcast sacred chanting or religious services. But the chiming of brass temple bells has not yet been drowned out by loudspeakers, street vendors, and automobile horns. Here, instead of "hello" or "namaste" the more commonly heard greeting is a religious salutation such as "Hari Om" or "Om namah Shivaya." Ochre-clad ascetics wander, usually alone and occasionally in groups, up and down the streets and along the riverbank. Renouncers who flock to pilgrimage towns such as Haridwar might choose to live in the open on the river's edge, in a cave or hut, in a monastery belonging to their order, or in an independent ashram.[2] The sights and sounds of Sadhubela's streets, even before one enters the private spaces of ashrams, suggest that this is a culture of sadhus.

Sadhu is a general term for ascetics or holy persons. Renunciation (*sannyasa*) is one specific form of Hindu asceticism, and its initiates (m. *sannyasi*; f. *sannyasini*) are the focus of this study. In terms of physical appearance, the most reliable indications of renunciant status are ochre-colored garments, identifying hairstyles, and other ritual accessories. Because some Hindu ascetics are visually very stunning and a few engage in sensational, even repulsive, forms of ascetic discipline, sadhus have served as a primary photographic trope of the mystical East. Photographic portrayals tend to feature those (male) sadhus with the most dramatic appearance: naked bodies whitened by ash, elaborate sectarian clothing, colorful body markings, and matted hair piled high on the head or hanging down to the waist or ankles. Equally familiar to Westerners are images of (again male) sadhus engaging in spectacles of the exotic: sitting in meditation with pots of fire on their heads, holding their right arms up for so long that they shrivel, performing feats with their penises to demonstrate their celibacy and power. These activities are stand-ins for the proverbial ochre-turbaned Hindu lying on a bed of nails (see K. Narayan 1993b). While such attention-getting forms of religious discipline do occur, they are not nearly as common as these images suggest. Because I believe that such photographs impede rather than aid understanding—and to protect the anonymity of my informants—I have not included photographs in this account.

If photographs were included here, they would probably be disappointing for their ordinariness. Both male and female renouncers may display shaven heads or, alternatively, piles of snakelike matted locks, and, for men, full beards.[3] A few of the women I met did have shaven heads or long, matted locks, but most had short cropped hair or long hair worn simply in a bun or braid. Hairstyles are sometimes accompanied by sectarian markings on the forehead and various other accessories such as wooden sandals, a rosary of *rudraksha* beads worn around the neck, a staff, a begging bowl, or a water vessel.[4] None of the women I interviewed wore the forehead markings associated with renouncers or carried these other accessories. Some went barefoot, but most wore either traditional wooden sandals or the plastic variety.[5] Even without these accessories, however, renouncers are not easily mistaken for lay Hindus. Female initiates are not required to wear any particular *style* of ochre clothing, but they do reject the jewelry and clothing that is considered not only aesthetically pleasing for female householders, but also morally good and auspicious. The lack of beauty-enhancing ornamentation on their bodies differentiates them strikingly from most Hindu women. They engage in typical ascetic activities: meditation, silence, study of scriptures, pilgrimage, advising of disciples, and worship of deities. They also perform stereotypically domestic activities such as cooking food, looking after neighborhood children, shopping, matchmaking, visiting friends, and supervising servants.

Sannyasinis represent a minority among Hindu renouncers, most of whom are men, and an even smaller minority among Indian women, most of whom are wives and mothers. Yet I believe their conceptual importance far exceeds their statistical presence because of the way they problematize standard representations of both religious renunciation and gender in Hindu India. Sannyasa, the ascetic tradition into which these women have been initiated, is seen by scholars and most Indians as a male tradition, and, in many ways, it is. Indian women have been represented as always domestic and dependent, and, indeed, most are. Yet women who refuse to conform to cultural expectations regarding marriage, sexuality, and procreation not only exist but are respected, even revered, for making these choices.

This book complicates standard representations of Hindu culture. If the information available about Indian women overwhelmingly "fits" our scholarly models, then we are left feeling that the lives of Hindu women are generally determined by social expectations and institutions. Women have little self-determination—their parents deciding how long they will study and whom they will marry, their husbands deciding whether they will seek employment or not, their mothers-in-law deciding how many children they will have, and their sons deciding how they will spend their older years. Scholarly and popular accounts most often identify the family, but sometimes the state, as the primary agent of control. Sannyasinis live on the margins of both family and state authority. Brahmanical Hinduism is also frequently and correctly identified as a source of patriarchy. Yet women renouncers have created opportunities for themselves within the most misogynous and brahmanical of Hindu ascetic traditions.

Westerners tend to overdetermine third world women's lives. In looking at them we see reflected back the free agents that we believe ourselves to be. This impression is reinforced by pervasive media representations of oppressed third world women and children and, sometimes, by anthropological analyses of social structures, laws, and apparently dominant ideologies. Moreover, many readers, in consuming ethnographic texts, see only what reinforces, and not what contradicts, their prior assumptions. Thus, the idea that third world people lead overdetermined lives is remarkably persistent. Here I demonstrate that Hindu women do sometimes determine their own lives in fairly radical ways—and I hope to do this without romanticizing them as mystic or feminist heroes, denying the reality of patriarchy, or elevating individual autonomy to the primary value by which we evaluate persons and cultures.

I have chosen to emphasize depth over breadth. Thus, while I interviewed nineteen female ascetics, and as many males, during eighteen months of ethnographic field research, I focused most of my attention on two women. Anand Mata left a husband and a successful career as a school principal to "take sannyasa" (that is, to be initiated into sannyasa) and now follows an ascetic path of meditative solitude. She lived in silence for many years, and, luckily for me, had just begun speaking again the year before I arrived. She refused to become a guru and take disciples, choosing instead to live alone in a small, quiet ashram. Although very serious about her own spiritual aims, Anand Mata was an insightful—and irreverent!—observer of the culture of sadhus. Baiji, as a young woman, resisted her parents' attempts to arrange her marriage, in order to pursue her spiritual interests. At a young age, she was initiated into sannyasa by a male guru and has become a guru in her own right with disciples and two ashrams of her own. Thus, while Anand Mata lives in someone else's ashram with other ascetics, Baiji is mistress of her own "home" and is surrounded by lay people, both employees and devotees. While Anand Mata leads a contemplative existence, Baiji's daily life bustles with religious, social, and charitable activities. While Anand Mata does not engage in much activity that is immediately recognizable as "religious," Baiji oversees temple worship, vedic rituals, the recitation of scriptures, and the feeding of other sadhus in great ritual feasts. My conversations with and observations of these two women form the basis for chapters 2, 3, and 4.

Social Involvement and Ascetic Withdrawal

One of the most interesting things about Hindu culture is the presence of a persistent tension between the value of responsible involvement with family life and the value of ascetic withdrawal from society in the pursuit of liberation. Thus, the ordinary goals and activities of getting married, nurturing children, respecting elders, eating well, maintaining good health, pursuing material prosperity, and experiencing sensual pleasure are valued as morally good. There is, however, another set of values that suggests: This is all fine, even ethically required, for ordinary people, but those who seek liberation will necessarily transcend these goals and activities; for them a different set of rules applies. This book is a meditation on the conflict between social responsibility and ascetic withdrawal. At times I will discuss this in terms of "worldly" and "otherworldly," which evokes a host of interrelated Hindu distinctions between worldly and otherworldly (*laukik* and *alaukik*), gross and subtle (*sthul* and *sukshma*), the seen and the unseen (*drishta* and *adrishta*).[6]

More specifically, this book is a meditation on this conflict from the point of view of women ascetics rather than women householders—and not just women ascetics, but sannyasinis. Ascetic traditions proliferate in Hinduism. Initiates into sannyasa see theirs as the most radical form of Hindu asceticism. It is defined in the negative as the giving up of household life and characterized by an absolute finality.[7] Thus, one conventional image is of the (male) renouncer who, in taking sannyasa, walks away from his family and never looks back. "Letting go" and cultivating a detached attitude is central to sannyasa; indeed, celibacy is important because it aids in the cultivation of detachment. Because of its emphasis on celibacy, vedic learning, solitude, and itinerancy, sannyasa is the form of Indian asceticism least hospitable to women. Despite the defining characteristics of celibacy and detachment, within contemporary sannyasa there exists a wide range of legitimate values, practices, and modes of interaction with laypersons. While most renouncers pass through an initiation ritual and are easily distinguishable from householders by appearance and place of residence, in general, the sociological indeterminacy of renunciation makes defining an ethnographic study of the subject especially problematic. To include women only makes this task more difficult.

Sannyasinis as an Analytical Category: Anomalous Women

Sannyasa is a tradition that was created by and for elite men. Women initiates may, but do not always, face opposition from their male peers in the world of ascetics. They may also, and most do, face opposition from family and friends when considering the option of renunciation. By rejecting the role of the good and virtuous wife whose life is devoted to husband and family, these women assert their agency. One need not seek out hidden and ritual social spaces to find evidence of their resistance to conventional gender expectations. They rebel against Manu, whose ancient treatise on correct behavior is said to provide "a direct line to the most influential construction of the Hindu religion and Indic society as a whole" (Doniger 1991:xvii). In *The Laws of Manu*, there is a frequently quoted statement: "A girl, a young woman, or even an old woman should not do anything independently, even in [her own] house. In childhood, a woman should be under her father's control, in youth under her husband's, and when her husband is dead, under her sons.' She should not have independence" (V. 147–48, trans. Doniger 1991). To what degree, if at all, do ideological statements such as this actually determine even upper-caste women's lives? As Narayanan writes, "while the Hindu tradition has used hyperbole in declaring the religious-legal texts to be an exposition of the Vedas, it did not mean that they actually *followed* all the rules." (1999:35). Sannyasinis lead unconventional lives but are respected by ordinary and even conservative people as sources of both spiritual power and everyday morality.

Is it *because* sannyasinis fit neither classical Hindu models nor sociological categories for analyzing Indian culture, particularly the gendered opposition between renunciation and householder life, that we know so little about their lives? This state of affairs is beginning to change as written accounts of female Hindu asceticism begin to be published.[8] Still, we know too little at this point to come up with much in the way of conclusive generalizations. I suggest that the category of sannyasini without further sectarian specification has no more sociological coherence than that of male renouncer (sannyasi). "[T]here is almost nothing one can say about female renouncer-ascetics that will apply to them all" (Denton 1991:221). How then do I justify taking sannyasinis as a subject of anthropological inquiry?

When I was a graduate student considering possible research topics, sannyasinis did not fit the standard anthropological categories through which I had come to understand Hindu culture. Both Hindu sacred literature and scholarly studies typically defined women in relation to men, as daughters, wives, sisters, mothers, and widows.[9] The feminine ideal most clearly defined in sacred literature, anthropological accounts, and popular culture is best symbolized by the modest and chaste wife Sita, heroine of the epic *Ramayana*, who voluntarily abandons the comforts and security of palace life to follow her husband Ram into the forest for fourteen years of exile. In Valmiki's popular and influential version, Sita suffers the injustices perpetrated on her by men with quiet and graceful dignity. Although this image of the ideal wife has not gone unchallenged, particularly in oral traditions, it still holds legitimacy in contemporary India. It is an ideal to which Indian women, especially upper-caste women, are often held and to which many aspire. For actual women, the positive aspect of this image of the ideal wife is her relationship to the material and spiritual well-being of a household. Even as the lawmaker Manu warned against independent women, he stressed that prosperity only comes to households where the women are honored and happy (III. 55–59, trans. Doniger 1991). The moral duty of women (*stridharma*) is to ensure the prosperity of their marital homes by performing domestic tasks skillfully, bearing and nurturing children, and worshiping their husbands as gods. In orthodox thought, the role of wife seems to be elevated above other female roles. I once heard that a sannyasini, in advising her female disciples to be devout wives, had said: "If you have only one glass of milk, should you give it to your husband or your child? Your husband." That the disciples related to me their surprise at this exchange suggested that it contradicted their own judgement. While brahmanical values that elevate a woman's husband above everything, including her children, may not be shared by women themselves, they send a clear message about orthodox expectations that, for women, the husband is supreme. The religious practices associated with Hindu women do seem to be oriented toward the household. The vows and fasts so important in women's religious practice are not unlike the austerities performed by renouncers, but householder women perform these fasts primarily for the sake of family members rather than for spiritual liberation (McGee 1991). Pearson (1996) suggests that this may be overstated and that women perform votive fasting rites (*vrats*) for other, more personal reasons as well, such as increasing personal purity and power or interacting socially with other women. Still, given the general female orientation toward home and family, women who opt for solitude, independence, and the full-time pursuit of their own spiritual aims do seem anomalous.

The anomalous status of female renouncers is suggested in the range of terms used to designate Hindu religious specialists. The grammatically feminine forms of masculine terms more often refer to the *wives* of male religious specialists than to their female counterparts in the vocation. For example, "*rishika*" refers to the wife of a sage (*rishi*) rather than to a female sage. "*Pandita*" designates the wife of a brahmin priest (*pandit*) rather than a brahmin priestess. Sinha and Saraswati note that a female *avadhut* (a particularly elevated category of Hindu ascetic) they met was called "Mataji" (Respected Mother) rather than "*avadhutini*" (the feminine form of *avadhut*) because the latter can refer to the wife of an *avadhut* (1978:73). There is a similar ambiguity in the term "*sadhvi*," the feminine form of the term "*sadhu*" (holy man); "*sadhvi*" can refer to a virtuous wife as well as a female ascetic. In recognition of this ambiguity most female ascetics I met used the masculine form "*sadhu*" to refer to themselves, sometimes tacking on "Mata" (Mother) if they wish to emphasize a feminine identity.[10] Following their usage, I use "*sadhu*" as a general category to refer to both male and female ascetics. "Mataji" is the most common term of address for female ascetics. The assumption underlying the use of terms like "*rishika*" and "*pandita*" is that a woman cannot stand alone. The term "*sannyasini*" is different. Since renouncers are by definition unmarried, "*sannyasini*" cannot possibly refer to the wife of a sannyasi. Perhaps for this reason, as I will discuss shortly, there is some confusion about the term.

As I first imagined this project, the existence and acceptance of female renouncers challenged the ideal image of "Hindu women" as always married and any simple notion of renunciation as either ungendered or hypermasculine. It was intriguing to imagine that solitary Indian women could actually *reject* marriage, as opposed to being widowed or unable to find suitable grooms, both of which signify pitiable states of existence. In this scenario, women renouncers could not be simply explained away as logical anomalies, social deviants, or conservative women who, in opting for an elitist and patriarchal tradition, suffer from false consciousness. Yet very little had been written about contemporary female ascetics, or, for that matter, about other intentionally unmarried Hindu women.

Although I am concerned here with rendering the phenomenon of female renunciation visible, I also risk making the tenuous assumption that sannyasinis are an already constituted group and appropriate unit of analysis. To assume outright that sannyasinis have more in common with each other than they do with the larger population of male renouncers might qualify as an example of discursive colonization of the material and historical differences among third world women, a colonization that assumes these women share identical problems, needs, interests, and goals (Mohanty 1984:334). Because the issue of sannyasinis as constituting an appropriate analytical category is a question rather than an assumption of this research, I approach sannyasinis in relation to both male renouncers and female householders. The term sannyasini does not refer to a group in the sociological sense of people who live or act together, as would, for example, the more specific "sannyasinis of the Juno Akhara" or "Sarada Math sannyasinis." During the course of my field research, I spoke with women from different sectarian backgrounds specifically in order to understand female renunciation in at least some of its diversity, yet I make no claim to offer a complete representation of the subject. In addition to gender and sectarian background, differences in education, material wealth, number and status of disciples are equally relevant in the world of renouncers, so I avoid giving one aspect of a renouncer's identity, such as gender, preeminence over other aspects across all contexts. Rather, the juxtaposition of women with different styles of renunciation is intended to make the most basic point that there is no such thing as a "typical" sannyasini. As I have indicated, it is difficult to generalize about Hindu renunciation because it is so loosely institutionalized. In order to obviate any assumption that it might be easier to generalize about female renouncers than about their male counterparts simply because they are women, I speak of "sannyasinis" as actual women with particular histories, not of "the sannyasini" as an abstract category. That a word for female renouncer (sannyasini) exists in Hindi and Sanskrit could be taken as sufficient evidence that the category is meaningful. But my discussions with people in Haridwar indicate that it is not a salient cultural category readily distinguishable from the male renouncer (sannyasi). In response to my queries about sannyasinis, people sometimes sought further clarification by asking if I meant "lady sannyasis" (lady male renouncers) or "sadhu matas" (ascetic mothers). A few wondered if I really wanted to meet widows. One orthodox Dashnami sannyasi, in a particularly hostile reaction, told me in no uncertain terms that female renouncers did not exist. In doing so, however, he was not doubting their existence so much as denying their legitimacy.

Another man, an elderly householder, wondered with more sympathetic concern how my learned professor in the United States could send me to study something that did not exist.

Rather than seeking an imagined unity in sociological terms, I have chosen to explore the meaning of sannyasa in the everyday lives of particular women pursuing diverse styles of renunciation. These women combine, with various emphases, the social roles and skills of a psychologist, medical doctor, mystic, social worker, priest, and mother. While female renouncers lack coherence as a group, the fact that they are women does color their everyday lives and identities in some very important ways. For example, their gender presents them with many specific problems in living and moving among men, such as the need to have a safe place to sleep every night. Moreover, the sannyasinis I met often seemed to identify with at least some of those values of the female householder that scholars have generally opposed to renunciation: fertility, health, prosperity, and nurturing.[11] Thus, I show that there is some degree of specificity to sannyasinis' lives as compared to those of male renouncers. Ojha points out a crucial difference between male and female asceticism in India: "[t]he male ascetic is a man who has made a choice between two ideals in life equally allowed for him. But the female ascetic is a woman who having renounced the single mode of life set for her adopts a behavior primarily intended for males" (Ojha 1981:256). For this reason, I have consciously decided to make gender issues central to my understanding of renunciation. As the following chapters make evident, my findings indicate that in some contexts sannyasinis ally themselves with female householders in opposition to all men, and in others they minimize the distance between themselves and their male peers by stressing their identity as renouncers.

My Own Not-Too-Straight Path to Sannyasinis in Haridwar

My initial fascination with sannyasa was fueled by the exoticism with which renouncers are often represented in the United States. Although I was born in the United States to immigrant Hindu parents, my upbringing was not particularly religious. As a child I experienced this as something of a lack. Christianity seemed alien, but I knew little about Hinduism. My parents immigrated long before the wave of South Asian immigration that began in 1965 and eventually led to the establishment of an infrastructure of temples, community centers, and diasporic public events in U.S. cities. I often note how young second-generation Indian students today seem so much more "Indian" than I ever felt. Aside from Indian food, Indian art, Indian habits of hygiene, and occasional trips to "the homeland" to visit much-adored relatives, there was little about my upbringing that was Indian. The music my parents played at parties was the Allman Brothers and Janis Joplin—never Bollywood songs or Ravi Shankar. They had Indian friends but were not immersed in a local

"Indian community." My brothers and I had no curfew and were allowed to date. There was no talk of arranged marriage, except among a few hopeful aunts in India. We were what an earlier generation of sociologists would have called "assimilated." I watched my first Hindi film as an adult and only enrolled in Hindi 101 as a sophmore in college.

During my undergraduate days studying religion and anthropology, when I first learned about sannyasa, it seemed like an extreme and dramatic version of lifestyles that had long fascinated me: self-sufficient and austere living in the context of homesteads and communes. Sannyasa is, of course, quite a different phenomenon. As Anand Mata once reflected, "I know I can solve all problems myself without guidance. This independence is not of the social type. In the West, they all look for independence from society and from rules of behavior. In *sadhana*, it is a spiritual independence. Don't depend on other people but leave everything in the hands of God. Some say we won't depend on God but on ourselves—this is the epitome of pride and ego." Still, like hippies and others in the United States who had chosen alternative lifestyles, sadhus were people who dropped out of mainstream society, and, in this sense, represented a form of protest and rebellion.[12] After spending a semester of my junior year in India studying Hinduism, I was convinced that developing self-control and detachment were the most important qualities to cultivate and that one did this by denying oneself what one most desired. I imagined fieldwork as my own experiment in austerity. This was the context in which I first decided to conduct doctoral research on Hindu renunciation: my general interest in asceticism led me to focus on women rather than the other way around. I realized the unfeasibility of a young, female researcher living among male renouncers, given their misogynistic and unsavory reputation. Ironically, by the time I finally arrived in Haridwar to research female renunciation five years had passed and, with those five years, my ascetic yearnings. I was no longer fixated on cultivating self-control and detachment and had promised to marry a man with no leanings toward austerity. My interest in Hindu asceticism had become more intellectual and less personal. After relating this story to Anand Mata, she commented that it was God's grace that had prevented me from living among sannyasinis at the time when I was most passionately interested in doing so. Had I been able to come immediately (rather than having to complete graduate coursework and obtain funding), she speculated, I might very well have taken sannyasa, but impulsively, without being fully "ripe." It would have been a mistake because I was young and lacked the full awareness and firm determination that are necessary to succeed on this path. What I felt in those early days, she seemed to be saying, was simply a mood of renunciation, which everyone feels from time to time. And, of course, that it did not last is proof of this. In Hindu India, the mood of renunciation is seen as a common response to emotional loss or disillusionment, but only rarely do such moods translate into actual renunciation.

My reasons for deciding to engage in research with sannyasinis in Haridwar rather than some other Hindi-speaking pilgrimage town were conceptual and pragmatic. It is often assumed by scholars and lay Hindus alike that most female ascetics are widows. Since Hindu orthodoxy requires that widows lead an ascetic lifestyle of poverty and austerity, but without the positive religious status of renouncers, it is reasonable to expect that many widows would turn to renunciation as a means to improve their status. However, even though Ojha worked in Benaras, a pilgrimage center that attracts large numbers of widows from Calcutta and elsewhere, she concluded that only a minority of female ascetics are widows (1981:279); my research in Haridwar further supports this conclusion (see also Caplan 1973:177). A widow's asceticism conforms to dharma, but a woman's taking sannyasa is a rejection of dharma (Narayanan 1993:281). Avoiding the confusion between widows and sannyasinis would be facilitated by avoiding those pilgrimage centers that particularly attract widows. Since Haridwar is not known for its population of widows, I expected (and later confirmed) that most of the solitary women there would be ascetics and would be viewed as such by others. In addition, Haridwar was a town of manageable size and my family had acquaintances there, which translated into a place to stay and some initial introductions.

The Personal and Particular

I highlight the human and personal aspects of renunciation and incorporate humanistic styles of writing. While I have not organized this text in terms of life histories, I have adopted other techniques of humanistic writing for my central ethnographic chapters: narrative form, reflexivity, and intense focus on two individual women. While I understand and accept some of the postmodern critiques of a humanism that renders social difference and power invisible, I must agree with Abu-Lughod's comment that we ought not to abandon humanism because it "continues to be in the West the language of human equality with the greatest moral force" (1993:28–29). Indeed, anthropologists who want their work to be accessible and widely read seem to find this familiarizing style particularly useful.

One of my reasons for this focus is that the activities, conflicts, and interpersonal relationships that fill renouncers' everyday lives have generally been absent in scholarly accounts.[13] What is most striking to me is the way in which sannyasinis' lives are simultaneously extraordinary and utterly mundane. Moreover, a similar combination of reverence and disinterest seems to characterize the way renouncers are treated by the general lay population. Stereotypically "saintly" activities such as a meditative trance or vows of silence may be viewed by lay observers with cynicism or simple indifference, while the most "ordinary" action or speech may be interpreted as mystical. In sharing the everyday lives of these women, I could not help but notice a down-to-earth quality that rarely surfaces in the more formal contexts that place them "on stage" as saints and gurus. Scholarly accounts of sannyasa tend to either emphasize the philosophical aspects of the tradition or its general sociological characteristics, leaving the reader with little sense of what everyday social life is like for a renouncer committed to attaining a transcendent ideal.

A second reason for privileging the everyday is that religious texts and abstract philosophical ideas are mediated by people and by practice. Scholars in religious studies have offered analyses of the textual and philosophical bases for Hindu ascetic traditions. What an intensely ethnographic approach to sannyasa can contribute to the study of Hinduism is an understanding of how abstract theological and philosophical ideas are interpreted by individuals and reenacted in everyday situations. Indeed, ethnography demonstrates the relevance of abstract philosophical concepts for contemporary people and everyday life. For example, my research suggests that the conflict between social responsibility and ascetic withdrawal is not simply textual, logical, or philosophical; it is emotional and social as well. In their study of Japanese religion, Reader and Tanabe write, "[w]e treat religion as a matter not only of doctrine and belief but of participation, custom, ritual, action, practice, and belonging. It is as much a matter of social and cultural influences and behavior patterns located in day-to-day concerns and the ordinary processes of life . . . as it is with ultimate concerns, theological explanations of the nature of the universe, or the destination of the soul" (1998:5–6). While highlighting the personal, I also reflect on the larger philosophical and sociological contexts in which particular lives are situated.

A third reason for focusing on the personal and the particular is that it best conveys the extent to which sannyasinis self-consciously reflect upon their own lives and culture, more so perhaps because they are, as women living in a man's world, relative outsiders in the world of sadhus. Dominant cultural models of Hindu renunciation are patriarchal, but there is growing scholarly evidence that ideologies about women found in sacred texts are unlikely to reflect the views of women themselves. Studies that give attention to the subjective life of Indian men and women contribute to debates in South Asian studies about the compatibility of individualism and Indian culture.[14] They also demonstrate that women's behavior and thoughts are not completely determined by dominant cultural models of renunciation and patriarchy and, more importantly, that women's behavior does not always reflect their subjectivity. Had I limited myself to formal or brief encounters with these women or to observations about their behavior, it would have been possible to leave Haridwar with an impression of sannyasinis as having internalized a patriarchal renunciant ideology to a much greater extent than indicated by their words spoken informally. As women, sannyasinis are expected to conform to certain social conventions regarding Hindu femininity that do not restrict their male counterparts. While the women with whom I worked did sometimes adjust their behavior to meet the demands of a patriarchal society by dressing modestly or, especially if young, living under male protection, they did not endow these restrictions with spiritual significance. It is also clear that they interpreted the misogynistic rhetoric of sannyasa as reflecting male insecurities and fears rather than female worth. That this sort of resistance to patriarchal meanings is neither new nor unique to independent female ascetics is indicated by research on women in contemporary and colonial India. In an essay written in the late 1800s, Tarabai Shinde accuses men of having the very vices they normally attribute to women. Though many of her female and male contemporaries were concerned with identifiable atrocities suffered by women, Shinde launched a critique of the ideological basis of patriarchal society by exposing men's stereotypes of women (Tharu and Lalita 1991:222–23). An emphasis on sannyasinis' words and reflections tells us that when they do conform behaviorally to society's gender roles by dressing modestly or traveling with others rather than alone, they often do so self-consciously and critically. They view the limitations placed on them as necessitated by imperfect social institutions rather than as signs of female inferiority.

A fourth reason to take this approach is that it allows me more adequately to represent the amorphous and anti-institutional quality of renunciation in general and female renunciation in particular. It is no easier to generalize about female renouncers, simply because they are women, than about male renouncers. Indeed, it is probably *more* difficult to generalize about a specifically female style of renunciation because sannyasinis seem to gravitate less toward established orders, since historically they have been excluded from the more institutionalized forms of sannyasa. Although sannyasinis do exist within the orthodox Dashnami Order and other monastic institutions, I suspect that the vast majority of female renouncers live quietly, independent of any sectarian structure in pilgrimage sites like Haridwar, Gangotri, and Benaras. It is likely that the rise in independent and charismatic Hindu gurus in India and internationally will bring more of these women into the limelight. They may live in large ashrams or tiny cottages, acquire a substantial following or live in solitude. They may devote themselves to charitable activities, practice meditation and austerities, give lectures, or do nothing that is "religious" in a conventional sense. A focus on independent sannyasinis conveys a sense of this heterogeneity.

In these accounts of everyday events and conversations with particular women, I aim to portray sannyasinis as persons rather than as cultural categories or receptacles of abstract philosophical ideas. Following the lead of other ethnographers who have responded to feminist and postmodernist critiques of anthropology, I reduce the level of abstraction and am more circumspect in generalizing about the "natives." In her work on Vodou, Karen McCarthy Brown offers a model of the kind of ethnography I aim to construct.

> My aim is to create an intimate portrait of three-dimensional people who are not stand-ins for an abstraction such as "the Haitian people" but rather are deeply religious individuals with particular histories and rich interior lives, individuals who

do not live out their religion in unreflective, formulaic ways but instead struggle with it, become confused, and sometimes even contradict themselves. In other words, my aim is to create a portrait of Vodou embedded in the vicissitudes of particular lives. (Brown 1991:14-15)

Renunciation is a difficult path full of obstacles and tensions. The agonistic aspects of Hindu renunciation are rarely portrayed in scholarly and hagiographic accounts, although they appear more often in popular culture. It is well known that Hindu folklore and oral traditions portray sadhus as powerful, but often greedy and lustful, figures (Bloomfield 1924; K. Narayan 1989). R. K. Narayan's novel *The Guide* represents sadhus more sympathetically, but as human and flawed. Except for fictional accounts, "the renouncer remains a figure whose existence comments on the human predicament but whose human thoughts and feelings remain opaque" (Gold 1989a:770). By featuring only two sannyasinis, I hope to convey not only their diversity but also a sense of their humanity.

Power and Representation: Epistemological and Ethical Considerations

My encounters with various male and female renouncers not only evoke the complex interaction of gender, power, and saintliness in the world of sannyasa, but they also address recent feminist and postmodern discussions of ethnographic research and writing. I have been concerned to represent, to some degree, the ideological range and variety of social behaviors that describe the phenomenon of female renunciation. Yet I make no claims of objectivity in the conventional sense of the term. Critics of Enlightenment philosophies have established that all perspectives are partial and have deconstructed strategies and discourses of writing that imply claims to universality and objectivity. While acknowledging the illusory nature of infinite vision or a god's-eye-view of the world, Donna Haraway has suggested that we retain the epistemological metaphor of vision as well as a usable concept of objectivity by insisting on the embodiment of all vision (1988:189). In other words, real objectivity means being clear about one's location rather than pretending to offer a view from nowhere. To this end, I have tried to contextualize my representations of particular sannyasinis as much as possible within the confining space of a book. For example, entire dialogues have been reproduced to allow the reader to see the context in which particular words were spoken. Providing a rich sense of context has also meant including myself in the text and choosing to write in a more personal voice. Behar writes,

[T]o assert that one is a "white middle class woman" or a "black gay man" or a "working class Latina" within one's study of Shakespeare or Santeria is only interesting if one is able to draw deeper connections between one's personal experience and the subject under study. That doesn't require a full-length autobiography, but it does require a keen understanding of what aspects of the self are the most important filters through which one perceives the world and, more particularly, the topic being studied. (Behar 1996:13)

Thus, I include myself in the text where I believe the information to be relevant for contextualizing the ethnographic situation and the manner in which sannyasinis' behavior and comments were a response to me. For some, no doubt, I will have gone too far in the direction of reflexivity and, for others, not far enough. Karen McCarthy Brown has eloquently asserted that putting herself in her field notes was not only a learning device and a way of staying honest, but also an acknowledgment that the intellectual labor of doing ethnography is a form of human relationship (1991:12). My decision to write in a personal voice is at once a strategy to highlight the personal and particular in my study of sannyasa and an epistemological message: all knowledge is situated.

Anthropologists now widely acknowledge that the power-laden interpersonal and international contexts in which the ethnographic enterprise exists have both theoretical and ethical implications, and until recently the emphasis has been on the researchers' position of dominance over their subjects as derived from colonial and neocolonial relationships of material and political inequity (Asad 1973; Clifford and Marcus 1986; Marcus and Fischer 1986). However, the work of women anthropologists clearly demonstrates that the position of women conducting research in patriarchal situations is never so simple, because gender hierarchies may crosscut other local and global inequalities.[15] In addition, they have described the disadvantages resulting from the expectation that women, especially young unmarried women, need to be protected from predatory males (Giovannini 1986:110; Golde 1986:5–6). Just as other women researchers have gained this protection by living with "respectable" families in the host society, I maintained my reputation by associating primarily with "respectable" sadhus. Commenting on the gendered tradition of anthropological fieldwork stories, Tsing (1987) noted that male scholars tend to highlight sexual activity and desire while women speak of constant and enforced prudishness.

At the same time, the ethical problems associated with the practice of first world women studying third world women are well known; they arise from the material inequalities that make such research possible and with the politics of representation. The debate about whether ethnographic methodology and feminist politics are compatible remains unresolved. Ethnography has been held up as a methodology particularly suited to feminist research, even more so for ethnography focused on the particularities of individual lives and incorporating women's own voices. In a well-known critique, Judith Stacey (1988) argued that, in the process of ethnographic practice and literary production, feminist scholars retain a privileged position, and this leaves informants vulnerable to betrayal. Indeed,

according to her, the more personal and intimate the information we obtain
about particular informants, the more likely we are to betray them in our writing. After all, the ethnographer is still the one to make decisions about what to
include in the text. It was only at the time of writing that I fully realized the
extent to which my focus on the personal and particular intensified the ethical
dilemmas of textual production. Patai (1991) has insisted that ethical research
on third world women by first world feminist scholars is not even possible, given
its dependence on material disparities. In the context of Haridwar, the
Sannyasinis I interviewed had more status and authority than me due to their
spiritual achievements. Moreover, their saintly status was due to voluntary austerity, and most had not experienced poverty or deprivation in their lives. Still,
in a geopolitical context, this does not change the fact that I could and did exit
"the field" whenever I chose. Addressing feminist anxieties over writing about
other, less privileged women, Ong has argued that these concerns, though valid,
fail to recognize the ways in which these women exercise power over the production of ethnographic knowledge by what they choose to tell, demand, and with-
hold (1995:353). Several sannyasinis, as will become evident, refused to become
my ethnographic subjects by claiming either silence or ignorance. That Anand
Mata who chose to remain silent for years, also chose to speak so articulately
and deliberately to a visiting anthropologist is a matter of some consequence.
Anand Mata recalls that, as someone who remained silent, she was often considered to be dim-witted, though one goal of her spiritual practice was to be
unaffected by this. She understands the problems of equating voice with subjectivity. Yet when someone who knows the power of silence speaks, her words
must be taken seriously. If her words have the power to revise Western construc-
tions of passive or resisting, but always domestic and dependent, Indian women,
then "the greater betrayal lies in allowing our personal doubts to stand in the
way of representing their claims, interests, and perspectives" (Ong 1995:354).

Work on female ascetics also poses new questions about ethical research.
Kirin Narayan (1989), Margaret Trawick (1990), and Karen McCarthy Brown
(1991) provided models for my project because they situate particular persons at
the center of their texts. Yet this humanistic orientation not only creates
increased risk of betraying informants, but it also conflicts with the goals of sannyasa. What happens when the person described in the text does not wish to be
so elevated? Renouncers are supposed to have neither personality nor autobiography. In sannyasa, "the adjuncts of the individual self's psychosomatic personality are to be stripped away" (Hirst 1993:129). Anand Mata once described her
decision to take sannyasa in terms of her refusal to submit to family pressure to
remain in married life, but she concluded with the following statement: "Even to
say 'I'll choose my own path' has ego. Pride and ego are the first and final problems one faces in sadhana. 'I' prevents us from total surrender." There is, then, a
fundamental contradiction between the goals of the women I interviewed and
my anthropological aims.[16] While renouncers are not supposed to seek the lime-

light or be concerned about reputation, reputation does matter, probably more so for women initiates, and the sannyasinis portrayed here are concerned with maintaining theirs. Intensely personal ethnography may at times conflict both with their need to maintain a good reputation as holy persons and with the renunciant ideal of having neither ego nor autobiography. In the world of ascetics, it is the job of disciples to construct personal biographies of holy persons through the medium of hagiography. Scholars, however, must retain a critical edge, even if they love and respect the people they write about.[17]

This has created so many dilemmas about what to include in the text that I have sat on this manuscript for several years (It is based on research conducted in 1989–91 and a brief visit in 1998). Having now decided to publish it, I have changed names and omitted some personal information to protect the privacy of my informants. While Anand Mata and Baiji are not seeking publicity and will not mind the use of pseudonyms, others, including both ascetics and disciples, may be offended by my refusal to publicize the accomplishments of ascetics and to give credit where credit is due. Disciplinary calls for increased accountability to those we study often seem to ignore the fact that the subjects of our research do not always share the same interests.[18] Since it is not possible to hide some identities and not others, all names have been changed. More important is the lack of other identifying information in this text. It is paradoxical that I have included lengthy dialogues and reflexive commentary while intentionally omitting other important information, such as names of gurus, in order to prevent identification. This was a compromise that enabled me to publish an ethnography I can live with. Some readers, specialists in the field, may see the lack of relevant information as a serious flaw, since, for example, ascetic lineages are a means of passing on particular kinds of knowledge. I believe that such omissions and changes allow me to write a more accurate and detailed account of people and events as I experienced them. If ethnography is a form of social and emotional engagement, this is both its weakness and strength.

Insiders, Outsiders, and Respectable Women: Some Limits of This Study

Debates about ethnographic representation intersect with commentaries on the epistemological, political, and practical significance of "native" and "halfie" anthropology. Before feminist and postmodern anthropologists made ethnography a subject of intense analysis, the relative advantages of insider and outsider positions were debated (see, for example, Srinivas 1976). More recently, by confessing to culture shock and informants' distrust or amusement, many anthropologists working in "their own" communities have succeeded in blurring the distinction between insider and outsider perspectives, thereby countering earlier assumptions that insider status is unambiguous (and even possible at all) or that it necessarily offers special access to ethnographic truth (Narayan 1993a; Abu-Lughod 1991; Naveed-I-Rahat 1991; Ong 1995; Lewin 1995; Behar 1996; Hsiung 1996; Slocum 2001). At the beginning of the twenty-first century, anthropology includes expats studying "their homeland," second-generation Americans "searching for their roots," and mission-educated aboriginals seeking to represent "their people" to the outside world. At the same time, the cosmopolitanism of the world's major cities makes my hip Indian cousins living in New Delhi unfamiliar with and disengaged from life in the ashrams where I stayed and more knowledgeable about American popular media than me, though I was born and raised in the United States. Family networks, travel, and media have made the Indian middle classes transnational. In some ways, sadhus have followed suit. Although globe-trotting, cosmopolitan Hindu sadhus are not the focus of this study and the lives of those featured here seem "traditional" and removed from urban middle-class beliefs and practices, Baiji and Anand Mata are modern women affected by larger economic and political processes. For example, Baiji's focus on social service and Anand Mata's attitude toward affirmative action illustrate trends and ideas that have developed in the last century. Their claim that all spiritual paths lead to the same goal and are in this sense equally valid is a central tenet of neo-Vedanta, which has come to stand for Hinduism (neo-Hinduism, that is) both in India and internationally; this version of Hinduism, largely shared by both Anand Mata and Baiji, is a result of India's interaction with Britain under colonialism and, since the end of the nineteenth century, with the United States (Jackson 1994; King 1999). Yet their aspirations seem only superficially affected by the "imagined possibilities" provided by a globalized world and its cosmopolitan experiences of cinema, video, restaurants, sports and tourism, even religious tourism (Appadurai 1991). The emotional ease of traveling between New Delhi and Virginia that I experienced contrasts with the schizophrenia that characterized my movement between Haridwar's ashrams and Delhi's middle-class and elite homes. I kept a suitcase with my city clothes at my aunt's home in New Delhi. I would arrive there in the morning by overnight train from Haridwar with bindi, plastic sandals, unfashionable *salvar kameez*, and hair that was always tightly braided and sometimes oiled, and emerge from my bath with jeans, T-shirt, and loose hair. This chameleonic pattern of transformation was amusing to all. Would my jean-clad cousins have felt more at home in Haridwar ashrams than I, just because they were Indian? The lines between insiders and outsiders are no longer easily drawn, if they ever were.

Karla Slocum (2001) agrees that identities should not be essentialized, but she also stresses that our politicized identities might motivate our research and that, for both professional and personal reasons, we may decide to render certain aspects of our identity visible in certain contexts. The *personal* offense I felt as a college student by stereotypes of Indian women was connected to my newly emerging Indian-American identity. More importantly, in order to construct an identity of a "respectable" young woman living among sadhus, I consciously highlighted certain aspects of myself (someone respectful of spiritual superiors) and not others (someone who cohabited with her spouse before marriage). Brackette Williams argues that ethnographers and informants are mutually constructed in the context of a range of identities that constitute the power relations into which an ethnographer enters; there is no identity for an ethnographer that exists autonomously of this (1996:92). As will become evident in the following chapters, sadhus and their disciples "translated me" (Williams 1996) into preexisting identities which included: American student who behaves too independently, daughter, girl from a "good Indian family," young married woman living among sadhus, Indian girl married to an American, and spiritual seeker who does not yet realize what has *really* motivated her to do this research! Chapters 2 through 5 illustrate these changing identities and how they shaped the data I gathered.

The fact that I stayed at a small ashram called Sant Kuti during my initial month of research colored everything that followed. I went there in the beginning not because there were any sannyasinis in residence, but on the advice of an uncle who, though living in Delhi, was a devotee of Sant Kuti's deceased guru and a member of its board of trustees. My study grew like a spider web from my relationships with the people of Sant Kuti. Prakash Mehra was a paying guest at Sant Kuti when I first arrived there, and, as a Ph.D. in Hindu philosophy, he took an immediate interest in my research. "Mehraji" introduced me to Anand Mata and Baiji, two of the central figures in my study, and to many other sadhus. That my contact with sannyasinis was always initiated by an introduction meant that, even as a foreigner who spoke imperfect Hindi, I was never a complete stranger, and this made my motives and character less suspect.

While there is no denying that such contacts provided ethnographic advantages, they also entailed disadvantages that were equally important in determining the limitations of this study. I felt constrained by different expectations and a stricter standard of behavior than might have been used to judge a total stranger, particularly a "foreign" woman. For example, certain physical and social spaces were off-limits to me. Foreign women are typically granted more leeway, as less is expected of them and less is at stake if they cross boundaries. At the same time, I was probably more sensitive to criticisms and less willing to transcend boundaries than a young woman more secure in her "Indian" identity might have been. I generally heeded the advice of those around me (such as the elderly "Mataji" who managed Sant Kuti) never to visit unfamiliar ashrams alone. I often traveled alone to meet someone known to me or even to shop in public bazaars, but going to strange ashrams by myself would raise suspicions about my character (read: chastity) and was considered unsafe. Initially, I constrained my own movement out of respect for those who, as informally appointed "local guardians," felt responsible for me. Still, I did so reluctantly, certain that they were overprotective. However, as I gradually realized that theft, embezzlement, rape, and murder were as much a part of life in Haridwar's

ashrams as in the secular domains of society, I began to internalize some man-
dates of respectable femininity.

Thus, with a few notable exceptions, most of the sannyasinis I met were
those my friends and relatives considered more or less respectable, whether they
personally admired them or not. I had observed from afar renouncers who
passed their days (and nights?) on the *ghats*, the paved steps that lined the banks
of the Ganges River. Mehraji and others assumed that many, if not most, of
these sadhus were unsavory characters whose primary spiritual discipline was the
smoking of hashish and that I would have little to gain from interviewing them.
The vast majority of such *ghat*-dwelling sadhus were men, though a rare, lone
woman could be spotted among them. Initially, I was eager to learn more about
these sannyasinis, and had they existed in groups segregated from the men it
would have been more feasible. However, my persistent requests to meet these
women and their male companions were consistently either dismissed as a waste
of time or politely ignored. Granted, I could have ventured out boldly on my
own to establish contact with these sadhus, but I felt such a move had the
potential to sabotage my reputation and my research. Moreover, the previous
year, while walking alone on the *ghats* in Benaras one day, my attempt to "make
contacts" with male sadhus was met only by catcalls from tall, naked men with
dramatic matted locks and eager grins. By the time I arrived in Haridwar the following year, I was acutely aware of both my limitations as a researcher and the
danger that sadhus could pose to my personal safety. Thus, without anyone willing to accompany me to meet strangers living on the Ganges' edge, I am not able
to say much about their perspectives.[19]

Not only did my local connections render certain types of social interactions off-limits, they in no way *guaranteed* that the sannyasinis to whom I was
introduced would welcome me or respond to questions. Theoretically speaking,
of course, renouncers are believed to have given up social relationships and obligations, so my family connections *should* have been irrelevant to them. That this
was not usually the case in my own experience lulled me into a sense of confident security that was occasionally shattered by encounters with particular
renouncers. Once, an uncle introduced me to two sisters, young women, who
lived together as ascetics in Haridwar. They were the sisters of a close friend of
his, a man whose son I had met in the United States when he came to study at
my university. The younger of the two sisters, who was home at the time of our
visit, greeted us warmly but evaded my uncle's requests that she speak to me
about her life. She indicated her disinterest in answering questions by remarking
that true devotion could not be expressed in words and by referring me to
another sadhu. "He is very knowledgeable," she said, "and can give you all the
scriptural references you need." I traveled to her place several times during the
next year only to find that she was out of town every time. I decided to try one
last time during my final week of research and found her at home. She greeted
me cordially at the door and, rather than inviting me in, disappeared for a

moment and returned with two folding metal chairs which she placed in the foyer right next to the door. Did she fear that I might pollute her home or that, if admitted, I might refuse to leave without an interview? During eighteen months in Haridwar, I had never been treated with such cold disinterest. After a few moments of courteous small talk there was a silence that should have been my cue to leave gracefully. Instead, I blurted out a request for an interview, as it seemed like the only legitimate excuse to stay a bit longer. She wanted to know what sort of questions I might ask and, as I tried to impress her, it quickly went from bad to worse. Finally, emotionally drained, frustrated at my failure to elicit any information, and remorseful about disregarding her privacy, I burst into tears. She took the tears as a sign that I wanted to take sannyasa rather than return to married life in America and proceeded to counsel me on the moral necessity of fulfilling one's family duties. I heard her out in defeated silence, accepted her blessing, and left. Even personal connections and relative insider status did not prevent me from sometimes feeling like a pariah anthropologist.

Clearly, the sannyasinis featured in this account were not only chosen by me for their articulateness, but were also self-selected. Attempting to elicit life-historical information from renouncers can be difficult, since they are not supposed to discuss their lives prior to initiation and may consider such questions insulting. Even though I spoke to sannyasinis with diverse styles of religiosity, the selection process could not be called random or objective. Some never let me into their lives, while others offered only scripted religious discourses. Many types, besides the *ghat*-dwellers, have been left out. This account, for example, includes no high-ranking sannyasini of the Dashnami Order, no sannyasini with transnational experience, and no self-identified tantric sannyasini. Almost all the sannyasinis mentioned here live independently or in nonsectarian ashrams. They fit the category of a generalized Hindu sadhu without clear sectarian affiliation, the type of sadhu often depicted in myth and popular culture. Had I chosen to study the women of a particular religious order, such as the female monastics studied by Sinclair-Brull (1997), rather than individual women from diverse backgrounds, I would be telling a different story about female renunciation. As it is, the sannyasinis I met were generally eclectic in their religiosity and often anti-institutional in their thinking, and this has significantly colored my perspective on the meaning of sannyasa. Not only are they independent women but also, for the most part, respectable women.

Despite the specificity and small sample size of this research, I attempt to make some general claims about female Hindu renunciation that I hope will be confirmed by future research. I argue that sannyasinis remain women after initiation, that they pursue an agency that is more practical than discursive, and that they transgress social norms and ideals but construct themselves as exceptions. Moreover, despite their celibate status, the primary constraint on their agency seems to be the threat of male sexual aggression. I also venture a few generalizations about Hindu renunciation. Sannaysa offers women (and men) the possibility for leading unconventional lives and is itself eclectic in both ideology and practice. Indeed, a dialogue between worldly and otherworldly (or between levels of reality) occurs within sannyasa, not just between renouncers and householders, and this is central to understanding both the relevance and irrelevance of gender distinctions in this domain. I suggest too that Hindu lay persons are concerned with evaluating the sincerity of renouncers and that this should prompt us to rethink the manner in which Hindu persons have been constructed as the Other of Western individuals. This book is about a handful of women renouncers, but it is also an exploration of Hindu renunciation and ashram life through the experiences of these women.

Chapter One

Gendering Hindu Renunciation

Hinduism has developed a wide array of overlapping categories of religious specialists, from married yogis and priests to celibate student-novices, each category representing one religious path (*marg*) among many. The habit of describing religious pursuits as a "path" is hardly unique to Hinduism, but the assumption that paths are plural and that their appropriateness is contextually defined is particularly Hindu. Although there is rivalry between followers of different paths, which gives rise to the notion of "higher" and "lower" paths, it is generally agreed that the paths lead to the same destination and, in this sense, are all legitimate, if not equal. The *Bhagavadgita*'s standard threefold division distinguishes the paths of knowledge (*jnanamarg*), action (*karmamarg*), and devotion (*bhaktimarg*), but these ideal types lose their heuristic value when they come to be seen as mutually exclusive and competing paths. Since the notion of paths is central to both philosophical and popular ways of understanding Hindu religious diversity, chapter 4 will explore in more detail its association with notions of movement or motion (*gati*), position or state (*sthiti*), time (*kal*), and the actor or vessel (*patra*). This metaphor of paths and journey help to explain why ascetics behave in such idiosyncratic ways and why sannyasa is eclectic without becoming an "anything goes" morality. Indeed, chapter 5 explores lay observers' concern with evaluating ascetics' sincerity and legitimacy.

It is also evident throughout the ethnography that renouncers communicate different kinds of messages to their interlocutors in different contexts. For example, what does the proclamation "in renunciation there is no male and female" mean and for whom is that message intended? What about the alternative message, "people should know the problems women face in sannyasa" (what Anand Mata said after reading portions of this book) or "women don't need sannyasa" (which was a comment made by several sannyasinis)? The contextual subtlety of these messages are crucial for understanding both the relevance and irrelevance of gender, the tension between worldly and otherworldly values, commentaries about hypocrisy and authenticity, and how renouncers interact differently with, and construct different messages for, lay and monastic disciples, anthropologists, and other sadhus.[1] All these are related to the notion of contextually defined paths.

Sannyasa as an Institution: Sociological Messiness

Sannyasa, as one possible path to liberation, is ideally a single-minded pursuit of spiritual liberation that demands a total and permanent break from the ordinary household interests and activities of the Hindu laity. As such, it is considered by its initiates to be the most intense (and the "highest") of religious paths. To take sannyasa is both a radical and irreversible move. One does not try out renunciation as one might experiment with hatha yoga, meditation, or the ritual worship of a particular deity. Thus, individuals must prove their readiness to a guru before receiving initiation into sannyasa. For initiates to fail in their vows and return to the very family life that they earlier renounced is a matter of serious disgrace. While sannyasa does not demand that its initiates take up any specific lifestyle or spiritual discipline, it does require that they permanently and totally give up their previous identities as householders. Household life is aimed at the moral and material prosperity of one's family, so householders are expected to be concerned with getting married, having children, earning money, offering hospitality to guests, performing ritual sacrifice, worshipping gods and ancestors, and generally following the rules of moral conduct (dharma) as defined according to social class, stage of life, and gender (obviously this is a high-caste construction of the ideal household life). The goal of following one's dharma is to ensure prosperity in this life and the next. Renouncers, by contrast, are concerned not with a good rebirth but with liberation from the cycle of birth, death, and rebirth.

According to sannyasa's Advaita philosophy one attains liberation when one's *atma* (individual soul) frees itself from the body in order to unite with Paramatma (Universal Soul) or Brahman (Ultimate Reality or Impersonal Absolute, not to be confused with the "creator" god Brahma or the caste status Brahmin). More accurately, *moksha* (liberation) is the realization, which can come gradually after decades of discipline or instantaneously in a moment of grace, that *atma* and Brahman are and have always been the same and that, ultimately, nothing else is real. In order to achieve this goal, renouncers adopt an attitude of indifference toward their parents, spouses, siblings, children, and family events such as weddings or funerals. Having conquered all passions, conventionally identified as lust, anger, desire, attachment, and ego, they remain always calm, unruffled by the events of the material and temporal world. Renouncers are expected to face whatever obstacles come their way without fear or frustration. This shift in mental outlook is accompanied by a change in social and legal identity. Initiates leave home, cease to recognize marital and family obligations, vow to remain celibate, beg for food, discard all possessions, abandon their means of employment, forfeit all legal claim to family property, and replace their birth name with one given by the guru.

While the classic renunciant profile still enjoys widespread currency *as an ideal*, it does not characterize the values, personal goals, and life experiences of most contemporary renouncers. Many subsist on food provided by ashrams rather than begging door-to-door. And most have some possessions, perhaps even possessions so valuable as homes and land.[2] More importantly, female renouncers, by definition, do not fit the image of the archetypal renouncer. That the initiation ceremony emphasizes the abandonment of Vedic ritual reveals that the archetypal renouncer described above is also a high-caste male since only they were qualified to perform the ritual in the first place. If women and low-caste men are forbidden from performing Vedic sacrifice, as they have been historically, they are not in a position to renounce it. Women, by definition, have an ambivalent relationship to the renunciant ideal and reject elements of it on both practical and ideological grounds. For example, considerations of safety and reputation mean that the solitary, itinerant lifestyle is particularly unappealing to women. It is not surprising that the women featured here speak from diverse ideological positions, including those of classical renunciant values, conventional femininity, and a modernized neo-Hinduism.

Even though sannyasa is a radical form of asceticism, within the category of renouncer the range of acceptable values, lifestyles, spiritual practices, modes of interaction with householders, and dress is so great that one can speak only tentatively of patterns and hardly at all of constants. This can be attributed to sectarian complexity, nonbrahmanical influences, and a tolerance for independent renouncers. The lack of sociological specificity is evident in many general studies of Hindu asceticism written from sociological and anthropological perspectives (Burghart 1983a, 1983b; Ghurye 1964; Gross 1992; Miller and Wertz 1976; Sinha and Saraswati 1978; Tripathi 1978). Depending on sectarian affiliation, renouncers may eat only what is received from begging (having vowed not to touch a cooking fire) or refuse to accept food cooked by others. They may follow elaborate rules of ritual purity or deliberately ignore them. There are few statistics about the general population of contemporary renouncers.[3]

Sannyasa as an Idea: Singular Aim

It is easier to generalize about the goals of sannyasa than about its sociology. The singular aim of sannyasa is, of course, the attainment of knowledge (*jnana*) or liberation (*moksha*). To this end, renouncers cultivate an attitude of detachment (*vairagya*) toward the transient world. To have *vairagya* is to remain indifferent to illness, pain, loneliness, sensual temptation, material goods, uncertainty, fear, and even insults. Thus, one sannyasini noted that cultivating detachment does not mean that one cannot experience pleasure or enjoyment. "If someone offers you an ice cream," she explained, "it is alright to enjoy eating that ice cream, but, having eaten it, you should not feel desire to have it again." A common theme in popular narratives about ascetic detachment is testing the ability of a sadhu to resist temptation. In the version narrated to me by one sannyasini, a sadhu sits in a meditative trance while some people who were evading work and had nothing better to do try to disrupt his concentration. "These mischievous loafers," she said, "dressed a prostitute to look really beautiful and sent her to his side . . . to degrade him. She sat beside the sadhu and tried to attract his attention by jingling her anklets and bangles. Suddenly, his eyes opened, and he said 'Mother, what do you want?' The prostitute was so surprised, 'No one has ever addressed me as mother,' she said, 'Everybody comes to me with lust in their eyes.' Immediately, she removed all her jewelry and pleaded, 'Make me your disciple. I was sent by those wicked, sinful people to degrade you.' The sadhu declined, told her she was pure, and instructed her to worship god. Eventually she too became a sadhu." In accordance with sannyasa's emphasis on celibacy and detachment, there are many stories about male sadhus who demonstrate their lack of desire by addressing a beautiful woman as "mother" and more humorous ones in which the male sadhu is less successful. Detachment is central to the definition of sannyasa. Indeed, this attitude is sometimes seen as a prerequisite for taking sannyasa rather than its goal. Several renouncers I met explained detachment using the metaphor of fruit ripening on a tree. A tree automatically drops or "renounces" its fruit when the fruit becomes ripe, while unripe fruit must be forcibly plucked. Similarly, persons who feel detachment toward worldly life simply and easily let go of it, since it holds no meaning for them. Such a person is "ripe" for sannyasa compared to someone who is still attached to family, sensual pleasures, possessions and status, and must, therefore, wrench themselves away from worldly life.

Spiritual liberation, conceived as escape from *samsara*, can be accomplished in various ways. Denton has noted an ambiguity in ascetics' use of the word *samsara*. "The word appears to have two different, overlapping meanings: on the one hand, it clearly refers to the cycle of life, death and rebirth that results in the repeated transmigration of the soul; on the other, it refers to the world of human relations which, from the ascetic perspective, is the foremost social expression of this cycle" (Denton 1991:215). Renouncers, then, seek eternal release from *samsara*, perceived as either the cycle of rebirths or social relationships, particularly family, that constitute worldly life. Burghart (1983a:642–43) has argued, contra Dumont, that ascetics define themselves in opposition to competing ascetic orders, not to householders. Moreover, ascetics view themselves as escaping the transient world of *samsara*, which they may or may not define as the social world of caste. Thus, individual renouncers might direct their attitude of indifference toward caste distinctions, family relationships, wealth, security, food, obligations, pride, or even the desire for liberation itself. This "contentless" definition of sannyasa is responsible, in part, for what I will argue is the "indeterminacy" of this tradition.[4]

Sannyasa as a Category: Restricted and General Meanings

In ordinary conversation, the word sannyasa has both a restricted and general sense. Its restricted usage refers to the Dashnami renunciant orders ostensibly founded in the eighth century by Shankara (but, see Hacker 1964:29). This monastic federation is divided into ten ascetic lineages, which have separate names but all trace their spiritual descent from Shankara (Dazey 1990:284). The ideological roots of the Dashnami Order lie in the philosophy of absolute monism, Advaita Vedanta, which posits the existence of an Ultimate Reality called Brahman that is without attributes or form. Corresponding to Brahman is the *atma* (individual soul) residing within each person, which originates from and, eventually (at the time of liberation), merges back into Brahman as a drop of water merges into an ocean. Those seeking advaitic knowledge need not practice the devotional worship of gods and goddesses so popular in India, since they see the self and its objects of devotion as ultimately the same.[5] Nor must they perform Vedic sacrifice since they do not desire the worldly benefits that Hindu householders hope to gain from sacrifice and since they have symbolically internalized the sacrificial fire. According to Dashnami renouncers then, the *atma* that resides within each person is one and the same as the abstract Brahman. A correlate of this philosophical belief regarding the unity of *atma* and Brahman is the idea that renouncers themselves are beyond all dualities, oblivious to distinctions of purity and impurity, pain and pleasure, wealth and poverty, female and male. Although British colonial and Indian nationalist discourses have tended to equate Advaita (or neo-Advaita) with Hindu thought itself, most Indian Hindus are not followers of this extreme, transcendent philosophy (King 1999:128–42).

How do Dashnami renouncers fit into the larger landscape of Hindu asceticism? Two of the most general sectarian categories divide Hindus into followers of either Lord Shiva or Lord Vishnu. Although there is evidence that Shankara and his immediate disciples may have favored Vishnu rather than Shiva, the entire Order has been regarded as Shaiva since the medieval period.[6] Lord Shiva, destroyer of the universe and patron deity of many contemporary renouncers, is himself the quintessential ascetic of the Hindu pantheon. He is frequently portrayed in the garb of a wandering ascetic, his body smeared with ashes and the Ganges River flowing from his matted locks.[7] Competing systems of Vedanta philosophy were established by Ramanuja and Madhava and offered alternative, Vaishnava forms of asceticism.[8] Since Vaishnava ascetics, who wear yellow or white, are usually called by other terms such as "*bairagi*" and "*tyagi,*" the terms "sannyasi" and "sannyasini," in their restricted sense, usually refer specifically to Shaiva renouncers.

Dashnami renouncers, as Shaivas, must be distinguished not only from their Vaishnava counterparts but also from other Shaiva ascetics. Nathapanthis (also called Kanphata Yogis) represent another major brand of Shaiva asceticism found primarily in North India. Influenced by Tantrism, they emphasize the practice of yogic postures (*hatha yoga*), seek to attain extraordinary magical and psychic powers (*siddhis*), and are commonly referred to simply as *yogis* or *jogis.*[9] Another variety of Shaiva ascetics is the Virashaivas (also called Lingayats). Most Virashaivas are householders, and they are located almost exclusively in Karnataka, South India.[10] Dashnami renouncers are more widespread and numerous than either the Nathpanthis or Virashaivas, and it is to them that the words "sannyasi" and "sannyasini" primarily refer. Other ascetic traditions are beyond the scope of this work.

Sannyasa, however, should not be completely equated with the Dashnami Order as represented by its monastic abbots, for the tradition has retained a high degree of philosophical and sociological diversity along sectarian lines. More importantly perhaps, it has also continued to allow the proliferation of independent renouncers who hold no substantial institutional or group affiliation. Those initiated into a Dashnami lineage need not maintain affiliation with the order. Moreover, it is possible (if not legally recognized) for one to simply don the ochre robes without formal initiation and live independently of a monastic center. Thus, according to Dazey, the centralization of the Advaita tradition is balanced by the decentralization of the wandering sannyasis (1990:308). Miller and Wertz note that solitary wandering ascetics are more likely to incorporate popular ideas and practices, in contrast to those who follow "pure" Advaita (1976:27). Focusing on independent, if not wandering, women renouncers reminds us that sannyasa is not essentially constituted of the Dashnami monasteries. Indeed, it suggests that sannyasa as it is practiced outside the monastic structures is an eclectic and dynamic contemporary practice.

In their more general meanings, then, the terms "sannyasi" and "sannyasini" refer to those ascetics who have rejected worldly and family life for the single-minded pursuit of liberation, even if they have not been initiated into one of the ten Dashnami Orders (though most have been). It is this general, nontechnical meaning of sannyasa that I intend when I use the word here. Shankara emphasized rigorous discipline, Sanskrit learning, and Advaita philosophy, and today's Dashnami renouncers often have a modern, secular education as well. This ideal has relevance beyond the strict boundaries of the Dashnami Order. "Sannyasis" and "sannyasinis" then, in popular usage, refer to renouncers who wear the ochre robes of Shaiva renunciation and *more or less* model themselves after the Dashnamis. They are expected to have renounced family life (both literally and emotionally), remain celibate, own few or no possessions, maintain a strict vegetarian diet, eschew liquor, follow some form of spiritual discipline or austerities, and embrace Advaitic monism. Renouncers outside the Dashnami Order may be independent or associated with an alternative monastic institution. The modern Arya Samaj and Ramakrishna Order, for example, have Dashnami origins, but their own interpretation of sannyasa and their own institutions; both initiate men and women into sannyasa and use Dashnami terminology. When referring to ascetic women who are not sannyasinis in this general sense, I identify them in terms of their particular status as religious practitioners, such as *brahmacharini* (female celibate student).[11]

A History of Tensions, Debates, and Compromises

Archeological evidence from the Indus Valley civilization suggests that ascetic practices on the subcontinent may date as far back as the third millennium B.C.E.[12] However, historians' primary source of knowledge about ancient Indian asceticism is scriptural rather than archeological, and religious texts indicate that ascetic practices flourished in northern India during the first millennium B.C.E. The corpus of ancient Sanskrit literature composed around this time indicates a wide spectrum of attitudes toward ascetic practices, ranging from outright hostility to glorification. The ideal of earlier Vedic theology was a married householder who studied the scriptures, fulfilled ritual obligations, and fathered sons, while the ideal person of the Upanishadic period was a celibate ascetic who shunned rituals and withdrew from family and society (Olivelle 1995).

The Vedic period (approximately 1500–600 B.C.E.) is associated with the earliest body of Indian literature known as the Vedas and the social dominance of the Brahmin or priestly class. Its system of beliefs, ideas, and rituals is referred to as "the brahmanical tradition," which has provided a systematic interpretation of social and religious behavior that many consider normative in India (Embree 1988:5). Its normativity, however, is a contested domain, since the voice of brahmanical Hinduism is by definition upper-caste and male. The main concern of Vedic religion was the proper performance of elaborate ritual fire sacrifices by highly trained Brahmin priests, the purpose of which was to ensure progeny and material prosperity for the patrilineal family. The earliest and most important of these texts, the *Rig Veda*, tends to refer to ascetics with words (*yati, muni, rishi*) that have connotations of magic, mystical rites, meditation and religious ecstasy, while later Vedic literature uses terms (*tapasvin, sramana, sannyasin, parivrajaka, yogi*) that suggest renunciation, the casting off of social obligations, a life of aus-terities, wandering, and the control of such bodily functions as breathing (Thapar 1984:67–68). The terminology suggests a historical shift in the purpose and meaning of ascetic practices, from an ancient magico-religious mysticism to something closer to the classical Dashnami ideal.

Toward the end of the Vedic period, texts began to appear in which Vedic ritual was attributed with symbolic meaning, and understanding this mystical meaning became even more important than actually performing the rite (Embree 1988:29). A collection of texts called the Upanishads were composed during a period of great social, economic, and religious turmoil on the subconti-nent and reflect a shift from Vedic ritualism to new ideas and institutions (Olivelle 1998:3).[13] They also represent a major challenge to priestly religious authority and contain philosophical speculations about the nature of the human soul and its relationship to the cosmos. The Upanishads reflect the perspective of sages rather than priests and, as such, provide a mystical interpretation of the Vedas. In addition to switching from a literal to a symbolic interpretation of ritual sacrifice, the Upanishads also represented a shift in ideas about rebirth and the doctrine of karma. Karma refers to the fruits of past deeds, both good and bad, that cause rebirth. While the Vedas taught people to perform meritori-ous and ritual acts in order to ensure prosperity in their next life, the Upanishads held out the possibility that people could eliminate karma altogether through mystical and ascetic practices and thereby attain eternal release from rebirth. As the final stage in the development of Vedic philosophy, the Upanishads represent the "end of the Vedas" (*vedanta*), so later philosophical schools of classical Hinduism that are based on the Upanishads are referred to as Vedanta (Embree 1988:29). In claiming superiority of ascetic practices over ritual sacrifice, the Upanishads provide the primary textual authority for con-temporary renunciation.

In general, the history of sannyasa can be seen as a continual process of dis-sent and neutralization, a tug-of-war between these two broad value systems central to Indian culture. On the one hand, an institutionalist orientation of brahmanical orthodoxy gives primacy to household and family prosperity, ritual sacrifice, Vedic learning, and the system of *varnashramadharma* (moral duty defined according to social class, life-stage, and gender). On the other hand, the otherworldly philosophy of Advaita Vedanta, as expounded in the Upanishads, emphasizes experiential and experimental knowledge over scholasticism and glo-rifies renunciation as the way to truth. Advaita insists on the unity of Brahman and *atma* and on the illusory, transient nature of everything else and thus encourages its adherents to ignore social institutions and distinctions (of social class, life-stage, and gender) as worldly, and, thus, ultimately unreal. Of course, as we will see, a dialogue between worldly and otherworldly realities occurs within sannyasa.

The Monastic Centers as Forces of Institutionalization

The parallel processes of domestication and dissent can be identified at the level of religious movements, particular orders, and individual renouncers.[14] Renunciation seems to have originated as an individual practice but has tended to become increasingly monastic over time. For most of its early history, argues Thapar (1984), renouncers typically wandered alone or lived in isolated caves and forests on the fringes of society. There was no organization to speak for their interests, provide them with food and shelter, or formulate rules of behavior. Indeed, such an institution would have seemed antithetical to renouncers of the ancient period, as the very purpose of sannyasa was to rise above personal interests, physical needs, and social mores. The gradual organization of ascetics into monastic orders during the first millennium B.C.E., following the rise in the numbers of ascetics, may have had several causes. On a practical level, Thapar points out, itinerant sadhus needed a place to live during the monsoon when flooding made travel difficult and sometimes impossible. Also, they may have sought an institutional base in order to counter the hostility of political elites, for kings and other authorities tended to view itinerant holy men as loafers who simply wanted to avoid social or political responsibilities. There was a rise in sectarian groups during the first millennium B.C.E., though many of these monasteries were connected to the heterodox sects of Buddhism and Jainism. After the first millennium C.E., the wane of heterodox movements in North India was accompanied by a rise in Hindu monasticism, specifically the Dashnami Orders (Thapar 1984:87–92). Thus, Hindu renunciation as a noninstitutional, even anti-institutional, religious practice dates back at least to the first millennium B.C.E., but it did not acquire an organizational framework until much later.

Thapar argues that the gradual monasticization of renouncers had the effect of moving some away from the ideal of the solitary wanderer, possessing neither wealth nor political interest. Donations of wealth and property made administrative duties necessary, and this inevitably led to more hierarchy within the order than had previously existed among renouncers. The material prosperity of the monasteries was furthered by their exemption from paying taxes, and those with rich endowments were especially likely to seek out a political role. In general, monastic institutions, emphasizing group action, discipline, and rules, were not appropriate places for those seeking absolute freedom defined in advaitic terms. Thus, Thapar argues, the evolution of renunciant institutions toward a greater participation in secular life was in a sense self-annihilating. Householders made contributions (*dan*) to renouncers and gained spiritual merit (*punya*) in return. Ironically, the donations were sometimes of a nature that enabled the monastery to exist independently, resulting in its increasing distance from the lay community. When this occurred, reciprocity decreased and the anti-institutional, world-rejecting quality of sannyasa was undermined. Thus, the renunciant sects themselves have changed over time, as the development of monastic institutions undermined sannyasa's tendency toward social protest (Thapar 1984:87–92).

However, the dissent-inspiring philosophy of Advaita ensured that sannyasa did not become completely controlled by monastic centers. When particular orders or individual renouncers were seen as having moved too far from the ascetic ideal, they were denounced, and sometimes individuals dissatisfied with monastic life took a solitary path in search of salvation. Even today it is not uncommon for renouncers to leave their sectarian institution for a lone path, and this move may involve an implicit or explicit critique of monastic and sectarian religiosity. Anand Mata, for example, left the camaraderie of fellow disciples in her guru's metropolitan ashram and began an intense discipline of silence and solitude. Baiji spent most of the year in her Haridwar ashram, heavily engaged in advising lay disciples, overseeing rituals, and organizing social service activities. However, she would leave this ashram periodically to spend time in a Himalayan ashram, almost, it seemed, as a way of renouncing her socially engaged renunciation. In the midst of the historical process of institutionalization, the idealized image of the solitary wanderer has retained validity and prevents sannyasa from becoming entirely institutionalized. The otherworldly advaitic roots of renunciation create a climate in which "walking away from it all" continues to have spiritual legitimacy. Through the centuries, the wandering ascetic who did not join any order and lived in isolation has remained the ultimate symbol of dissent. Today there is an acceptance of independent renouncers who reject institutional affiliation, although, as will be discussed in chapter 5, this acceptance is tempered by a cynical popular discourse warning of thieves, megalomaniacs, and sexual predators posing as ascetics. Thus, in the midst of increasing institutionalization, the countervailing advaitic tendency continually deconstructs social institutions and distinctions.

Rethinking Analytical Oppositions

These competing pulls of transcendent Advaita ideology on the one hand and social engagement and institutions on the other have been mapped onto the distinction between sannyasa and household life (*grihastha*), such that renunciation is understood as the rejection of the goals, values, and practices of household life. Dumont and Heesterman were among the first to seriously analyze renunciation in sociological and indological terms. Dumont (1980) posited a dialectical opposition between Brahmin householder as exemplar of the interdependence of caste society and renouncer as exemplar of the individualism of sannyasa. True individualism, according to Dumont, has no place in Indian society (defined as a system of interdependent and hierarchical castes) and, thus, can only exist outside of society in the world of renunciation. Accordingly, the Brahmin householder and the protesting renouncer represent mutually exclusive, if complementary, worlds. Although Dumont himself was not concerned with the role of gender in this model, logically speaking, women would be associated exclusively with householder life even if they do not exemplify it.

As both an indologist working from texts and a structuralist concerned with grand civilizational issues, Heesterman (1985), unlike many critics, approaches Dumont on his own terms. Heesterman's understanding of Hinduism highlights Vedic ritual rather than caste. In a critique of Dumont's opposition between the Brahmin and renouncer, Heesterman argues that the *ideal* Brahmin is one who *renounces* priesthood and ritual, so that the Brahmin's true role is renunciation rather than caste-imbedded priesthood. More importantly, he argues that renunciant values are inherent in Vedic ritual rather than anti-brahmanical. While Heesterman provides a convincing critique of Dumont's opposition between Brahmin and renouncer, his model nonetheless proposed another unresolvable conflict—between the atemporal order of renunciation and the sociopolitical realm of change. Thus, renunciation is still opposed to society, at least at an ideological level, and it remains absolutely transcendent, unchanging, and individualistic. The renouncer is seen as "turning his back on the world" and "leaving the world for good" (Heesterman 1985:4–5).

While the exact terms of their oppositions differ, both Dumont and Heesterman assume not a distinction but a fundamental ideological opposition between an otherworldly renunciation and the social world, the latter essentialized as caste by Dumont and kinship by Heesterman. Most scholars agree that household life, as the center of kinship and material concerns, does in some sense stand for the Hindu social world. That the householder and renouncer follow incompatible sets of values has also been widely accepted in the scholarship of India, though some scholars have brought attention to the ways in which Indian thought has attempted to resolve the contradiction (see, for example, O'Flaherty 1981:78–79). The householder-renouncer opposition has become central to anthropological and indological understandings of Hindu culture. Imbedded within this opposition as it has come to be used is the following set of analogies:

$$\begin{array}{ccc}
\text{Renouncer} & :: & \text{Householder} \\
\text{Otherworldly} & :: & \text{Worldly} \\
\text{Ascetic Withdrawal} & :: & \text{Social Engagement} \\
\text{Male World of Asceticism} & :: & \text{Female World of Domesticity}
\end{array}$$

Focusing on sannyasinis requires disentangling this dichotomous framework, which renders them logical impossibilities. Although my intent in conducting this research was to dispense with the structural framework altogether, my observations have led me to take a less radical stance: to speak of tensions rather than oppositions and to retain distinctions while separating analogies. While there is evidence for positing these two lifestyles as logical and mutually exclusive opposites, especially when talking at the level of abstractions, highlighting individual lives not only suggests a distinction rather than an opposition but also brings into focus unrecognized aspects of the practice and interpretation of sannyasa by contemporary initiates. We see, for example, that renouncers may in fact maintain connections with their families, although the nature of the relationship changes once they take sannyasa. Similarly, we observe that managing an ashram is not unlike managing a home. We learn too that while renouncers do not explicitly labor for wages, many freely discuss the reciprocity that exists in their relationships with householders. That this relationship can sometimes get perilously close to wage labor is a frequent subject of humor and sarcasm when, for example, disreputable renouncers are dubbed "professionals" and their activities referred to as "setting up shop." As the work of other ethnographers has also suggested, the competing ideals of social involvement and ascetic withdrawal are more accurately understood, not in terms of absolute opposition, but difference (Burghart 1983a; Narayan 1989; Gold 1989a; Sinclair-Brull 1997). "Tension" conveys a sense that competing pulls are not simply logical or philosophical, but emotional and social as well. Renouncers exist in society, but are not supposed to be *of* it. This simple fact creates not only dilemmas that must be negotiated but also ironies central to a renunciant way of life.

My second claim is that the tension between engagement and withdrawal exists *within* sannyasa, not just between a socially engaged householder life and renunciant withdrawal. Sannyasinis speak in both otherworldly and worldly voices, and not as if the latter were simply a corruption of the former. They may perform Vedic ritual, worship in temples, acknowledge the importance of social distinctions, and involve themselves deeply in the social concerns of householders, though their attitude toward these activities is expected to be different, detached, since it is informed by Advaita philosophy. "Ironically, the act of renunciation may in fact push an ascetic into more extensive social involvement than if he or she remained a layperson" (Narayan 1989:80). The social involvement of particular renouncers varies in both nature and degree, but it was not seen by the women I met as antithetical to renunciation. Social involvement was not necessarily "selling out." At the same time the tension here is real. For example, when householders view a particular renouncer as especially detached, and spiritually elevated, they seek to honor him or her by offering worldly and spiritual authority, personal adoration, and material comforts—all of which may present dilemmas for the renouncer. As Van der Veer has noted for Ramanandi sadhus, "[t]he more liberated he is from the restraining societal and physical bodies thanks to his ascetic feats, the more he will be surrounded socially by ascetic and lay followers" (1987:684). While renouncers' social activities and relationships may be seen by some as a corruption of authentic renunciation, it may also, and with equal legitimacy, be seen as integral to spiritual discipline. For example, achieving the Advaita ideal of seeing no difference between oneself and others may cause one to feel the suffering of others as if it were one's own and, perhaps, to become involved in their worldly problems in order to alleviate suffering. In other contexts, Advaita ideals may lead one to refuse to become involved, throw all social and material distinctions into question, and affirm the superiority of experiential knowledge over ritual and book learning. Just as renouncers may feel a sense of social responsibility, so too do many male and female householders aspire to cultivate detachment within the contexts of pilgrimage, devotional ritual, or the intense sociality of Indian family life (Gold 1989; Madan 1987; Daniel 1984; Pearson 1996). The difference is that for renouncers it is their primary goal, but the tension between these alternative goals is one that both ascetics and householders must negotiate.

Olivelle describes this tension from a textual perspective: "Attempts to blunt the opposition between domesticity and celibate asceticism were at best only partially successful" (1995:542). I explore how it is manifested and dealt with in the everyday lives of particular women renouncers. The apparently conflicting ideals of engagement and withdrawal represent ends of a continuum and the sannyasinis I met struck their own compromises between them. Although the particular expression of these ideals may have changed in the last century, it has historical precedence in the parallel tendencies of monasticism and dissent previously discussed. More attention to the range and diversity of renunciant ideologies and practices, and the contradictions resulting from competing aims, helps to counter both romantic and ethnocentric stereotypes that portray renouncers as either transcendent, serene saints existing outside society or corrupt frauds driven by economic and political self-interest.[15] Since sannyasa is informed by both Advaita philosophy and monastic institutionalism, I distinguish between these two strands *within* renunciation rather than opposing otherworldly renunciation and worldly society. For this reason, I speak not of householder and renouncer, but, rather of engagement and withdrawal, worldly and otherworldly, or, depending on context, the institutions of brahmanical orthodoxy and the transcendence of Advaita.

Finally, this tension is assumed to be gendered in predictable ways. Until recently scholars have taken for granted that women are always associated with household life and ascetics are always men, or, if not actual men, then symbolic males. Interestingly, Olivelle (1995) details an argument from the epic *Mahabharata* that reverses the ordinary gender associations of the conflict. The argument is between the famous king Janaka and a female ascetic named Sulabha who hears the news of Janaka's claim that he has attained liberation without abandoning his throne or household life. Sulabha wanted to test Janaka's claim, so she used her yogic powers to enter his body.

> Janaka goes on to admonish Sulabha about the impropriety of her entering his body. Taking her to be a brahman, Janaka asserts that she has thus created a confusion of castes. He then inquires who she is and where she comes from. In her response, Sulabha points to these questions as demonstrating Janaka's lack of true knowledge. A man who is liberated would not ask such questions. Sulabha thus exposes the fallacy that a householder, in this case a king, can acquire the liberating knowledge without abandoning home and family. (Olivelle 1995:546)

This scriptural passage offers a critique of the analogies that equate maleness with asceticism, even if it retains the equation between withdrawal and genuine knowledge. Actual sannyasinis at times deconstruct even the latter.

Female Renunciation: Legitimacy and Historicity

The Upanishads' turn away from ritual toward contemplation, meditation, and asceticism had positive and negative implications for women. According to Katherine Young (1987), if ancient Vedic religion was centered in the home and oriented toward fulfilling people's desire for children, material prosperity, and long lives, women as wives and mothers were crucial to the family's success. Moreover, their participation in Vedic fire sacrifice (as wife of the sponsor) was considered necessary to maintain cosmic order. Thus, even if subordinated to men, women were central to Vedic religion.[16] While one might expect that the Upanishads' new emphasis on meditation and ascetic practices, over Vedic learning and ritual, would have had a positive effect on women's religious status, the new approach was in fact androcentric in its goals and represented a critique of family and household life. Serenity Young observes that asceticism's androcentrism and emphasis on celibacy often "leaves women with the rather tiresome and religiously paralyzing role of sexual temptress"(1994:73). Katherine Young notes that religious and social changes also led to increasing educational disparities between men and women, and by the first century B.C.E. women were equated with low-caste Shudras and denied access to Vedic learning. Women came to be associated with both the household and ignorance, and it was assumed that women as a class aspire to a good rebirth rather than to the higher aim of liberation from the cycle of rebirths (K.Young 1987:69 and 2002:90–91). Insofar as these changes undercut the authority of priests, they also created new opportunities for those persons endowed with spiritual insight, which included some priests but also kings and women (Jaini cited in S.Young 1994:76). Thus, as will be discussed below, learned and possibly ascetic women appear in scripture.

Classical Sanskrit texts have much to say about who is eligible to take sannyasa, and, according to Olivelle, only when these discussions about eligibility focus on internal dispositions like detachment rather than external qualifications like Vedic learning are women included. When the question is addressed from the point of view of external, social qualifications the main point of debate is caste rather than gender. While all brahmanical authorities opposed the initiation of Shudras and outcasts, there is no consensus on the issue of whether only Brahmins or all twice-born men[17] should be allowed to take sannyasa (Olivelle 1977:33). Nor is there agreement, across historical periods and textual traditions, about women's eligibility for initiation.

Olivelle stresses the importance of distinguishing between the legality of female renunciation, its historicity, and its legitimacy in the eyes of dharma (1984:113). Dharma, usually glossed as "duty," is understood to refer to Hindu rules of right behavior that maintain the moral order of the universe. The attitude of the Dharmashastra literature toward female renunciation is more implicit than explicit. [These texts address every detail of the ideal life of Hindu men and women and, significantly, were considered by the British to be the most important and reliable source of Hindu law and custom.] Theoretically, women were unfit to renounce for the same reasons that low-caste Shudras were prohibited, since later brahmanical sources often equated women with Shudras:[18] neither were entitled to Vedic initiation or Vedic study, two basic prerequisites of sannyasa according to the Dharmashastras. The classical initiation ritual for sannyasa symbolizes an internalization of the Vedic sacrifice, so that, from that point on, the renouncer makes offerings to the internal atma rather than to the sacrificial fire. McGee (2002) has problematized accepted ideas about the fact of, and possible reasons for, women's ineligibility for Vedic learning and ritual in early Hinduism. Still, according to classical orthodoxy, women were prohibited from independently performing Vedic sacrifice, and excluded from undergoing the initiatory rite of sannyasa. Moreover, the Dharmashastras clearly state that the proper role of women (stridharma) is to be under the protection and control of men throughout their lives. That renunciation implied freedom and independence would in itself render it inappropriate for women. Classical Hinduism posits four stages that a man passes through during the course of his lifetime: celibate student, married householder, retired hermit, and renouncer. Classical thinkers viewed the ashramas (life-stages) as the appropriate sequence of stages in the life of a high-caste male, and excluded women from all except that of married householder.[19] However, even in the Dharmashastras, which as a whole prohibit female renunciation, it is written that a widowed queen, if she prefers, may renounce rather than be maintained by the new king (Olivelle 1984:114-5). Moreover, the Yatidharmaprakasa, a treatise on renunciation from within the tradition of Dharmashastra, admits that women are entitled to renounce (Olivelle 1977:34). With some exceptions then, brahmanical thought as expressed in the Dharmashastras generally considered female renunciation to be illegitimate (Olivelle 1984:114–5; Chakraborti 1973:94; Rukmani 2002:xi).

While Hindu law was derived from religious concepts of right behavior, it was never identical to those concepts. Dharma describes the rules of proper conduct according to the dominant Hindu moral order. "But the rule of dharma can only become a rule of law by a process beyond the expression of it, a process which enables it to enter society armed with a power of constraint which is not inherent in it" (Lingat 1973:xiii).[20] Actual laws relating to renunciation, and specifically female renunciation, did exist in early Indian history. The ancient lawmaker Manu had a low opinion of female renouncers and imposed a small fine on those who secretly conversed with them. The political theorist Kautilya legislated against initiating female ascetics (Chakraborti 1973:94–98). That he imposed a minimal fine on those who had sexual intercourse with a female renouncer indicates that he shared Manu's low opinion of such women. In contrast, Vi and Narada considered sex with a female renouncer as a crime equal to that of violating the teacher's bed (Olivelle 1984:114–15). Of course, that there were laws regulating female renunciation allows us to infer that it did exist.

As Rukmani notes, "there are plenty of examples both in the Epics and in literary works that tell us of the presence of women *saṃnyāsinīs*" (2002:xi). Although it can be inferred that female renouncers were a visible presence in ancient times and that they have existed throughout Indian history, little is known about their numbers in the past or what their lives were like. King (1984) and Ramaswamy (1997) see widespread social changes during the last hundred years or so as having made sannyasa more accessible to contemporary Indian women. Since some previously all-male monastic institutions have begun to admit women during the last two centuries and since modern times have seen a growth in women-only monastic institutions, I concur that there are probably more sannyasinis today than in the past. In the final analysis, whatever scholars might say about the historicity of female renunciation is speculative. Still, given the three obstacles that faced women interested in the ascetic life—their sexuality, the cultural emphasis on marriage, and the solitary nature of ascetic life—it is remarkable that there were any at all (S. Young 1994:75).

Colonial-era reform movements and the secular Indian women's movement have had significant reverberations in the area of religion. During the late-nineteenth century and early-twentieth century, both foreign missionaries and Indian nationalists, including reformist sannyasis like Vivekananda and Dayananda, criticized orthodox attitudes toward women and promoted women's education in secular and religious fields.[21] As part of his social program to uplift the poor masses for the sake of India's renewal, Swami Vivekananda promoted women's access to secular and religious education, insisted on a separate and independent monastic center for women, and felt that sannyasinis had an important role to play in strengthening national life (King 1984:75). Ursula King notes that gradually women have been allowed to learn Sanskrit, thereby gaining access to sacred knowledge. Late in the nineteenth century, the Arya Samaj revived Vedic ritual and granted women the right to perform it (Ibid.: 73–74). The Arya Samaj justifies women's access to Vedic study and ritual as a return to an original, golden Vedic era in which both sexes were equal and educated in Sanskrit. Following the wishes of Swami Vivekananda, the Ramakrishna Order established Sarada Math as a monastic institution for women, to be legally independent from its men's counterpart but run along parallel lines; in 1959 eight women were given initiation into sannyasa with full rites, as practiced by the Ramakrishna Order (Sinclair-Brull 1997:74–75). Women's self-understanding in modern India includes leadership in women's organizations, social service roles, higher education, monastic training, and participation in ritual (King 1984). Even if women's emergence into public roles of religious leadership has been linked to masculine projects, women became active agents in this process (Falk 1995). Several sannyasinis I met expressed their awareness of the secular women's movement in India and their agreement with its goals.

Not Just Sita: Alternative Models of Femininity in Hindu Scripture

Feminist scholars have had much to say about what are admittedly the most widely circulating models of Hindu femininity, including Sita and Draupadi, and have debated the feminist possibilities of these figures (Mankekar 1999; Sunder Rajan 1999). Hansen's essay on heroic women (1988) and Oldenburg's work on the courtesans of Lucknow (1990) show that alternative, if less accessible, models of femininity have existed in Indian history. In my conversations with sannyasinis, the names of other, less-known, female figures consistently came up—women attributed with spiritual knowledge and power and not identified primarily as wives and mothers.

Two women who were learned, and possibly ascetic as well, appear in the first Upanishad, the *Brhadaranyaka*. Findly (1985) offers a complex analysis of the philosophical tournament in which the learned woman Gargi emerges as a prominent figure. The tournament occurs in King Janaka's court on the eve of the historical decline in women's intellectual life and the shift from ritualism to contemplation. King Janaka offers a prize of enormous quantities of cows and gold coins to whoever among the Brahmins present can demonstrate true knowledge of Brahman. As the teacher Yajnavalkya asks his student to drive the cows home, the other Brahmins present become angry at his presumptuousness. By turn, each poses a question to Yajnavalkya to determine whether he is indeed the most knowledgeable among them. In the ensuing interrogation, Gargi, the only one to speak twice, distinguishes herself as the most astute, challenging, and learned of Yajnavalkya's philosophical interlocutors. Gargi is the one to affirm his true knowledge, and the other Brahmin men accept her evaluation. While Findly offers a subtle analysis of the literary and philosophical agenda of the text's composers and questions whether it should be considered feminist, she concludes that, in the figure of Gargi, the Indian tradition affirms "women as productive colleagues in the on-going search for truth" (1985:53).

Maitreyi, one of Yajnavalkya's two wives, appears in the *Brhadaranyaka Upanishad* as well (II.4.1–13 and IV.5.1–15, trans. Olivelle 1998). Of his wives, according to the text, Maitreyi takes part in theological discussions while Katyayani is knowledgeable in conventionally feminine matters. When

Yajnavalkya is about to renounce home and family for the life of a wandering ascetic, he calls Maitreyi to make arrangements to divide his wealth between his two wives. Maitreyi asks him whether all the wealth in the world would bring her immortality, and he replies that one cannot achieve immortality through wealth. "What is the point of getting something that will not make me immortal?" she retorts. "Tell me instead, sir, all that you know." Pleased, Yajnavalkya proceeds to instruct her with a philosophical discourse. While there is no evidence that Gargi and Maitreyi were ascetics rather than simply philosophers, several sannyasinis I interviewed held them up as exemplary women ascetics.

In the *Yoga Vasistha*, when a sage narrates a story to Ram about a royal couple, the queen Chudala emerges as a remarkably atypical devoted wife (VI, trans. Venkatesananda 1984).[22] We learn that the noble king Shikhidhvaja and his wife Chudala were devoted to each other and enjoyed the pleasures of palace life. They became learned in all fields of knowledge and began to study spiritual texts. Chudala, in contemplating the inertness of the physical body, the sensual organs, and even the intellect, arrived at the realization that the self is pure consciousness. Observing her to be enlightened and resting in peace, the king remarked: "You appear to have regained your youthfulness and you shine with an extraordinary radiance, my beloved. You are not distracted by anything at all, and you have no craving. Yet, you are full of bliss. Tell me: is it that you have drunk the nectar of the gods? Surely, you have attained something which is extremely difficult to attain" (Ibid.: 291). She responded with a discourse on what she had learned from the scriptures, but, unable to understand, he simply laughed, calling her childish and ignorant. Queen Chudala pitied him for his inability to understand, but continued to go about her work in the palace. They lived this way for some time (Ibid.: 288–92).

Meanwhile, Queen Chudala gained psychic powers that enabled her to travel through the sky, oceans, and earth and to enter into such substances as rock—without ever leaving the side of her husband. She moved with celestial beings and conversed with enlightened sages. Despite her efforts to enlighten him, King Shikhidhvaja remained ignorant, and she thought it unwise to display her powers before him. While continuing to perform his royal duties as his ministers advised him, the king gradually descended into delusion and grief. One day he asked Chudala permission to go to the forest and live as an ascetic. She replied that forest life is fine for old age, but that household life was appropriate for people of his age. "When we grow old," she exclaimed, "both of us shall leave this household life and go to the forest! Moreover, your subjects will grieve over your untimely departure from the kingdom" (Ibid.: 301). Dismissing her as childish and unsuited to the difficulties of ascetic life, he suggested that she stay back to rule the kingdom. Later that night while she slept, he quietly left the palace. When she woke and discovered that he had left, she flew through the sky and spotted him wandering in the forest. She used her psychic powers to see everything that would happen in the future; then, without making her presence known to him, she returned to the palace (Ibid.: 300–02).

Chudala ruled the kingdom and Shikhidhvaja roamed the forest for eighteen years. At that point she learned through psychic powers that her husband's mind had matured and that it was time for her to help him attain enlightenment. Observing her husband from the sky, she was saddened to see him looking so emaciated and lonely in his foolish pursuit. Fearing that he would again reject her as an ignorant girl, she appeared before him in the disguise of a young male Brahmin ascetic named Kumbha. The king was delighted and offered flowers of worship to his visitor. In this guise, Chudala instructed the king through a series of parables that illustrated the foolishness of his ascetic yearnings. She pointed out that he had renounced everything except ego and the very trappings of asceticism (his cottage, staff, deerskin, rosary). He was so worried about his own austerities, Kumbha said, that the *spirit* of renunciation had left him. Hearing this, the king piled up all the material objects associated with his asceticism and lit a bonfire. Even then she insisted that there remained one thing yet to be renounced. Certain that she was referring to his body, he prepared to destroy it as well. She intervened and corrected him by suggesting that he must abandon the mind (*chitta*), which means the idea of the "I" itself and "even the notion 'I have renounced all'" (Ibid.: 313). He now understood and, like her, became radiant with enlightenment. At that moment, before Shikhidhvaja could offer flowers of adoration, Kumbha vanished. Leaving her disguise Chudala returned to the palace, and Shikhidhvaja retreated into deep meditation (Ibid.: 302–24).

Chudala returned in the guise of Kumbha after three days and used her psychic powers to awaken him. Together they roamed the forest for eight days, until, again, Chudala left to discharge her royal duties in the palace. She returned to the forest again as Kumbha and sorrowfully told the king that a sage whom she had encountered on her journey and angered with her teasing cursed her; the curse was that Kumbha would transform into a woman every night. But then, she contemplated aloud, she should not grieve, for this does not affect her inner self. Shikhidhvaja agreed that it did not matter if her body became female every night, for her real self was the soul. So Chudala lived with her husband as the young male ascetic Khumba during the day and as the beautiful Madanika at night. After a few days she said to him that she felt she should live as the wife of a worthy husband. "I wish to marry you," she said, "and enjoy conjugal pleasure with you. This is natural, pleasant, and possible" (Ibid.: 329). So they lived as friends during the day and made love on a bed of flowers at night. After several months of this, she decided to test her husband to make sure he was not attracted by temptations of pleasure and created two illusions with her magical power. In the first, the chief of gods Indra appeared before them, praised Shikhidhvaja, and invited him to heaven. Shikhidhvaja's reply proved he was untempted by pleasure: "I am happy wherever I am because I desire nothing"

(Ibid.: 330). In the second illusion, Chudala wanted to ascertain whether he would succumb to the dual forces of repulsion and attraction. Thus, she created a young male lover even more beautiful than her husband and a fragrant bed of flowers. When the king completed his evening prayers and looked around for Madanika, he found her seated on the bed in a passionate embrace with her lover. The two lovers appeared to be so immersed in passion that they were oblivious to their surroundings. Shikhidhvaja was unmoved and turned to go. When the couple noticed him, he said only, "Pray, let me not disturb your happiness" (Ibid.: 331). When the king thus proved that he had transcended both lust and anger, she revealed to him her true identity as Queen Chudala. He entered into deep meditation and witnessed all that had transpired since he left the palace. Emerging from this, he embraced Chudala fervently with a commentary on how devoted wives strive to enlighten their husbands and, because of their love for their husbands, they achieve what even the scriptures, guru, and mantra are unable to achieve. Because a wife is everything to her husband, he declares, she should be always adored and worshiped (Ibid.: 325–32). Even though this story seems to offer a critique of the practice of renunciation in that Chudala achieves enlightenment without ever leaving the palace or her husband and convinces her husband to renounce his renunciation, numerous sannyasinis mentioned Chudala's name to me. Significantly, both Anand Mata and Baiji urged me to read this particular text.

While philosophical women were most frequently mentioned in my interviews with sannyasinis, other women ascetics and saints also exist in history and legend, although only a few are well known. The bhakti saint Mirabai is believed to have been born in the fifteenth century to a royal family in present-day Rajasthan. Declaring her love for Lord Krishna, she refused to consummate her marriage to a prince and instead took up the life of a wandering mendicant (Mukta 1994). Mahadeviyakka was a twelfth-century Virashaiva mystic and bhakti poet from Karnataka. She was initiated into Shiva bhakti at age ten and betrothed herself to Shiva. It is likely that she married, according to Ramanujan (1973), but later left her husband to wander naked, clothed only by her hair. Legend has it that she died in "oneness with Shiva" (Ramanujan 1973:114). Andal was a ninth-century Tamil saint who dedicated herself to the god Ranganatha and refused to wed anyone else (Madhavananda and Majumdar 1982:301–03). History tells us that the legendary figures of Mirabai, Mahadeviyakka, and Andal were all bhakti poet-saints who took a path of emotion-filled devotion to a god envisioned as a true husband.[23] Even though bhakti (unlike sannyasa) explicitly elevated women and outcastes, the asceticism of these women nonetheless resulted in their "social alienation" (Ramaswamy 1997). References to extraordinary women in scripture, such as Chudala, do not constitute proof of the historical existence of such women, but they suggest that female asceticism was seen as legitimate, at least by some. Moreover, while most of these women in scripture, myth, and legend are identified as philosophers, ascetics, poets, and saints—not sannyasinis per se—the sannyasinis I met refer to them to legitimate their own choices.

Sannyasa as a Site of Undetermination

Sannyasa has gained a reputation for being an archaic institution that promotes Hindu orthodoxy and plays a conservative role in society. This reputation is not unfounded if we look at the beliefs and activities of Dashnami monastic abbots. In the 1920s, the abbot of Puri Math opposed Mahatma Gandhi's legislative attempts to abolish untouchability (Cenkner 1983:132). In the 1970s an abbot, again of Puri Math, rose to national attention by establishing an organization against family planning (Ibid.: 1983:125). More recently, a Dashnami leader of Kamakoti Pitham condemned the changes in personal law proposed by women's groups, argued that women were barred from inheriting property on the basis of their ineligibility to perform the rites for ancestors, and dismissed the concepts of personal freedom and fulfillment as foreign (Robinson 1999:136–37). Clearly the Dashnami Orders have furthered a conservative agenda of classical education, priesthood, the use of Sanskrit language, and even caste distinctions (Cenkner 1983). This conservative reputation has only been intensified by sadhus' leadership in the nationalist movement since the mid-1980s.

It would be foolish to deny evidence that the Dashnami leadership has been both unconcerned with and overtly hostile to the interests of most women. However, if this is a self-evident view of sannyasa, it is also a partial view. I have argued that the practice of sannyasa is not defined by the authority of Dashnami monastic centers, have pointed to anti-institutional tendencies within sannyasa, and have noted the prevalence of independent renouncers affiliated loosely or not at all with a monastic institution. But more importantly, equating sannyasa with orthodox elements in the Dashnami Order blinds us to the existence of female and independent renouncers. A woman taking sannyasa is a transgressive act and a good place to explore issues of women's agency. I would like to suggest that renunciation is (at least potentially) a "site of undetermination" and, as such, it is a place where "agencies slip through the structures—in new situations, at transitional moments, or in liminal areas; those factors which allow women to act differently, independently, or even contrary to the demands of structured relationships" (Sangari 1993:872).[24] Feminist scholars have shown how important it is for us to extend the definition of politics in order to validate women's political activity, resistance, and protest, which often lie outside the domain of organized politics, group structures, and group consciousness (Moore 1988:179). Feminist scholars' interest in "sites of undetermination" converges with anthropologists' critique of holism that emerged in the 1980s.

Appadurai, for example, argued that a holistic conception of culture has led to India being defined by caste and hierarchy and that this has blinded scholars to the diversities and indeterminacies of social life in South Asia (1986:758). Similarly, in her reflection on the contributions of the subaltern studies project, Veena Das observed that the analytical tools of anthropology consist of "concepts that can render other societies knowable in terms of 'laws,' 'rules,' and patterns of authority" and preclude analyses of transgressions, disorder, and violence (Das 1989:310). Accordingly, the emphasis on order and constraint makes it difficult to recognize the subject in theories of social structure and social action (Ibid.:311).

In a parallel effort to historicize "culture" in India, scholars working in the area of post colonial theory have demonstrated that both academic and popular understandings of the systematic nature of Indian culture are the direct descendents of colonial efforts to define "tradition," religion, and social identity for legislative and political purposes (Mani 1990; Narayan 1997; Dirks 2001). Considering the phenomenon of female renunciation offers a critique of the way in which anthropology still, despite postmodern and feminist critiques of holism and coherence, tends to represent the lives of people in other cultures as overdetermined. There is no institutionalized role for women in the world of sannyasa, and, in choosing this path, women defy normative expectations of marriage and motherhood. For these reasons, the lives of women renouncers can bring into focus the cracks and leakages in India's social structure and gender ideologies. I probe the contradictions that might allow women, particularly women from religious and high-caste families where sadhus are respected, to transgress boundaries of gender.[25]

Two peculiarities of sannyasa converge to make it a space that offers women the possibility of "slipping through the structures." One is the contradiction between sannyasa's elite brahmanism and the philosophy of Advaita. Advaita, as I have indicated, promises the possibility of transcending all dualities, and it is the conventional wisdom that renouncers seek to transcend the body. However, transcending the body means more than simply ignoring physical needs like eating or sensory distinctions like hot and cold. It means ignoring moral and social distinctions as well. The renunciant ideal of being indifferent to social differences ("treating everyone equally") is simply one expression of a more general value that Advaita Vedanta places on transcending distinctions and dualities. Renouncers are expected to ignore differences among others and, in their self-perception, to identify with their inner *atma* rather than their external, transient form. The abstract philosophy of Advaita is self-consciously expressed in the everyday behavior and speech of contemporary renouncers when, for example, they ignore distinctions between purity and pollution by taking food from a low-caste household, claim to feel the pain of others as if it is their own, or announce that in sannyasa there is no male and female. There exists an "intrinsic tension between the teaching of Advaita Vedanta which proclaims absolute freedom of the Spirit including the transcendence of all finite human institutions, and the monastic organization which is the custodian and exemplar of this teaching. In a very real sense, the Dashnami Order contains within it the seed of its own transcendence" (Dazey 1990:313). Because of this dynamic, sannyasa offers women important opportunities for transgression.

A second and related characteristic that renders sannyasa a potential site of undetermination is that the social world of sannyasa operates on a free market model without any authoritative hierarchy. The current Dashnami monastic heads are not like Popes charged with the responsibility for determining the saintly authenticity of particular holy persons. There are little in the way of institutional constraints on who can call herself a sadhu or wear the ochre robes of sannyasa. One implication is that there is space for independent renouncers who reject institutional affiliation; indeed, such independent and charismatic gurus are becoming increasingly popular in India and internationally. Many are women. Sannyasa's privileging of Advaita philosophy and its lack of centralized institutional authority combine to create possibilities for women to lead unscripted and unconventional lives. The next three chapters will present Anand Mata and Baiji. I believe that their lives illustrate not only the undetermined potential of sannyasa but also the manner in which renouncers speak about gender and other matters from both worldly and otherworldly perspectives.

Chapter Two

Walking a Tightrope: Renunciation as Love

M y first encounter with Anand Mata occurred eight months before I began my formal period of field research. I stayed at Sant Kuti during that weekend visit to Haridwar and again the next year during my first month of research. An elderly resident named Mehraji took an interest in my research project. I enthusiastically accepted his offer to introduce me to "one very good sannyasini" who had taken a vow of silence (*maun*) that lasted ten years and had just recently begun speaking again. Anticipating my first meeting with a female renouncer, my imagination conjured up an image—gleaned from scholarly as well as popular representations—of a fiercely independent, rigidly disciplined woman, face framed perhaps by the fearsome and dramatic matted locks I had come to expect, living as a recluse on the fringes of society.

The next morning Mehraji and I traveled to Gomukh Ashram where Anand Mata lived. We arrived to find a *satsang* (religious assembly) in progress, so we joined the small group of people listening to the animated lecture of a bespectacled swami. I was about to seat myself at the rear of the women's side when a matronly middle-aged woman smiled sweetly and gestured for me to sit in front of her so that I might see better. It was only when the lecture concluded and Mehraji got up to greet her that I realized this short, ordinary-looking woman with a pleasant face was Anand Mata. Her right eye continually strayed

47

to one side, as if it had a will of its own. A wisp of hair escaped the pale saffron scarf that covered her head; the hair was neither matted nor shaved, just hair, beginning to gray. I was introduced as so and so's niece and a student who wanted to write a thesis on "lady sannyasis." She uttered a bemused, noncommittal "Oh?" and smiled indulgently. Then she slipped on a pair of wooden sandals and the clicking of her feet led us up the narrow stairway to her rooms above.

Ignoring her protests that our feet would be cold, Mehraji and I respectfully removed our sandals at the entrance before seating ourselves in the aluminum lawn chairs that were arranged around a small wooden table in the center of the room. I stood and unceremoniously offered the bag of oranges I had brought as an offering for Anand Mata, then watched Mehraji present his fruit with grace and reverence. He told her of my desire to ask a few questions, and she agreed to be interviewed. The day before he had insisted that I speak to her in English. "She is educated and fluent in English, so you can interview her in your language." It was clear that he preferred to communicate with me in English, as it signified our erudite status. When I asked Anand Mata which language she would prefer, she said "Hindi, of course." I proceeded to ask a few of the biographical questions I had prepared, to which she gave short but thoughtful replies. As we spoke she seemed oblivious to the birds that fluttered in and out of the windows industriously attending to the construction of a nest in a corner of the room. Although her humor, patience, and informality put me at ease immediately, Mehraji and I, having arrived unexpectedly, did not stay long that first day. When planning our next visit, we expressed concern about interrupting her *satsang*, and she laughed, "Don't worry about *that*. I only go because it is expected of me, so your being here will provide an excuse for me not to attend!"

Her Story: From Social Activism to Detached Solitude

Before describing my subsequent encounters with Anand Mata, I will briefly outline her past as she described it to me during our first interviews. Although Anand Mata's recent spiritual life is characterized by meditative solitude, this period of her life is almost a complete reversal of her earlier social activism in the area of girls' education in western India. Anand Mata identifies herself prior to renunciation as an "extrovert" and describes sannyasa as a turning inward. She was born into a Brahmin family strongly influenced by the reformist, service-oriented thinking of Mahatma Gandhi. Her family became prominent in the fields of politics and education in the 1950s when the nation was still in its infancy and politics was respected as a form of patriotic service. Her maternal grandfather, who was reputed to possess both spiritual wisdom and skill in astrology, looked at the signs surrounding her birth and predicted that this child may go in the direction of sannyasa, but no one paid attention to his prediction at the time.

Though Anand Mata was a well-rounded child with diverse interests, what she calls "the spirit of surrender" was highly developed in her from a very young age. She recalls that while worshiping Shiva, she ignored both the instructions of her mother and the example of her older sisters regarding what sort of requests to make of the deity: a long life, a good husband, many children. This stubborn refusal to include such demands in prayer had to do with her understanding, even at a young age, that Shiva knew better than she what she needed in life. If she did not know what was best for her, then how could she possibly ask for it? On one occasion, her obstinacy in this matter, perceived by her mother as childish impertinence, provoked an angry reprimand and a slap on the head. Even though Anand Mata emphasizes that all mothers deserve only love and respect, she insists that in this instance she was right and her mother wrong. Most sannyasinis I met recall at least a few such instances when their spiritual beliefs or aims directly conflicted with the interests of family or society.

Anand Mata's marriage to a Jain, a friend of her brother's, was a "love marriage" that lasted many years. She agreed to marry this boy, she says, because he was so persistent in his attentions that she felt her refusal would leave him utterly dejected. "I will marry you," she finally told him, "but I don't know how long I will remain in householder life (*grihastha ashrama*)." Her family was unenthused about the match, but did not oppose it. The marriage was a happy one. Anand Mata founded a school for girls based on Gandhian principles and, though she and her husband managed it together, she earned a higher salary as the school's principal. Devoted to social activism, to her pupils, and to the orphaned niece and nephew she and her husband raised, Anand Mata did not crave children of her own. She expressed her willingness to have children if her husband desired them, but only on the condition that he earn enough money to support the family so she could stay home. He insisted that children were unimportant to him. Much later, as she began to move in the direction of *sadhana* (spiritual discipline), he suddenly began to express a strong desire for children. At this point she knew that he wanted a family only to bind her to him, so she refused.

When in her early thirties, she began to realize that her inner cravings were not suited to the environment in which she lived. Around this time Anand Mata became friendly with an older woman who introduced her to *sadhana*, but because of her husband's disapproval she broke all ties with this woman, whom she still views as her first guru. Soon after, she and her husband began regularly to attend the lectures of a prominent swami, the man who would eventually initiate her into sannyasa. Her husband's early enthusiasm for the guru's teachings began to wane along with his interest in a religious disciplinary regime. Since he felt threatened by his wife's increasing involvement in *sadhana*, it came as no surprise to her when he started to criticize this guru as well. Influenced by the teachings of her guru, she began to feel the need to leave home to live in the guru's ashram. She gently ("with love") rejected her husband's initial attempts to convince her to stay at home and, much later, his offers to provide financial support for her renunciant life. Anand Mata's natal relatives and friends opposed her asceticism for different reasons than her husband, who simply feared losing her, and her in-laws, who wanted to assert their authority. As followers of Gandhi and social activists themselves, they felt that social and political service was morally superior to the renunciation of worldly life. Rather than leaving suddenly and without explanation, she felt compelled to first convince family members of the sincerity and wisdom of her choice. She thus defended her decision in long, heated debates until, finally, her relatives offered their blessings. For her, sannyasa represented a radical withdrawal from family, social, and political involvement.

After a few years of ashram life, Anand Mata transferred all her wealth and property to her husband of eighteen years and was initiated into sannyasa. She spent five years learning meditation and Advaita philosophy, and helping in the ashram's administration. Since her guru attracted foreign disciples she interacted with people from many countries in a cosmopolitan environment. As the ashram expanded, her organizational and leadership skills proved useful. But the moment she received instructions to travel and help set up a new ashram in the United States, she felt an urge to leave her guru's side and withdraw into deep sadhana. She emphasizes that she left with her guru's blessings, that he understood she had learned a lot under his guidance but was now ready to move on, and she interprets his willingness to let her go as a sign of his authenticity as a true guru.

Leaving the ashram was followed by a period of mental confusion. Anand Mata consulted some fifty sadhus at the 1974 Kumbh Mela,[1] many of whom advised that she take a vow of silence to expedite the transformation of her active, extroverted nature by focusing inward. One of these sadhus brought her to his ashram in Haridwar where she lived for the next three years; he became her third guru. Under his tutelage she undertook a vow of silence, the first six months of which involved remaining in a room alone with her eyes covered in such a way that she could only see her feet to walk. This is called "stone silence" (patthar maun). She met no one and ate the food left outside her door only if hunger demanded. While only the first six months were spent isolated and blindfolded, the silence itself lasted ten years. For much of this time period, although silent, she assisted with running the ashram and, when necessary, communicated via writing. During the initial period of stone silence sadhana, Anand Mata's family did not try to contact her, even when her mother became seriously ill. When her mother died shortly after falling sick, Anand Mata's relatives brought the cremation ashes to Haridwar and performed the immersion ceremony in her presence. She had already achieved a state of detachment (vairagya) toward her family. "Whenever my relatives came to meet me," she said, "I was polite but felt no special affection for them. They are perceptive people; eventually they realized that their visits disturbed my sadhana, and they reduced the visits to a bare minimum." After three years in this guru's ashram,

Anand Mata accepted the offer of two rooms in the small, unstructured Gomukh Ashram where she still resides today. The ashram's founder had, in his will, granted her the legal right to occupy these two rooms for the rest of her life. When we met she was in her late fifties and spoke with intensity and eloquence, but never in larger and more formal public contexts.

Getting Acquainted

Anand Mata says that in the beginning she spoke to me only because I was connected to Sant Kuti Ashram, whose founding guru she had known, and because I had been introduced to her by Mehraji. Otherwise, she declared, if some girl had arrived at her doorstep to ask questions for a thesis she would offer only cryptic, monosyllabic answers in order to be rid of her as soon as possible. Anand Mata, as is considered appropriate for a sadhu, is not in the habit of talking about herself. And although she was polite and responsive from the first time we met, I realized only later that she never said more than was necessary to answer my queries. Months later, after concluding that I had come not only to gather material for a thesis but also to fulfill some personal quest, she deliberately and generously began to take on the task of educating me as if it were not only her desire but her duty as well. In refusing to be interviewed or "refusing the subject" (Visweswaran 1994:60), some sannyasinis objected either that my scholarly search for knowledge was too worldly (they were not interested in helping a girl obtain a degree) or the quest was impossible (I could not comprehend their experiences through interviews). A few stated flatly that they had no knowledge to offer, which is usually an assertion of humility rather than ignorance.

Anand Mata, when introducing me, would often say, "You cannot tell by looking at her, but this girl was born and raised in America, learned Hindi only after growing up, and is about to marry an American boy; yet she has come to study sadhu *matas* (holy mothers) of India!" According to initiates, predictably, sannyasa represents the very essence and pinnacle of Hinduism, so my decision to study this ascetic tradition was indicative of some insight on my part. In order, I think, to indicate my family's support for my marriage to a white American, it was often mentioned that we had planned a Hindu wedding and that both our families would attend. Anand Mata once noted with approval that the scarf never once slipped from my head when I was before a sannyasi. "Even our Indian women must keep pulling it up as it slips." Comments such as these conspired to construct my reputation as a well-bred Indian girl from a good family rather than a western female of dubious moral standards. "She asks such deep questions and listens with such interest," she often remarked; "I fear that by going on doing this research she'll eventually *become* a sadhu." In lame attempts to honestly present my scholarly project as an intellectual one I would explain that my upbringing was not at all religious, to which the reply was usually a reference to the miraculous effects of the mental impressions (*samskaras*) of previous lives. Among the unmarried holy women I knew, there was a general sense of happiness, even relief, to learn that two months into my field research I would go to Bombay to be married and would return to Haridwar with a husband. It was acceptable, even virtuous, for a young woman like myself to study sannyasinis, as long as I did not wish to become one.

The fact that sannyasinis tend to uphold the classical system of life-stages, which limits renunciation to the final years of life, and discourage other women from following their example has been interpreted as a sign of orthodoxy. However, if we mean by "orthodoxy" some sort of blind allegiance to a classical system of beliefs that was unsympathetic to women, it is a misnomer. One reason female sadhus tend to dissuade others from following their example is that it is contrary to the ideals of sannyasa to recruit followers. Rather than the guru "making" a disciple, in the ideal situation it is the guru who is somewhat reluctantly recruited. So the fact that female sadhus tend to dissuade others from following their example may be viewed by their peers as a sign of authenticity rather than of orthodoxy. In addition, there is a strong belief among sannyasinis that, while they themselves may be exceptions, it is important for ordinary people to first experience marriage and family life before they can succeed on the difficult path of celibacy and detachment. If someone proves herself to be an exception to this rule, it is explained with reference to the experiences of past lives. While they may be revered as exceptions, renouncers are not held up as figures to be emulated, and this is true for both male and female sadhus. This reluctance to encourage others to follow their example also reflects an awareness of the possibility that momentary personal problems or loss may inspire a mood of renunciation in anyone, but to take sannyasa without being fully prepared or "ripe" (*pakka*) can be downright dangerous. This is particularly true for women because, as will be discussed in chapter 6, the obstacles they face in renunciation are many. It is not surprising then that the irony of my own situation, perched on the threshold of married life yet living among sadhus, was an endless subject of commentary and joking; it expressed a very serious tension.

Thus it was with both compassion and trepidation that Anand Mata admitted me into her world. Her trepidation had to do both with the discomfort of putting her private life into a public arena and with the uncertainty of where it might lead me. Becoming my "informant" was her considered decision. Our first official interview on a bright winter morning focused on the reasons for women's exclusion from sannyasa and lasted several hours. We paused for lunch when the ashram gong sounded from below and returned to our discussion after eating. In the midst of a speech about the virtues of maternal love, she jumped up and exclaimed, "Speaking of which, I haven't even fed my children coffee yet! Interview is finished for today; now it is time for coffee." Mehraji was about ten years older than her, yet he called her Mataji (Respected Mother) rather than Behnji (Sister), the term he used for other older women; his use of this term expressed his regard for her and was an apt response to her motherly attitude toward him. We followed her into a small back room adjoining the hall where she received people. It was barely large enough to accommodate a single bed, a two-burner gas stove, a couple of buckets of water, cooking utensils, and other personal belongings. Everything from the rug to the bed sheets to the dish rags were in shades ranging from pale peach to bright orange. The intimacy of this small, lived-in room contrasted strikingly with the austerity and expanse of the hall. Here Anand Mata fed us sweet, milky coffee with lots of cream and a variety of snacks, while hardly eating anything herself.

During the first months of research Mehraji and I continued our weekly visits to Anand Mata and, initially at least, I was grateful for his company. The manager of Sant Kuti, called Professor Singh (because she was a retired physics teacher), did not consider it safe for me to travel to Gomukh Ashram alone even though it was only a distance of a few miles. Mehraji was an appropriate escort for my ventures on public transportation to unfamiliar ashrams. During those early interviews, he was also helpful in translating words I did not know, supplying textual references, and elaborating philosophical concepts that came up. Gradually, though, he faded into the background. He had his own reasons for accompanying me, and these may have been related to the prestige of associating with "an American research scholar" (as he liked to introduce me). Yet also, he came along because he was, in his own words, a spiritual seeker and scholar. He considered it a privilege to participate in these "*satsangs*," as my interviews with sannyasinis were often characterized. He had known Anand Mata for years, but never intimately, and through these meetings he came to respect her immensely. After our visits to other sadhus he would inevitably provide lengthy commentary on their hypocrisy: "So and so only travels around lecturing to collect contributions (*dan*)." He shared the conviction with many Hindus, householders and renouncers alike, that the vast majority of sadhus are "professionals" who take up renunciation as a business, as an easy way to make a living. "They accumulate disciples and travel around giving lectures as a form of advertising," he laughed. "They all do this to make a living; Anand Mata is the exception." He believed that genuine saints did exist but that discrimination was needed to distinguish them from the frauds, a topic I'll return to in chapter 5.

Throughout the first few months of these visits, Anand Mata and I played a game such that after each interview she would pronounce, "So now your work with me is complete," and I would shrug or smile vaguely but always return with more questions or simply to visit. She answered my queries thoughtfully and patiently, yet always behaved as if she expected them to be the last. I wondered whether she truly hoped the interviews would end so that I might leave her in peace or whether she was somehow testing my persistence. Gradually, as my Hindi skills improved, I stopped conducting recorded interviews. Also, as the nature of our talks became more personal, the interview format became unnecessary as an excuse to visit. For her, the "interviews" (defined by the presence of a tape recorder) contained information for my thesis while our "talks" had the more important goal of personal growth. Even in the "official" recorded commentary, Anand Mata continually subverted patriarchal rhetoric by, for example, attributing women's exclusion from sannyasa to male fears of women's superior ascetic abilities. Off record, she would describe personal experiences or defend unorthodox opinions, but always self-consciously and always with some didactic intent. She was willing to confide in me, I believe, because I was a relative outsider and because my relatively neutral position vis-à-vis local ashram politics made it possible for us to discuss events that were not public knowledge, especially once she began to trust my discretion. Perhaps another reason was simply that few people had ever been so intensely interested in and had taken so seriously every word she uttered. Yet she felt I would benefit from her knowledge in some deep way, or in her words, that I was "capable of digesting it." Occasionally, she prefaced her comments: "This you may not understand now but keep it in the back of your mind for later," or "This is not for your thesis, but so that you will understand." Increasingly, she began to offer unsolicited information or direct me to topics she considered important. I began to seek her advice on personal dilemmas and intellectual confusions, and within a few months the distinction between what was for my thesis and what was for me became hopelessly blurred.

Anand Mata became the center of my field research in more ways than one. She was what anthropology calls a "primary informant," the native who takes a reflective stance toward her own culture and who assumes the task of educating the ethnographer. Wary of the dangers of assuming female solidarity, I nonetheless choose to represent what could be read as just another "myth of rapport." Feminists have had much to say about the romance of ethnographic intimacy. While Stacey (1988) argues that feminist anthropologists conducting research on women are especially susceptible to the "delusion of alliance," Tedlock (1995) associates the ethnographic "myth of rapport" with a masculinist, poised self-image. While narratives of alleged solidarity may very well be fictions, the more pressing question for me is whether they reinforce hierarchies by erasing differences between women. I visited other sannyasinis and ashrams but would return to Anand Mata periodically to report my discoveries and seek advice, so she became a guide in my journey into the world of sadhus. Although her interpretive interventions are clearly marked in this text as her own voice, throughout this book mine are intertwined with hers.

From Interviews to Participant Observation

After ten months of weekly visits, Anand Mata actually invited me to stay with her for a couple of weeks. For her, the seemingly mundane events of my stay formed the basis of any education she could impart to me. My observations and conversations offer not only a portrait of her daily life but also some under-standing of what sannyasa meant to her. They led me to conclude that, even though her chosen path was one of solitude, she believed that renunciation demanded a deliberate approach to social relationships with the dual, and gen-dered, aims of treating others with compassion and avoiding exploitation.

I had been visiting Gomukh Ashram regularly for several months before finally meeting Swami Visvanand, the Dashnami sannyasi who headed Gomukh Ashram. Though based in Haridwar, he spent much of the year on the move, wandering, like the classic renouncer. On one of my weekly visits he was in town, so Anand Mata introduced us. Swami Visvanand was young for a man of his prominence. During that brief meeting, I learned that he took sannyasa at the tender age of thirteen. He had toured India twice on foot and had performed severe austerities (*tapasya*) of sitting daily in the hot sand from sunup until sun-down. He used to sit in the sand, he told me, with a 40-liter pot of water that he drank during the course of the day. "I felt cold as ice inside, and sweated a lot." He likened his condition to that of a refrigerator which needs heat to cool itself and which lets out a lot of heat as well. "But the sand underneath me remained cool," he said. "A man used to come for *darshan* (auspicious viewing). He removed his shoes from far away, and would jump and come running because the sand was so hot! But then I would take some of the sand from beneath me and the man could sit on it." Because of his austerities, his knowledge of philosophy, and his skill at lecturing, Swamiji was respected in the renunciant community.

Anand Mata arranged an interview for later that week, and Mehraji and I returned to Gomukh Ashram on the appointed day. Anand Mata wanted to know what questions I had prepared for Swamiji; she had introduced me to other sadhus but had never before quizzed me about what I would ask. She seemed concerned that I impress him or at least refrain from offending him and, perhaps, embarrassing her. The three of us walked over to the new addition to Gomukh Ashram where Swamiji and several other male sadhus stayed. We found Swamiji seated in the lotus position on a wooden bed taking his midday meal in the shade of the courtyard. Anand Mata was deferential and gestured unobtrusively for me to sit on the floor; Swamiji acknowledged our presence with a silent nod and went back to his lunch. Mehraji and I made ourselves comfortable on the floor while Anand Mata sat in a chair opposite him. He wore a bright orange lower garment (*lungi*) and shirt (*kurta*) stitched from the finest cotton. We waited qui-etly while he slowly finished his meal and downed a glass of milk. After washing his hands and seating himself comfortably on the bed, he asked me how I had become interested in this topic. Responding to a seriousness in his demeanor which suggested that whatever occurred here must be profound, I answered that I was motivated by a respect for the renunciant life and a concern for the advancement of women. This satisfied him and I went on to ask a few of the more philosophical questions that interested me. The interview went well and when I ran out of cassette space, Swamiji said that we could meet again.

Even though he was much younger than her, Swamiji was not as deferential to Anand Mata as she seemed to be to him. He called her "Ma" which is the more intimate form of "Mother" while she called him "Swamiji." Explicit rules regulating interactions between men and women may exist in particular Hindu sects, but they do not exist in any formal sense for sannyasa as a whole, because there is no institutionalized role for women. I was later to revise my interpretation of Anand Mata's deference to Swamiji that day after seeing them interact in other contexts. She frequently criticized or scolded him like a child, though never in public. For example, when he decided to get a television for the ashram, she rebelled, warning him that she would keep pulling the plug out so that no one could watch it. He never did get the television. Anand Mata's voice carried moral authority with Swamiji, and she used her influence freely. Eventually, I began to see her deference to him on the occasion of that first interview less as an expression of simple gender asymmetry and more as an effort on her part to create a formal atmosphere appropriate for the interview and to guide my behavior so that I (as a householder and young woman) might show the proper deference to Swamiji. Anand Mata was well aware of the fact that I was new to the world of sadhus and would behave according to her cues. In effect, through her own deferential behavior, she was saying: "Swamiji is not like me, so don't make the mistake of being as casual with him as you are with me."

A few months after this meeting with Swamiji, Anand Mata and I discussed the progress of my research. She was pleased that I was collecting interviews from different types of sannyasinis.

"So now, aside from me, you have one orthodox Mataji who runs her own ashram, one reformist Arya Samaji, and then one who is involved in politics. Perfect! We are all going on paths involving very different types of *sadhana*, so you can see the different problems each must face."

"Yes, my research is going well," I said. "But . . . well . . . I was thinking that after Peter returns to the United States in July I would like to live with different sannyasinis rather than staying in a separate home or at Sant Kuti." Since returning to Haridwar after our marriage, Peter and I had lived in town, in the ancestral home of one of my relatives.

"That's an excellent idea, since you will only see one side from interviews. To really understand sannyasinis you must live with them day in and day out. Very good. You can come and stay with me for a while also if you want to." I was delighted. I wanted to stay with her, but hesitated to make such a request. During the last ten months of visiting Gomukh Ashram I had never known anyone to stay with her; in fact, people who came from out of town to meet her stayed at a hotel or another ashram. As a contemplative, independent sannyasini, she seemed content in her solitude. Anand Mata, as if reading my mind, gave an explanation.

"I had not offered before because of the poor bathroom facilities, but now you know what to expect. You can stay with me in my rooms, or in the new addition there are rooms which offer more comforts and better bathing facilities."

"No, I want to stay with you in your rooms."

It was settled. After going to Bombay, and then to Benaras to spend ten days with another sannyasini, Uma Giri, I was to return directly to Gomukh Ashram to stay with Anand Mata.

It was August when I returned. My first day at Gomukh Ashram, a steady stream of people came to meet Anand Mata for various reasons. This in itself was interesting because she was so emphatic in her refusal to become a guru and take on the responsibility of intimate involvement in disciples' lives. A guru-sister (female disciple of the same guru) from South India had come to visit for the day; they talked excitedly for hours like two schoolgirls catching up on old friends. I sat with them for a while before going out to run errands and then returned to make tea for the three of us. Later, after the friend left, Anand Mata opened the dusty padlock on a door I had never noticed to a reveal a small room. As if made for a resident anthropologist, it contained an aluminum cot, a small writing table and one chair. The only other object in the room was a por-trait of an elderly couple that hung askew on a wall, and I wondered if these might be her parents. Weren't renouncers expected to renounce their families? Some days later, when I was bold enough to ask, she seemed amused: "Oh that? I do not know who it is; the photo was hanging there when I first came to this place." Not only did she not hang the photo on the wall but she didn't even bother to take it down.

Because the room's window had no screen and the door that led into Anand Mata's hall was usually left open, a cool breeze drifted in from the Ganges and I slept soundly that first night. We both awoke around a quarter to six in the morning and I made tea. I clumsily took on the tasks of making tea, serving refreshments to Anand Mata's guests, and cleaning up afterward as these are appropriate ways to express respect for a sadhu. For her to continue to serve me, a householder, would have signified a reversal of proper relationships between sadhus and laypersons. Anand Mata protested in the beginning but seemed comfortable with my performing these tasks; in fact, when other visitors came for an afternoon they often did the same, particularly the women. Swami Visvanand was to give a lecture that first morning at seven on the request of some guests, a group of pilgrims on their way to Badrinath. Anand Mata pre-ferred not to give religious discourses, which generally bored her, but sometimes attended the lectures of others to show respect. We quickly bathed and dressed, then walked over to the new addition. Swamiji spoke poetically, with a deep voice and long, deliberate pauses, and kept returning to the point that, ulti-mately, one must travel alone on the path of *sadhana*.

Visitors who found me living with Anand Mata made little attempt to con-ceal their curiosity. Prompted by one of these moments, Anand Mata told me that she never had "guests" and that I was the first person she had brought to stay with her in her rooms. She only invited me, she said, because my goals were "top," my behavior was good, and I didn't mind following the "formalities" of the ashram such as sitting on the floor and keeping my head covered in front of male sadhus. Her earlier reference to the minimal bathroom facilities as the reason for not inviting me sooner had been a facade; she had simply not known me well enough to invite me to stay. More than a simple white lie, though, it was also a test. She said that if I had indicated a desire to stay further away in the new wing of the ashram because of its modern bathing facilities, she would not have let me come at all, simply because she did not wish to be responsible for my safety. Luckily, I had indicated a desire to stay in her rooms. Moreover, after observing my behavior in the ashram and during the first interview with Swamiji she felt assured that I would be polite but distant in my interactions with unfamiliar men, sadhus and householders alike. She repeated on and off during the next two weeks that she had never allowed anyone to stay overnight in her rooms. By way of explanation as to why she made an exception for me, she returned to her "motto" again and again: "I have no hard and fast rules."

The second morning was more relaxed and our long conversation while sipping hot tea from steel glasses came to characterize our mornings together. That particular day we drifted onto the topic of what time a sadhu wakes up in the mornings. I mentioned that I had been sleeping very well, too well, in my new room.

"That's good," she said. "I have never understood what it is that sadhus have against sleeping. After all, unless one's eyes are fully open one cannot do *sadhana*."

"What is the reason that most sadhus rise at 4 A.M.?" I asked.

"Yes," she replied. "It is a time that is neither night nor day; it is the most peaceful and quiet time of the day, and the atmosphere is pure, so it is the easiest time to do *sadhana*. This ashram gives more freedom to its residents and does not have a lot of rules. This is why I stay here."

Many ashrams did indeed have rules requiring residents to rise at a given time, attend worship services, or follow a particular guru, while Gomukh Ashram did not even have its own temple much less rituals of worship. In fact, Anand Mata's life at Gomukh Ashram was so unstructured that soon I found myself losing track of the days, not knowing what date to write on a letter or in my journal. It was startling when I stared at my calendar one day and realized that it was useless since I neither knew the day of the week nor the date. My time with Anand Mata was fluid, without schedules or appointments. There was no daily prayer, no ritual, no activity that was obviously "religious." This posed a stark contrast to daily life in the other ashrams where I stayed with specified times for waking, worship, and meals; Hindu ritual practice requires strict attention to the calendar. Anand Mata was often busy with the accounts or some other ashram responsibilities but felt that strict adherence to schedules was an obstacle in the type of sadhana that she called (using the English) "total surrender." For example, she was in the habit of fasting for Shiva's birthday but felt that it made no difference if she failed to do it one year.

Anand Mata had introduced me to other sannyasinis in the neighborhood whom I visited whenever she was occupied. I also became friends with Sushma, an unmarried working girl who lived nearby with her family and visited Anand Mata several times a week. When she came over, Anand Mata would often insist that Sushma and I sit down and chat while she prepared refreshments. Sushma was in her late twenties, pushing the limits of marriageable age by Haridwar standards. In spite of her insistence that she wished to remain single and pursue a career as a clerk, her family continued the search for a suitable boy, and Anand Mata agreed that she should marry. Although Sushma never expressed any interest in becoming a sadhu she had asked Anand Mata for advice in *sadhana*. Anand Mata was willing to provide spiritual guidance but did not encourage Sushma to go in this direction. In fact, one day I was sent by Anand Mata on a match-making mission. Unbeknownst to Sushma I took her to meet a handsome, young yoga instructor who had recently come to ask Anand Mata's advice on his decision to enter married life. We were sent on the pretext of delivering a message from Anand Mata. She hoped that Sushma would marry and was disappointed that our efforts that day proved unfruitful. Through Sushma I began to realize that, even if sannyasinis discourage other women from taking sannyasa, they nevertheless play a very important role in the lives of householder women, as spiritual and moral guide, nurturer, confidante, and mediator in family disputes. Anand Mata firmly believed that, rare exceptions aside, it is best to marry and experience "the pleasures of worldly life" before taking the path of renunciation. She attributes her own success in renunciation to the fact that she had already enjoyed a happy marriage, prestige, and wealth earlier in life and was thus no longer attracted to those things. The spirit of renunciation is thought to be inspired by the fulfillment rather than the denial of worldly desires, and this is the common sense wisdom that still gives the classical system of life-stages popular legitimacy.

As Anand Mata and I chatted while resting one afternoon I mentioned that a skinny sannyasi who had been in the ashram since I arrived gave me the creeps, that he stared at me sometimes. Upon hearing this she laughed out loud. "So you want to live in ashrams, huh? Of all the sadhus around here you will find maybe five who are really doing *sadhana*. Many of them take sannyasa as young boys because of poverty or to escape hard labor. In this life everything is free. But they do not have detachment (*vairagya*); they still have anger, desires, and lust. Forget the young ones, even those who are eighty, ninety years old still have a desire for sex. That is why it is best to first experience all those pleasures fully, because only after experiencing something can one truly renounce it."

That she was always wary of others' motivations became evident to me on several occasions. Though the ethos of her *sadhana* is "total surrender," Anand Mata surrenders to Paramatma rather than to any human being. For example, I mentioned to her that a local shopowner, an acquaintance of my aunt, had offered to escort me to the isolated cave dwelling of a particular sannyasini after I mentioned wanting to go there. Anand Mata refused to let me go with him, saying she did not trust anyone without knowing them intimately. She will not even sleep outside on the verandah or with the doors open at night, no matter how hot it is. "I have more trust in householders than in sadhus. Before coming here I used to imagine how wonderful it would be to live in Haridwar among the *rishis* and *munis* (sages and hermits). While I *have* seen the highest peaks, I have also seen the lowest of the low." An incident she recalls painfully occurred many years ago: one night she went to throw some leftover food off the roof into the alley for stray animals. When she looked down she saw a middle-aged swami whom she had known for years copulating with a small cow. She was so upset from this sight, she said, that she almost fainted; it was not the expression of a deviant sexuality that disgusted her so much as the hypocrisy of a supposedly celibate sadhu led to such extremes by his sexual desire. She cried and cried that night, wondering why she had come here to live among sadhus and what she had expected to find. Such stories, whether directly or indirectly experienced, are important in shaping the beliefs of sannyasinis and in their reluctance to encourage young women to venture onto their path.

My Story: Gender, Power, and Saintliness

Hearing Anand Mata's comments about the darker side of renunciant life, I became quiet. When she asked me what was on my mind I said I was thinking of my trip to Bombay and Benaras. At her prompting, I proceeded to tell her the story of my visit with Uma Giri and why I did not stay for ten days as planned.

I had originally met Uma Giri at Sant Kuti in Haridwar, when she was passing through on her way from her home base of Benaras to Badrinath. She had invited me to come and stay with her in the small Benaras ashram where she lived. Uma Giri refused to marry, she said, and had lived in her parents' home until age forty-two when she finally took sannyasa from the Dashnami sannyasi for whom this ashram had been built. After he died, she was allowed to stay on there. She was educated and literate in Hindi. Although she seemed to be respected by the people at Sant Kuti and in the Benaras ashram where she lived, she had no lay disciples. Yet, she was gregarious and female householders in the neighborhood brought her offerings of food and cloth from time to time; in fact, her courtyard seemed to serve as a gathering place for neighborhood women. She was the only woman living in an ashram among male ascetics, though her room was a little separated from the others by a small courtyard. She rose at four every morning to meditate and then collect flowers for the morning worship. Because the ashram food did not suit her stomach, she had a stove and cooking utensils in her room to prepare her own midday meal, which was the only one she ate. She spent a surprising amount of time looking after Chotu, the three-year-old daughter of a neighborhood priest. Perhaps she was looking after Chotu more than usual because the girl's mother, Radha, was pregnant with her second child and needed rest.

One day, Uma Giri and I had been talking in her room when there was a loud knock on the door. I opened the door and there stood a tall sannyasi, an imposing figure in the small entrance area.

"Is Mataji here?"

"Om namah Shivaya, Maharaj!," she greeted him with a smile. "You have come."

"I arrived last night," he said.

As we stepped outside into the courtyard Uma Giri introduced me to her guru-brother Maharaj, and I bent to touch his feet. He spent a month each year in Haridwar, she said, and several months here in Benaras. Although he was clearly younger than her, his gray hair and beard seemed incongruous with his radiant skin and youthful posture. She told him about my project and suggested that I might interview him. "Yes, of course," he said, "go ahead." I fetched my tape recorder and sat at his feet for a philosophical discourse.

He came again the following evening and sat in a lawn chair in the courtyard next to Uma Giri. I was inside Uma Giri's room feeding tea and biscuits to Chotu. As soon as the child heard Maharaj's booming voice she started whining and trembling as if with fear. As Maharaj and Uma Giri spoke in the courtyard, he kept calling out loudly to Chotu, but the child refused to go to him. My efforts to coax her into going out to greet Maharaj were met with looks of terror that I found very disturbing. Aware of the child's discomfort, Uma Giri suggested that I take the child home to her mother—that she must be tired. I came to know later that Maharaj had twice picked the girl up by her ears! He finally stopped this tormenting practice only when the girl's grandfather, a respected yogi who lived in the neighborhood, intervened. He warned Maharaj that the child was a *kanya* (virgin), a goddess, and should not be maltreated.

Maharaj came to Uma Giri's room for some reason or another at least twice every day while I was there. To show respect I interviewed him whenever he offered. One day, Uma Giri went to a *katha* (an event in which a mythological story is read aloud to an audience), while I stayed back to prepare vegetables for our lunch. When Maharaj came over looking for Uma Giri, I informed him that she had gone to the *katha* but did not invite him to sit down. He hesitated at the door and then left. He came again later that afternoon, when Uma Giri and I were playing in the courtyard with Chotu. In his presence our conversation always became more formal and more focused on religious matters. While Uma Giri was helping little Chotu squat over the outside drain to urinate, he said to me, "You should do *jap* (the silent reciting of a mantra)." I responded without thinking that I had no mantra, not intending to imply that I bemoaned the fact that I did not have one. He suggested that I ask somebody for one. Having no desire to seek spiritual guidance from him, I threw a glance toward Uma Giri who was busy with the child and had her back toward us. He nodded in affirmation, indicating that I could ask her for a mantra. I congratulated myself for escaping an awkward situation and promptly forgot the matter. It was disconcerting, then, when he returned the next day and inquired, "Have you asked Mataji about the mantra?"

"No, Maharaj. I did not get a chance."

I then turned to Uma Giri to explain.

"Yesterday Maharaj suggested I do *jap*."

She looked at Maharaj and said, "Why Maharaj, you know that I do not give mantras." Then she looked me in the eye. "What do you need a mantra for?"

I shrugged my shoulders, embarrassed, and said to both of them. "Since my family is Arya Samaji, perhaps I should just recite the Gayatri Mantra if I feel the need for it." Maharaj responded that the pronunciation should be perfect. I, in a desperate attempt to end the conversation diplomatically, told him that I would learn it from Mataji, but he persisted.

"You *both* come and learn it. Mataji, you should learn it too."

"I have no need to learn any mantra," said Uma Giri, "but Meena should think about it and, if she wants to do it with full faith, only then she should learn it."

"Mataji, you recite the Gayatri Mantra so that I can check your pronunciation."

She clearly did not want to. He finally compelled her to do so and then proceeded to correct her pronunciation. This was an attempt to humiliate her and thereby demonstrate to me that he was more learned and, perhaps, a better guru. His efforts to pressure me into learning a mantra were also disconcerting. But of course I continued to treat him with respect. This mess resulted from my unwillingness to offend him, because I recognized that my behavior was a reflection on Uma Giri and the ashram manager who had allowed me to stay. But my cultural ignorance was also to blame. In approaching sadhus, most Hindus understand the fine line between respect and reverence; one can demonstrate respect, for example, without touching the feet. I thought of myself as an independent person, not easily manipulated into doing things against my own will, but I was also a young female householder in confrontation with an older male saint of good repute. My experiences with Maharaj made me acutely aware of the social skills sannyasinis require to negotiate everyday relationships that are imbued with power and define reputations.

"Actually, Mataji, I am a bit upset about something," I said when we were alone.

"Tell me."

"I do not want to learn the Gayatri Mantra from Maharaj."

"Good, then don't. We'll think of some excuse, but don't worry about it. He knew very well that I would not give you a mantra and so he assumed that you would naturally return to him for the mantra and thereby become his disciple (*cheli*). Then it would begin. He thinks you have money. Moreover, you live abroad, and he has ambitions of going abroad. He is trying to trap you into becoming his disciple." While I knew that receiving a mantra was part of being initiated by a guru, I never suspected that simply learning a mantra, outside the context of ritual, could constitute this initiation.

She continued: "As soon as the question of your learning a mantra came up, I knew that Maharaj had started spinning his web. I could also see that he was just waiting for an opportunity to get you alone without me around so that he could trap you. That is why, when Chotu had to urinate I didn't take her to the latrine but, rather, had her pee over the outside drain—I didn't want to leave you alone with him. And it was exactly at that moment when my attention was diverted that he asked you about the mantra. I knew it would happen so I was watching his every move. The day I had gone to the *katha* he came here looking for me. The fact is that he knew very well that I was at the *katha* and came thinking that he'd get a chance to talk to you alone. But since you did not respond or invite him to sit down, he left. When I went to him later and asked, 'Oh, you didn't know that I'd gone to the *katha*?,' he claimed to have forgotten. The wife of the ashram's manager had also remarked to me that he had come in my absence. She was warning me to look out for you because she knows him too well. I've noticed that if there is some function, Maharaj will keep getting up and leaving. He will be watching whatever girl he is interested in at the time, and when she gets up, he'll also get up. It happens every time when he is here. That is why it is better if you are not here for the anniversary celebration next week. He will use that as an opportunity to entrap you because I will be busy. Can you understand why you should leave earlier than intended?"

The tension between Maharaj and me began to feel like a fencing match, infinitely graceful yet deadly serious. The next day, the day before I was to leave the ashram for Haridwar, these antagonisms reached their climax. Uma Giri, the ashram manager's wife, the neighbor Radha and little Chotu were all in the courtyard; the mood was light and filled with laughter. When Maharaj strode into the courtyard and parked himself in an empty chair, the mood became serious. He was accompanied by two of the other sannyasis who lived in the ashram on a more or less permanent basis. As new initiates they were both very deferential to Maharaj, although he was not their guru. At Uma Giri's prompting, I scurried inside to bring some fruit for Maharaj, and while I was in the small room peeling apples he yelled, "Will it take long Meena?" The tone and sheer volume of his command infuriated me, as if he wanted the whole world to hear him order me around. After distributing some of the fruit and eating the rest, he looked at me and said simply, "Water." I had several times brought a glass of water for him from the tap near the entrance gate; it was the water he preferred for drinking. This time, however, upon returning with the water, I was horrified to see that he merely wanted it to rinse his hands without having to get up. It was a service I was happy to perform for a few sadhus, but I felt manipulated by Maharaj. At that moment it seemed to be a service one should expect only from one's own disciple, and this is perhaps why his demanding it of me at that moment before many observers seemed so powerful. When he left after eating the fruit I did not touch his feet.

Uma Giri offered her commentary after he left. "He wants to show in front of other people that you respect him and will dance around his orders. Such an educated and well-bred girl running to satisfy his needs—it will make others think he is something great! The other day, he asked me loudly in front of the other people at the *satsang*: 'What about Meena's mantra?' Now he just wants a chance to meet you alone because he thinks that it is only my presence that prevents you from responding to him. You see, if you were his disciple, he could go to Haridwar looking for you and could demand a car, an airline ticket, or whatever he wants. He sees you as a golden bird and fears desperately that you might slip through his clutches."

I decided to make the implicit explicit. "Does he also exploit women sexually?"

"Yes, he does have relationships with girls." She explained that he had tried to have such a relationship with Chotu's mother Radha when she was expecting Chotu, but Radha refused. This is why he was so cruel to the child.

Maharaj came over to Uma Giri's courtyard again in the evening after everyone had left. He seemed mellow, less aggressive somehow. I merely bowed my head to greet him, having stopped the practice of touching his feet that morning to communicate my distance. Uma Giri said that as I walked back and forth across the courtyard, taking dishes to the tap to be washed, his eyes were on me to see if I would stop. I did not and neither did she invite me to join them. That he had decided to retreat became clear in the way he spoke to me. When the dinner bell sounded and I came to ask if I should bring food for him, he said to me, "Child, take your food." His addressing me as "Child," a term with strongly protective rather than predatory connotations, and his gentle tone left me speechless. At that moment I knew that we had made our peace. Uma Giri confirmed my reading of his statement later when we were alone. "He got the message (*Voh samjha*)," she proclaimed, but she wondered aloud why he relented so suddenly. My ceasing to touch his feet no doubt played some role. However, she also remembered then that he thought I was closely related to a particular woman he knows, who is a trustee of an ashram he visits (though it was actually a very distant relationship) and thus did not want me to leave angry. He feared for his own reputation. The dynamics of my relationship with Maharaj were neither simple nor unambiguous; after all, even if I was young and female I still had Uma Giri, family connections, and class status on my side.

Early the next morning, before departing for Delhi and then Haridwar, I offered Maharaj some fruit and *dakshina* (payment for spiritual services) and began distributing the envelopes of *dan* to other residents and employees as householders do when they leave an ashram. The look on his face was memorable; he was very surprised that I was leaving. Fifteen minutes later, when we were back in Uma Giri's room, she was summoned by Maharaj. As she predicted, he wanted to know why I had decided to leave earlier than planned and if I had given any complaint. She insisted that I was very happy here in the ashram and had no complaints.

Hearing this long story about Uma Giri and Maharaj, Anand Mata was quiet for a moment and then exclaimed, "You see, this is why I was worried about your staying with other sannyasinis. And even about bringing you here to stay with me." She leaned forward in her chair and said very seriously, "Listen carefully to what I am going to say."

"Many sadhus develop a thirst for power and wealth, once they get a taste of it. . . . These people can stoop so low, you cannot imagine! As my Guruji used to say, when people perform austerities they do get more power but the inside *vrittis* (dispositions created by actions in previous lives) do not change, so that the newly acquired power just goes to fulfill the desires that are already there. So if these sadhus have the desire to dominate, they become much more dangerous than ordinary people seeking power. So that Maharaj took the first step by offering his help in giving interviews. I have seen this over and over again. The second step in this exploitation is for the person to treat you as someone important. The third step is . . . if you do not respond to them, they will start to ignore you. This is where many girls fall. If a girl desires attention or likes that feeling of importance then she will fall here. The fourth step, if the third does not succeed, is that they will start speaking badly about you. I am sure that Maharaj knows a lot of people in ashrams you have visited here in Haridwar. He could easily say to people, 'You know that American girl from Sant Kuti visited Uma Giri in Benaras—she is not good (*voh tik nahin he*).' Even that little, coming from a prominent sannyasi, could ruin your reputation! I am sure he thinks you are very *bholi-bhali* (naive, simple-minded)."

I was exasperated at having been called *bholi-bhali* so often. "Why does everyone think me so simple-minded?"

"Well you are obviously not because you can understand a lot of 'psychology' and can see the hypocrisy in people, but you don't let it show on your face. You still treat them with respect." Anand Mata agreed that it would have been wrong for me to openly insult Maharaj. But she also pointed out that there are polite ways to rebuff a sadhu . . . by greeting them perfunctorily with a bow of the head rather than touching the feet or by accepting their *prasad* indifferently with one hand rather than reverently with two.

Anand Mata and I remained lost in our respective thoughts for some time. Then I asked if all this exploitation would still take place in an ashram with only women. "There are many ways to exploit . . . for money and work. There may be some big Mataji, and another sadhu may get her to keep a girl for him. So the girl maintains a good reputation while he gets his pleasure. The head, whether male or female, must still run an ashram, and one needs money for that. There is also a lot of homosexuality. When I used to be shocked by the corruption, my first guru used to scold me, demanding to know why I was so horrified and did I think everyone in the world was good and did I expect everyone to follow my standards? She told me not to worry about the rest of the world, to just make my own life good.

"It was only because I had trust in you that I kept you here with me," she said. "I would not allow any *bholi-bhali* girl to stay with me here. Also, you've come to do research and you have the discrimination to know what should and should not be printed. And you are seeking something personally, not only for your degree. For these reasons I brought you here." I confessed that I now realized that there was a certain pragmatic wisdom at the heart of Manu's statement, in his classical treatise on proper behavior, that a woman should never be independent. These being words I had always despised, I could hardly believe I was speaking in their defense now . . . not so much in their defense as with an understanding of the fear created by the pervasive threat of sexual aggression.

Anand Mata replied, "Everything the *rishis* and *munis* wrote was based on their experience. It is practical advice."

"Yes."

"But we must remember that there can always be exceptions and that is how you see people like me and other sannyasinis. We are exceptions."

When to Say "How Does It Concern Me?"

As Anand Mata and I were discussing my visit to Benaras again the next morning, the doorbell rang. I quickly covered my head with a scarf as I made my way to the door, then flipped the latch and pulled the doors open. There stood Swami Visvanand, the head of Gomukh Ashram. Rather than waiting for an invitation, he strode swiftly into the room, his movement pushing me out of the way with a force that was almost physical. Anand Mata, who had gone to get her headscarf, emerged from her room to welcome him. He sat down and, after I had served some fruit, made it clear that he was available for questions if I had any. Swamiji offered himself up for a "*satsang*" and, though not in the mood, I managed to come up with a question.

"Swamiji," I inquired in a deferential, if strained, voice, "how can we overcome feelings of anger?"

"If one does not feel power (*adhikar*) over others then one cannot feel anger," he announced with finality.

I persisted. "But Swamiji, I may get angry to see someone harm another person."

"That is compassion because you see something and wish that it were not so."

Anand Mata interrupted, explaining to him that the emotion is in fact anger in the latter case. "We should be concerned only about our own actions, not those of others," she stated. "Then we will not feel anger." When I asked if this type of anger could actually be a form of intolerance, a desire to control the actions of others, she agreed immediately. One purpose of all her years of silence was to overcome feelings of anger, to learn, for example, how to accept insult without reply or resentment. In transcending anger about, say, the exploitation of women, Anand Mata did not deny its existence or refuse to mitigate the suffering it caused. When I inquired about the appropriateness of sannyasa for women Swamiji responded predictably:

"For a sannyasi there is no male or female."

"But then why do so few women take sannyasa as compared to men, Swamiji?"

"There is a difference in tendency. Women are more dependent by nature."

Anand Mata retorted immediately, "Society has *created* a tendency in women so that they themselves want more dependence."

"Swamiji, do you have any disciples?" I asked.

"I have thousands of disciples (*chelas*) but no special ones. I don't consider anyone a disciple, but if someone comes and tells me they want to be my disciple, then I do not refuse."

Anand Mata said to Swamiji, "Seeing her lifestyle (*rehen-sehen*) and hearing her questions, I fear she will become a sadhu."

"She has *surya-guru*," he said matter-of-factly.

"But you haven't even seen her palm, Swamiji."

"I can see it in her forehead."

Noting the blank look on my face, she explained that *surya-guru* is a very auspicious astrological sign. She held out my palm for him to see.

"She should show it to me later, not now, sometime in the morning between nine and ten." On his way to the door, he stopped, turned around, and held out a one rupee coin toward me. I hesitated. Anand Mata urged me to accept this "special and great *prasad* (blessed object)." As I took the coin and bent to touch his feet, Swamiji placed his hand on my head and murmured some blessing.

After he left, Anand Mata informed me that Swamiji did in fact have disciples and that there is a reason he did not want to tell me about them. "He has given sannyasa initiation to three people." She went on to explain the reasons for a heated argument she had with him the day before, part of which I had overheard. Swamiji and his main disciple Mukhtananda had come over to persuade her to tell the skinny sadhu (the shifty-eyed one I had complained about) to leave. He had not done anything wrong, but they did not like him. She, however, was resolute in her refusal, pointing out that they were the ones who had invited him to stay in the first place and now they wanted her to take the responsibility of kicking him out. She mocked them for their weakness, for hoping to be able to tell people, "Ma said he was bad so we are putting him out," and thereby use her name to lend moral authority to their action. She was adamant that if they wished to expel him they should do it quietly and fairly, rather than making it sound like a punishment since the man had not done anything wrong. "You are more guilty than him," she told Mukhtananda, "for wanting to put him out in such a manner." She insisted that it was their problem and expressed her displeasure at their cowardly attempt to involve her in it. Now I understood why the two men left so sheepishly that day.

She grumbled to me that this sort of thing happens from time to time, but that she will not allow others to compel her to do such things. When the disciple left and Anand Mata was alone with Swamiji she warned him, "Since Mukhtananda is your disciple you should educate him. His behavior is very bad and he is in the habit of insulting people. If you don't teach him to behave properly the bad reputation will only come on you."

Upon hearing this, Swamiji became very concerned. "When you saw his behavior, Ma, why didn't you reprimand him?" he implored in a quiet voice.

"He is not my disciple and I am not here to educate him. How does it concern me (*Mujhe kya lena dena*)? My only responsibility here is to look after the accounts; I am not even a trustee." She often used this phrase "How does it concern me?" to express her disdain for and distance from a person or situation.

Swamiji had also expressed his concern, Anand Mata told me, about what sort of impression I might get overhearing these arguments. She told him flatly, "Since Meena is doing research she should see both sides. She knows the problems that sannyasinis face and I do not wish to hide anything from her." Swamiji was planning to host a meditation retreat the following week and wanted to get Anand Mata involved in organizing it. She promised to attend but refused to take on the responsibility of organizing events or looking after the guests. He pleaded with her by stressing her talent for organization, but to no avail. "After this retreat," he had said, sullen and defeated, "I just want to go wandering." She advised him, in a stern tone, to stay around to supervise the construction of a new addition and temple that he was having built, especially since there was a shortage of hands around the ashram. "I don't feel like wasting my energy (*shakti*) in this," he lamented. "I want to go live in the jungle for four months."

"He sounds like many men who want to have a nice home without the mundane work of running it," I mused.

"Yes, this is how they try to exploit women."

That evening, I brought groceries so that we might enjoy a respite from the tasteless ashram fare. As I sat down on the low stool to begin preparing the food, Anand Mata received the message that Swamiji wanted to see her. She returned twenty minutes later and said that some of the organizers for the

Ramjanmabhoomi movement had come to discuss political strategies. The movement to build a Ram temple in Ayodhya on the very spot where an Islamic mosque stood was at the center of communal violence that plagued parts of North India during the period of my research. "I refuse to get involved in such games," she said. "When I tried to tell Swamiji that Muslims are also *atma* (that is, the same as us), he said 'No, they are the enemy.' They are also against Harijans."

Although Anand Mata comes from a family deeply immersed in Congress Party politics and was asked to stand for election in her state legislative assembly at the time she was considering sannyasa, she now considers politics and elections to be "mere drama." When she consulted her first guru about whether to run for election or to take sannyasa, the female sadhu had said that self-respecting women should not get involved in state politics due to the high level of corruption. Anand Mata says that, seeing the condition of present-day politics, she made the right decision. She insists that her disinterest in politics is not because of her sannyasa, but rather because of the degraded state of electoral politics. She does not support sadhus' increased involvement in Hindu nationalist politics. Anand Mata is convinced that the Indian leadership must have the foresight to allow freedom of religion in the country and proclaimed this openly to peers who were sympathetic to the Hindu nationalist cause.

My final day at Gomukh Ashram was a bit sad, as I would have liked to stay longer. Since I was headed to Sant Kuti and Anand Mata also wanted to visit someone there, we decided to travel by scooter together later in the afternoon. As we sipped our morning tea, the mood was reflective. "I have never talked so intimately with anyone before," she mused. "I will miss you when you leave. Usually people come, have tea, and go, and I do not feel much." I too had spoken of things I'd never discussed before. The intimacy of our discussions had to do, of course, with our particular personalities, but I believe it was also facilitated by the ethnographic context that brought us together. As an ethnographer and stranger I was simultaneously very interested in her views and a relative outsider to her immediate social world. I believe that it is due to a similar combination of engagement and detachment that sannyasinis play such an important role in the lives of ordinary women. Anand Mata once narrated an incident about a young widow who swept floors and washed dishes in an ashram. Frightened by the unwanted advances of the ashram's new manager, she came sobbing to Anand Mata, lamenting that she didn't want to be exploited by a man since she had four children to raise. Diplomatically, Anand Mata managed to save her from that man in such a way that no one lost their prestige.

"If a working woman faces such exploitation," she said to me, "you can imagine what a sannyasini must face. Now you can understand what has made Jayashri Mata [a neighborhood sannyasini who was considered to be crazy] the way she is. And seeing what all a girl doing research here must face, you can imagine what problems face a sannyasini living here. That Maharaj you met in

Benaras is still nothing; he backed off easily. There was a family that used to go to a particular sannyasi for many years. He is over seventy years old and the head of a big ashram. The daughter had been going there with her father since childhood. Then the father died. One day the girl's mother sent her to deliver food to that sannyasi. He instructed her to put it in his room. When she went to leave the package in the room he followed her in there and locked the door behind him. Luckily, the girl had her wits about her. She used to ask me what to do if she ever found herself in such a situation and I would outline various options for her. She said to him, 'Swamiji, what are you doing? Everyone will know. If you want me to be with you I will since you are my guru, but I'll come back another time.' In this manner she got out of there and came straight to me in tears."

Although Anand Mata would say "How does it concern me?" when being pulled into something she did not wish to do, she also willingly intervened in people's lives. As will be described in chapter 6, she assumed some social risk by encouraging one young divorced woman discreetly and without her family's knowledge to pursue a relationship with a boy Anand Mata deemed suitable. It was necessary to do this, she felt, because the future happiness of this girl was at stake. An action motivated by love and compassion was always morally right in her view, even if it conflicted with society's conventions; in this limited sense renouncers are indeed beyond the morality of ordinary Hindu society. There was another young woman who, Anand Mata suspected, was using her visits to Gomukh Ashram as an excuse to rendezvous secretly with a boy who lived nearby. In this case, Anand Mata's disapproval was absolute. She felt the affair was not in the girl's best interest, did not like being used as a facilitator for such deceit, and was concerned that her own reputation was being put on the line. Here, love and compassion demanded that she try to stop these illicit meetings, but she did not confront the girl immediately for fear of losing her trust. Many women come to Anand Mata when they need a sympathetic ear, when they are looking for advice rather than condemnation, and she goes to great lengths to support and nurture them. Rather than talking about this in the more common idiom of *seva* (service to others) she used the idiom of love . . . love as the top priority, love as the only thing that ultimately exists.

That morning (we were to depart in the afternoon) Anand Mata's guru-brother Madhav Bhai and his family came to visit. They would come about once a month, traveling by bus from their home an hour away and always spending the night in a rest house for pilgrims before returning the next day. Although they did not come for any particular purpose except to be with her, she would advise them on everything from employment to child-rearing. Madhav Bhai was very curious about me and about life in America. As Anand Mata napped on the rug with his children and wife, we chatted in the other room. He was the son of an astrologer and, after asking my birth date, proceeded to tell me some very specific things about myself. Later, he told Anand Mata that, in comparing her birth date and mine, it was destined that she and I should become close. He looked at me in wonder and said, "I have never seen Ma be so intimate with anyone." His wife laughed at his disbelief, while Anand Mata teased him for being jealous.

Later in the afternoon Madhav Bhai and I sat talking again while the others rested. He was informing me how women were once oppressed in India but how that is no longer the case. My disagreement led to a heated argument, and Anand Mata stirred from her nap just long enough to remark that women have a long way to go in India. Next we argued about the controversial issue of reservations (something like affirmative action policies in the United States) for Backward Classes. When he expressed his opposition to reservations of any sort, Anand Mata sat upright to explain that we must at least give them (people of Backward Classes) a chance even if it means that there may also be some harm done in the process; such unpopular views revealed her Gandhian background. I do not know if Madhav Bhai actually changed his opinion, but he nodded affirmatively as she spoke and refrained from expressing any disagreement. Although Anand Mata refused to call anyone a disciple and Madhav Bhai had been initiated by another guru, he clearly regarded Anand Mata as an informal guru. One time, when we ran into Madhav Bhai's close friend and *guru-bhai* on the street as he was on his way to visit her, the man laughed out loud, fell to the ground in a full prostration on the street and clasped her feet, then stood back up and hugged her. His deference to her was a reflection of her spiritual status, but that deference was characterized by affection and intimacy rather than formality.

Madhav Bhai's wife and I made tea since our projected time of departure was approaching. As we all sat around the small table in the hall, cups in hand, Anand Mata turned to Madhav Bhai and said, "I feel sad. Of course sadhus should not feel sadness, but today our daughter is leaving." She had always addressed me as "daughter," and the departure of a daughter (usually at the time of marriage) is a sad event. I reflected on all that I had learned during the last two weeks and of how I had savored our conversations. For Anand Mata, educating me about sannyasa did not mean teaching abstract philosophy, meditation, or ritual worship; rather, it meant instructing me how to negotiate social relationships so as to maintain my own integrity without harming others. This is what she meant by love, the compassionate love that was the goal of her *sadhana* and did not conform to hard and fast rules of right and wrong.

On our journey to Sant Kuti, we dropped off Madhav Bhai and his family at the bus stand and declared our farewells. As soon as the scooter began to move again Anand Mata clasped my hand and remarked that she would remember these last two weeks. She likened my research to walking a tightrope. "You have done a lot of *sadhana* in previous lives. You have walked a very fine wire without falling into any sannyasi's clutches and without angering anyone either. . . . You will be successful in life. I am now confident that you have the ability to survive any crisis in life. No matter how strongly I feel about someone I try to be neither overconfident—since we never know what Paramatma will do—nor too hopeless about that person, no matter how bad they seem. And I can see that you have the same attitude. You have experienced here in a few months what you would have gotten in ten years back in America!" I was saddened at the thought of leaving her for a new sannyasini I hardly knew and a new ashram with unfamiliar ways.

When we arrived at the gate of Sant Kuti, Professor Singh and another elderly lady, "Masiji," rushed out to greet us. Masiji, looking at my feet, announced with a big smile that Anand Mata had made me into a sadhu starting from the bottom up. I looked down to see my own unadorned feet (devoid of nail polish and toe rings) in the hideous but cherished ochre-colored, plastic sandals which Anand Mata had presented to me upon our parting, apologizing that it was the only thing she had to give. The *salvar* (loose pants) I wore that day also happened to be of a salmon shade, close enough to saffron that, from the knees down, I did in fact look like a sadhu. This was cause for alarm. I did not want to become a sadhu. To the others, aware of my husband awaiting my return to the United States, it signaled that I was dangerously close to retreating from the duties of a female householder. The uncomfortable irony of a recently married woman dressed like a sadhu, when the householder's ethic demanded that she be ornamented in bright colors and shimmering jewels, was greeted by loud howls of laughter that I found strangely soothing.

Walking a Tightrope

What I gained from my two weeks with Anand Mata was some understanding about the way in which she attempts to imbue her life with the spirit of bhakti. For her, Paramatma is love and should color a renouncer's every thought and action. There are many different emotions that in India might be translated as love, including *moh*, *mamta*, *prem*, and *karuna*. During the course of our interviews, Anand Mata made a clear distinction between *moh* (attachment) and *mamta* (parental affection) on the one hand and *prem* (love) and *karuna* (compassion) on the other. "A mother typically loves her child because of *mamta*, while the guru's love for a disciple is full of *karuna*," she explained. One difference is that *mamta* can never become hard or stern (*kathor*). "If a child asks his mother for something that she considers harmful," continued Anand Mata, "*karuna* (compassion) will cause her to deny him that thing. But if she is motivated by *mamta* (affection) or *moh* (attachment), she will feel helpless and give in to the child's desire. Say a child with bad teeth requests a toffee. Under the influence of *mamta* or *moh*, the mother may give him a toffee, even secretly, behind the father's back. *Karuna* would never permit such an action, so it has a tinge of cruelty. The guru always appears slightly cruel to the disciple because she will forbid anything that might take the disciple away from her *sadhana*. It is not that the guru has no love (*prem*) for the disciple, but her love is so full that she protects the disciple from harm. If the mother is also a guru she will lovingly explain to the child why he cannot have a toffee, then if explanation fails she will resort to *karuna* and simply refuse to allow it. We think there is a lack of love here, but that is not so. Perfect love has a place for *karuna*, because the lover, in spite of an unfavorable reaction from the beloved, will deny that which is harmful. This is the subtle distinction between the two types of love." Thus, the guru's love may have an outward expression of cruelty.[2] While an outward display of anger may be necessary at times, as in scolding a small child, it should never be felt inside. According to Anand Mata, if the goals of bhakti, loving devotion and fervor, and those of sannyasa, detachment and indifference, seem to conflict, it is only in the lower forms of love. The highest form of love is compassion, a love imbued with detachment.

It was compassion, simultaneously detached and loving, that motivated her to protect the reputation of Swamiji by not criticizing him in public and by advising him to educate his disciple, to instigate an affair for one girl and discourage the budding romance of another, and to take on the responsibility of aiding an aspiring anthropologist. Having renounced worldly life, Anand Mata nonetheless lives in society, and this means she must strike a delicate balance of spiritual and pragmatic goals. Her refusal to condemn anyone absolutely is founded in her knowledge of the abstract idea that everyone is Paramatma, and her *sadhana* of "total surrender" to the forces of Paramatma implies an understanding that we do not control our own destinies. At the same time and on a more pragmatic level, she asserts that women have had to suffer because of their greater spiritual strength and capacity for surrender. "Women," she says, "know the art of surrender. This art was exploited by men, and women out of magnanimity did not complain about this treatment for a long time." As a social critic and pragmatist, she recognizes the necessity for people, especially women, to escape exploitation and maintain personal dignity in the face of power inequalities while simultaneously striving to fulfill their worldly needs, such as holding on to a job or collecting information for a thesis. Ensuring that one's every word and action is informed by all of these goals requires a delicate balancing act in which priorities shift but are never suspended entirely. It is not surprising then, that she likened my encounter with Maharaj in Benaras as walking a tightrope. Curiously, it was the success of this balancing act that led her to announce with such confidence not only that I had performed *sadhana* in previous lives but also that I could handle any, yes, any, crisis in life. For her, the ability to negotiate social relationships without ignoring spiritual or pragmatic goals was at the very heart of sannyasa. And it was a form of *tapasya*. The central lesson she tried to impart to me, a young female householder, was the importance of approaching social relationships with a combination of compassion, personal dignity, and pragmatism. To have simply rid myself of Maharaj's attentions by ignoring or insulting him was not an option for both otherworldly and worldly reasons. The importance of treating Maharaj with respect was due partly to my own need to maintain a decent reputation in order to conduct research and to Uma Giri's need to live with him in the same ashram. But also, it was simply that he (a respected sannyasi), like the shifty-eyed sadhu (a nobody), deserved to be treated with compassion. Her emphasis on treating others compassionately, even while acknowledging their weaknesses and protecting herself from their mal-treatment, was evident also in her attitude toward Jayashri Mata.

Jayashri Mata was a ninety-year-old sannyasini living near Gomukh Ashram and generally considered to be crazy. This reputation was earned by her cer-tainty that people wished to harm her and by her habit of yelling at neighbors for no apparent reason. The fact that she lived alone was not reason enough for criticism, though it may have contributed to her reputation. She did nonsensical things like put great effort and some money toward building a shack that would keep her neither warm nor dry. Although she owned an eight-foot square cot-tage and a small piece of what was now prime real estate, she lived there in a state of destitution. When Anand Mata gave her an old woolen rug one winter, Jayashri Mata said it was too good to use and packed it away. She agreed to spread it on her cold cement floor only when Anand Mata threatened to take it back and give it to some poor sadhu who would use it. Anand Mata also tried to convince her to sell half the land and then use the money to subsidize a nutri-tious diet, but she refused. In spite of the woman's irrational and sometimes mean behavior, Anand Mata did not simply dismiss or make fun of her as Swamiji did. He was amused that I spent any time with her at all. While I was visiting the old sannyasini one day a neighbor dropped off some *prasad* wrapped in a leaf that he had brought from the temple. While Jayashri Mata was engrossed in lecturing me about the importance of celibacy (even in marriage), I was distracted by a trail of ants that had discovered the blessed sweets and alerted her to this minor crisis during a lull in the conversation. "It doesn't matter," she said, "they are also devotees of Bhagwan. I'll just brush them aside when I need to eat some." On another visit I watched as she poured half of her meager day's supply of milk into a bowl for two cats. When I reported these inci-dents to Anand Mata she emphasized the compassion behind Jayashri Mata's mental imbalance. "See," she said, "if she had received the proper guidance she could have reached a very high state."

Treading the path of sannyasa as a bhakti-oriented person involves imbuing one's life with the spirit of compassionate love. What is striking about Anand Mata's style of renunciation is the apparently unlikely combination of other-worldly, transcendent withdrawal from the social world and a devotional atti-tude that colors the negotiation of everyday social interactions. This combination requires daily decisions about when to get involved, in the hope of alleviating suffering or providing spiritual guidance, and when to say "How does it concern me?" A related challenge facing Anand Mata is how to treat those around her with compassion without giving in to demands that might encroach either on her dignity as a human being or on her spiritual needs. Adhering to these goals requires discrimination and intelligence, according to Anand Mata, but the goals themselves are not ultimately incompatible.

This particular tension between personal spiritual needs and compassion for others is expressed dramatically in her very decision to renounce. Anand Mata once narrated the story of Buddha's departure from home: "After obtaining realization Buddha went back to the palace to beg alms from Yashodra, the wife he renounced. Buddha knew that she would demand an explanation from him. And he knew that he would have to give her an answer since he had committed an injustice by running off in the middle of the night, without even telling her he was leaving. When Buddha arrived at her door Yashodra said, 'Before I give you alms please answer two questions for me. The principle (*tattva*), the truth, which you went to the forest to find, could you not have obtained that here in the palace? And since you left without telling me, does that mean you had no trust in me? If you had told me I would have let you go.' Buddha said, 'I'll first answer the second question. My leaving without saying anything did not mean that I had no trust in you; I did not trust myself. I knew that if I had asked you, you would have agreed with whatever path I had chosen. But facing you and speaking with you would have broken the firm determination (*sankalp*) that had arisen within me. It is because I did not trust myself that I left quietly. And the second question. . . . The self-knowledge that I obtained in the forest was present in the palace then and is present even now. You were not an obstacle in my path, but for me it was necessary to wander. It was because of my own weakness that I could not obtain it here.'"

Anand Mata told this story as an illustration of the pain and hardship women must suffer because of their capacity for surrender. Implied was a critique of the way Buddha left home, without compassion or regard for his wife's feelings. In comparing this story to Anand Mata's own departure from householder life (narrated to me months earlier), the differences are significant. Even in renouncing one's family, according to her, it is important to do so with compassionate love. She could not leave without first persuading family members that her decision was both wise and sincere, otherwise it would have been too cruel. And when she decided to take a vow of silence, she went to her relatives one-by-one and informed them of her plan. She neither forbade anyone to visit her nor showed any special affection for them when they did visit, so eventually they themselves stopped coming. She tried to minimize the suffering caused by her renunciation; yet she did not give in to relatives' attempts to dissuade her from doing what she needed to do. For Anand Mata, the very act of renouncing is fraught with tension between the compassionate love emphasized in bhakti and the detachment of sannyasa.

Sannyasa as Love

According to the *Bhagavadgita* the path of bhakti emphasizes the emotional, karma the practical, and *jnana* the philosophical or reflective aspects of the human approach to the divine. Anand Mata considered herself to be oriented toward bhakti, and one reason she left the ashram of her second guru was that she realized his emphasis on *jnana* or philosophy was incompatible with her own bhakti nature. As Potter notes, bhakti implies taking an informal attitude toward ritual and an intensely personal attitude toward devotion. More important than the form of worship is its spirit, which should be playful, random, and expressive (Potter 1991:40). Anand Mata valued the knowledge contained in scripture but felt that one should absorb the spirit of texts rather than engage in intellectual debate about their meaning. For her, Paramatma *is* love (*prem*) and the meaning of bhakti *sadhana* is to permeate one's every thought and action with Paramatma, with love. Much has been written about medieval bhakti female saints who dedicated themselves to a god envisioned as husband or lover. Anand Mata's devotion, however, was not directed toward any particular deity through ritual worship, as indicated by the absence of religious imagery in her rooms. Rather, it was a diffuse sort of devotion or "total surrender" that is thought to arise from the knowledge that Paramatma is everywhere and is everything.[3] When I met Anand Mata for the first time and asked if I should leave my leather purse at the door (since leather is ritually polluting), she replied, "If I see that leather purse as Paramatma then how can I forbid its presence?" Devotion to Brahman can be in *saguna* form (with qualities or attributes) or *nirguna* form (without qualities or attributes), and Anand Mata's comment can be interpreted as either. Because Paramatma is *manifest* in the leather, this can be understood as *saguna*. However, since Paramatma is manifest in the leather in the same way that it is manifest in an image of a deity, this can be seen as *nirguna*. *Saguna* and *nirguna* are philosophical distinctions that are common in everyday usage, though the distinction is not always clear-cut. Either way, this habit of seeing the divine in all living and insentient beings is a kind of bhakti informed by Advaita.

Dazey writes about the apparent contradiction in the Dashnami Order between a professed Advaita that elevates knowledge above all else and the prevalence of conventional devotional practices (1993:147). Shankara's writings suggest that he viewed bhakti either as a discipline that can prepare one for knowledge, or, in its higher stages, as identical with this same knowledge (Alston cited in Dazey 1993:152). According to Dazey, the object of devotion becomes, in the final state of realization, nondual. In the committed form of renunciation that emerged in the late nineteenth and twentieth centuries, bhakti is reinterpreted to mean social service. Here, prayer and ritual worship that is focused on a deity is only one form, and indeed a lower form, when compared with the more direct "service of God in man" (Swami Akhandananda cited in Dazey 1993:164). Anand Mata does not engage in "service of God in man" in the sense of being devoted to social service; indeed, this is what she left behind in taking sannyasa. However, emphasizing diffuse "love" over "devotion" is compatible with advaitic goals; this interpretation is unusual but not entirely idiosyncratic (see, for example, Hatley and Inayatullah 1999:143–44). People expect renouncers to embody the teachings of Shankara and thus to be emotionally aloof. This is what separates them from other kinds of ascetics, particularly Vaishnava bhakti ascetics, but Anand Mata was both aloof and emotionally engaged.

The final stage of religious life, for Anand Mata, is not to love objects or persons or gods but to become love itself. This love is both transcendent and manifest in everyday life, because the distinction itself dissolves. At this final stage, bhakti combines with the detachment of sannyasa. These two seemingly contradictory but transcendent goals of love, which draws one into social relationships, and detachment from those same relationships, dovetail with more pragmatic concerns in the everyday life of Anand Mata and other sannyasinis. Since this is an abstract love that needs no object, it follows that whatever Anand Mata does is *sadhana* because it is done with love as the goal. This includes what are normally considered to be mundane activities, including the negotiation of everyday social relationships.

Chapter Three

Real Saints Don't Need Sleep: Renunciation as Service

I had been living in Haridwar almost a year when Mehraji, the man who introduced me to Anand Mata, shifted from Sant Kuti to a significantly larger ashram not too far away. Rishi Ashram was presided over by a sannyasini called "Baiji." She had invited Mehraji to live in her ashram and manage one of its charitable projects in exchange for room and board. Even before meeting Baiji I knew that she was a very different sort of sannyasini than Anand Mata. Aside from the fact that she had an ashram of her own, one (male) monastic disciple, and many lay devotees, Baiji was reputed to be a strict, rather orthodox guru. In person, she was soft-spoken and quick to smile; she wore ankle-length robes and covered her short hair only for warmth in the winter. On our first meeting, she not only agreed to be interviewed but also warmly offered me a room at Rishi Ashram so that I might see for myself what life there was like. By the end of my stay in Haridwar, I had spent more time with Baiji than with any other sannyasini.

While Anand Mata claimed to be following the path of devotion, Baiji consistently refused to define herself according to any particular sect or path. Indeed, her religiosity crossed several conceptual boundaries. For example, it was not that she considered the distinction between bhakti, karma, and *jnana* to be meaningless but that she followed all three paths rather than any one of them. Also, Baiji was considered "orthodox" by many who knew her because of

79

her initiation by a Dashnami sannyasi, her knowledge of Sanskrit scriptures, and her meticulous attention to ritual; and yet she also emphasized the social service characteristic of modern renunciation. Another distinction blurred in Baiji's religious life is that between worship of an abstract divinity without form (*nirguna*) and *saguna* worship of personalized deities. Baiji's disciples often discussed this in terms of the parallel distinction between *nirakar* and *sakar*. Devotional worship is particularly associated with the Puranas, texts which contain stories about the personalities, lives, adventures, and family life of gods and goddesses. Devotion to a personal deity is not generally associated with sannyasa (and some would find it antithetical to sannyasa), even though many renouncers participate in *puja-path*. Rishi Ashram housed both a lavishly maintained temple for the worship of personal deities and a sacrificial altar for the performance of fire sacrifice (*havan*). My observations of religious life in Rishi Ashram supported Baiji's self-proclaimed eclecticism.

Her Story: From Arya Samaj to Devotional Worship

As with Anand Mata, Baiji's present religious life is hardly a simple continuation of her upbringing. While both sannyasinis give importance to having grown up in religious households and in the proximity of saints, each has made a rather profound philosophical break with her past. Baiji was raised in a staunch Arya Samaj family that performed Vedic ritual daily and rejected the worship of images, but she now performs Vedic sacrifice as well as *murti puja* (the worship of icons) with apparently equal fervor. Her ashram maintains a large temple housing icons of Shiva, Vishnu, the Goddess, and their various incarnations. The brightly painted and ornamented deities are worshiped through song and prayer (*prarthna*) for an hour and a half each morning and evening. The deities are offered incense and flowers, fed whatever is cooked in the ashram, bathed, and put to sleep at night. In addition, special *pujas* to major deities are performed on astrologically appropriate days of the week.

The Arya Samaj, a revivalist sect founded in the late 1800s by the sannyasi Dayananda Saraswati, aims to rid contemporary Hinduism of its "corruptions" (worship of icons, untouchability, ignorance of sacred texts) by returning to Vedic culture. The Arya Samaj valorizes such brahmanic ideals as vegetarianism, Vedic ritual, and Sanskrit study. It also, however, criticizes brahmanic orthodoxy's definition of caste as a status one is born with. Instead, it considers caste to be an achieved status in the sense that any person who upholds brahmanic ideals in their daily life is a Brahmin, regardless of birth status. According to Baiji, her father was a devout Brahmin (and his name indicated he was Brahmin by birth) who practiced Ayurvedic medicine (an indigenous Hindu system), and their household was run according to brahmanic ideals. She describes her paternal grandparents as yogis who meditated each day for long periods. During childhood, she and her siblings woke before dawn each morning to meditate, perform fire sacrifice, and recite the Gayatri Mantra; only upon completion of their religious duties were the children given breakfast or allowed to leave for school. These habits of religious discipline, she says, were so ingrained in her personality that when the turning point came in her life she instinctively went in this direction.

A central belief of the Arya Samaj is that religious and educational equality of the sexes characterized ancient Hinduism. Consistent with this, the Arya Samaj has historically encouraged both secular and Sanskrit education for girls in an attempt to improve the status of women. Also, both male and female members of the order are allowed to take sannyasa provided they are initiated by a guru of their own gender. Because Baiji was raised in an Arya Samaj atmosphere, when she began to desire a spiritual teacher she naturally imagined her future guru as a woman ("a Yogi Mataji") rather than a man. So it came as a surprise when, at age twenty-two, she dreamt that a man put his hand on her shoulder and promised to teach her. She had not told anyone of her deep longing for a guru. Her father was in the habit of asking about his children's dreams each morning and when she related hers, he replied, "If you have decided about the path you must follow; then you will certainly meet him. . . . Who is that man?" She did not recognize the person in her dream but replied that, from his appearance—he was wearing a white shirt and waistcloth—it looked as if he had come from the region of celestial beings (*divyalok*). His face was imprinted on her memory.

Six months later, the young Baiji and her family met a swami while visiting Haridwar, and even though his voice sounded familiar she did not recognize him at first. When he offered to take her father to meet a saint who lived deep in the forest she insisted on tagging along with the men. She asked the forest-dwelling saint if women could become yogis, and his reply was unambiguous: "Never." Just as the absoluteness of his answer began to sink in, and with it a feeling of despair, says Baiji, the swami who had escorted them into the forest put a hand on her shoulder and said, "Get up my child; I will teach you," *exactly* as it had happened in the dream six months earlier. It was then that she realized he was the man who would be her guru. The next morning, and much to her family's chagrin, Baiji stubbornly refused to leave for the bus station until "Swamiji" kept his promise. At that moment, though, he was seated in meditation and therefore unavailable, and, with the bus about to leave, a battle of wills between Baiji and her father was imminent. Just then, Swamiji broke his meditation and called her and her father into his cottage. There he instructed Baiji to meditate on a certain mantra and sent her home. From then on, she began to meditate and keep periods of silence while living at home.

According to Baiji, it was through the meditation she practiced at home that she began to move toward the path of knowledge (*jnanamarg*) by understanding Vedanta philosophy intuitively rather than through the study of texts.[1]

Swamiji had her keep a spiritual diary and, through it, he monitored her progress. Once Baiji and her family went to Haridwar to meet Swamiji with the idea that she would stay on for a while, but he was not there when they arrived. So, instead, Baiji stayed at the ashram of a local sadhu, Swami Ramanand, whom she had met through Swamiji on a previous trip to Haridwar. It would be safer, she was told, than staying alone at her guru's ashram. During this stay with Swami Ramanand she met a visiting *avadhut* who lived in a Himalayan pilgrimage town and eventually became her second guru.[2] "Avadhutji" formally introduced her to the philosophy of Vedanta and instructed her to memorize texts in the Nyaya and Vaisheshika philosophical systems [which emphasize the use of logic in the pursuit of liberation (Embree 1998:298)] and several Upanishads, which she did. Eventually, she went to Uttarkhand where Avadhutji lived and remained there for several years, practicing *sadhana* under his guidance, until poor health forced her to return to the plains.

When I first met Baiji she was almost seventy and had had many bouts of illness. Yet her smooth skin, gleaming white smile, bright eyes and abundant energy made it difficult to think of her as elderly. Her short, cropped hair was more black than gray and her movements quick, strong, and confident. A sadhu's youthful appearance is taken by many to be a sign of spiritual power. Baiji spent most of her time at Rishi Ashram but visited her smaller, older ashram in Uttarkhand twice a year. Her circle of over thirty disciples was primarily composed of male and female householders who lived with their families. Ved Brahmachari was her only ascetic disciple who had devoted himself full-time to spiritual discipline rather than taking up family life.[3] He was a middle-aged man, some twenty years younger than her, who lived at Rishi Ashram and still wore the white robes of celibate studenthood.

Mistress of Rishi Ashram

While Gomukh Ashram, where Anand Mata lived, provided little more than shelter and two basic meals a day for its residents, Rishi Ashram felt more like a community. All residents, including servants, *pandits*, disciples, and guests received three full meals as well as morning and afternoon tea (or milk for children, sadhus, and some elderly people) from the kitchen, and even packed-lunches when necessary. There were no cooking facilities in individual rooms. Baiji did not require attendance at religious functions or allegiance to her religious teachings. Yet, while a few residents such as Mehraji followed their own gurus and spiritual traditions, most visitors came to Rishi Ashram solely to be near Baiji, either to seek her advice and blessings or simply "to serve." She was not only the ashram's spiritual leader but also and unambiguously its administrator. Not all gurus are as involved as Baiji in the mundane details of managing their ashrams. Baiji made all final decisions on matters of food, finances, medical treatment, ritual protocol, and interpretation of scripture. This is not to say that her power was absolute, as her devotees had a great deal of influence, but that she was the center of all activity.

The charitable activities of Rishi Ashram also made the place busier, louder, and more cluttered than any other ashram I had visited. The ashram provided room, board, a small allowance, and in some cases a college education to five or six young *pandits* from poor villages. In return, they maintained the temple, performed ritual services for Baiji's disciples, and helped with other chores around the ashram. The ashram also ran a small clinic for Ayurvedic medicine, offered sewing classes to neighborhood girls, and founded clinics and schools in remote mountain villages. These services were offered to the poor free of charge. The extent of Baiji's involvement in these various projects was evident in the clutter that filled every inch of her ashram. In the hall there were huge sacks of grains and vegetables, bottles of pickles, tins filled with sweet and salty edibles, bolts of cloth, and straw mats spread out on empty floor space and covered with chopped greens for dehydrating. Along the walls were rows of sagging shelves filled with Ayurvedic health tonics, multiple copies of the *Bhagavadgita*, and years' worth of accounting ledgers. Baiji's involvement in charitable projects required her participation in a wide range of what are normally considered to be worldly activities, such as negotiating with merchants to obtain cheap cloth for the sewing school, planning meals, hiring teachers and doctors, and recording financial transactions.

In addition to the charitable projects, another reason for Baiji's marked involvement in worldly activities was her circle of devotees. Anand Mata, too, was involved in the lives of householders, but the guidance she offered was more a by-product of her *sadhana* than the purpose of it. For Baiji, providing guidance and other forms of service *was* her *sadhana*. I met some of Baiji's followers several months earlier when I visited the ashram to attend a reading of the *Ramayana*. That day Rishi Ashram was filled with fashionable, denim-clad children educated in Delhi's elite English-medium schools. Their mothers sported short hairstyles and gold bangles. Although Baiji herself spoke no English, many of her closest followers were as comfortable with English as they were with Hindi or Panjabi. The husbands were educated, some abroad, and were generally successful in business. Though not all of Baiji's disciples fit this elite class profile, those who formed the core of her following did. They were the disciples who would host Baiji when she visited the city. And, of course, it was their wealth that built Rishi Ashram and supported its various charitable projects.

Ritual activities were equally central to the daily functioning of Rishi Ashram, and they too involved Baiji in worldly matters, as she had to purchase ritual objects, prepare special foods, and plan what should be given in *dan*. She looked after the *pandits* by arranging their daily food, providing education, and even disciplining them. They were, after all, young men and had to be instructed to clean their rooms, behave with proper decorum, and attend to their studies. Moreover, many rituals were sponsored by householder disciples for specific worldly purposes: to mark a death anniversary, to celebrate an engagement, or to seek divine intervention in resolving some crisis in health or employment. Baiji's devotees saw her involvement in worldly activities as *seva*. She offered food, shelter, and knowledge to me as a form of *seva*, so that I might be helped in my endeavor to write a thesis and serve as a conduit for what she considered to be Hinduism's highest truths.

Learning to Participate in the Life of Rishi Ashram

An insightful sannyasini once remarked to me that an ashram is usually exactly like the homes of its trustees. That observation was on my mind the evening I arrived at Baiji's ashram for my first ten-day visit. I already knew something about Baiji's disciples, having met several of them during the *Ramayana* reading I had attended several months earlier. The wealth and aesthetic of Baiji's disciples were embodied in the building. It was modern, yet elegant in design. The outside walkways were smooth, made of polished stone rather than rough cement, and the external walls were coated with a tasteful whitewash instead of the more popular pastel blues, pinks, and yellows. These were the most superficial markers of the economic class of Baiji's followers.[4] As soon as I slipped through the ashram gate, the gatekeeper took my bag and led me to the rear entrance, the one for daily, informal use. I left my footwear among the clutter of sandals outside the door and stepped onto the cool, slightly sticky stone floor of the deserted dining area. The lack of natural light made the gray interior look even grayer. Within seconds, Baiji appeared, greeted me, and instructed the gatekeeper to show me to my room, informing me that the bell would sound for the evening meal around eight o'clock.

Upstairs, the long, unswept hallway lined with padlocked doors indicated that the ashram was relatively empty. The rooms were new and inviting, each furnished with a ceiling fan, a bed, a tiny bedside table, a straw mat for the floor and a single, naked light bulb. I was delighted to discover the luxury of a private bathroom, inside of which was a tap for bath water, two plastic buckets (one for fetching hot water and the other for mixing it in with the cold), a tiny sink, and a western-style toilet, the type, no doubt, that one would find in the homes of Baiji's urban disciples. I recalled the large and crudely constructed dining table, covered with a plastic tablecloth, that dominated the main room outside the kitchen. Though dining tables are a standard piece of furniture in middle and upper-class urban homes I had never seen one in an ashram. In ashrams (except some catering to Westerners) it is customary to sit cross-legged on the floor for meals. Those who are either socially elevated or too arthritic to sit on the floor might be seated on a low stool with their food on a higher stool or small table in front of them. The large, communal dining table surrounded by chairs was a sign of the influence of Baiji's urban devotees.

Meals also followed a schedule more typical of urban households than of Haridwar ashrams. That first night, the dinner bell rang at nine o'clock rather than eight. As it turned out, such late dinners were usual for Rishi Ashram. Since the *pandits* were always served first, guests second, the cooks and other workers, including Baiji herself, frequently had dinner as late as ten o'clock. I came downstairs at the sound of the bell to find the *pandits* in the middle of their dinner, seated on the floor in two rows. I was instructed to sit at the table, with Mehraji and a visiting disciple whom I called "Vimla Auntie." Baiji was not eating because of an upset stomach but sat at the table anyway to give us company and to supervise our meal. She served us a soupy chutney that she had concocted to use up the large quantities of ripe guavas recently donated to the ashram.

After eating, the four of us remained at the table chatting while the cooks served themselves and sat on the floor mats, long since vacated by the *pandits*, to eat. It was past eleven when we finally rose from the table, each of us washing our own utensils and then retiring to our rooms. Baiji had informed me that the morning bell would sound at 3:30 to rouse the *pandits* so they could fire up the wood stove to heat water and bathe before the 6:00 prayer session, but that I could come down whenever I was ready. "Breakfast is at nine," she said. I rarely attended the morning service (few people did) but joined the evening prayer session (*prarthna*) most days and participated in a variety of ashram activities: performing *puja* along with everyone else, sitting through hours of readings, engaging in religious discussions. Taking my lead from the other householders, I performed *puja* to the *pandits* after attending any special ritual that they performed; this typically involved sprinkling flower petals on their heads, touching their feet, and giving each a token amount of cash.

While all this activity in the temple was important, the transformation of my status from a "guest" and outsider to an integrated, if temporary, member of the ashram resulted more from my involvement in ordinary activities than in specifically religious ones. I trace the development of this new role to my fifth day at Rishi Ashram. I had come downstairs some time before dinner to find Baiji and several *pandits* engaged in the task of hand-stitching thin mattress pads from rough, old burlap bags. A new gardener was recently employed by Baiji after his wife came begging for a job; Baiji came to know that the couple and their infant were sleeping on the wooden beds provided to them without anything underneath for warmth and padding, and though it was only September the nights had been cold and damp. She turned to me and smiled, "Burlap is supposed to be very warm. When somebody sends *dan* here nothing is wasted." The burlap bags had arrived at the ashram containing gifts of grains and vegetables. Baiji kept the sacks, sure that she would eventually find some use for them. And rather than simply handing the sacks over to the couple to fashion some sort of mattress for themselves, she saw to it that they were made neatly and durably.

Until that evening my offers to help in the kitchen had been rebuffed, and, being unsure of orthodox rules governing food handling and preparation, I did not insist. Rules of purity and pollution were closely observed at Rishi Ashram, and, having already been reprimanded for ritual gaffes more than once, I wished to avoid further embarrassment. Stitching burlap, however, did not seem to be a task requiring either purity or skill. After much insistence, Baiji finally allowed me to help, remarking, "What will Mehraji think that I am making you do this dirty work?" Since Mehraji had introduced me to Baiji, I was generally associated with him. As an educated gentleman, he helped Baiji by running errands and doing administrative chores. But, in keeping with Indian attitudes about the lowliness of manual labor, he did no such work around the ashram aside from cleaning his own room, dishes, and clothes, which are the basics required of everyone. Because of my association with Mehraji and my status as an American ("but from a good Hindu family"), I was placed in the category of one who did no manual labor. My participation in the hygienically, if not ritually, dirty task of stitching dusty old burlap bags marked a turning point in my status and my experience of Rishi Ashram. The next evening I found myself helping Vimla Auntie iron the doll-like garments for the temple deities, whose clothes were changed twice a month. Since there were sixteen *murtis* in the ashram's temple and each outfit consisted of several articles of clothing, it was no small task. Gradually, as I learned the proper way of doing things and as others felt more comfortable requesting my help, I became increasingly involved in a wide array of chores, particularly those of food preparation.

One afternoon I emerged from my room at teatime to find several people gathered in the kitchen. There was a lot of work to be done, they said, so I gulped my tea, performed a purificatory rite by rinsing my mouth with water, and joined the others in the kitchen. The two cooks were called "Lakshmi Behn" and "Sita Behn," "Behn" being a term for "sister." Lakshmi Behn had just returned from vacation and was thus new to me. She would only allow me to help after one of Baiji's disciples convinced her that I was in fact "one who worked" (*kamkamevali*); even then she decided that it was fine for me to chop carrots but unacceptable for me to do the dirty work of cleaning mud-encrusted potatoes. By the next week, however, she was more than willing to hand me a large bowl of muddy potatoes for scrubbing.

The amount of time and attention devoted to food at Rishi Ashram seemed equal to that in any Indian home. Baiji was praised for making delicious dishes from what is considered waste vegetation, such as the leaves of zucchini plants or banana peels. "Baiji lived in the forest in Uttarkhand doing *sadhana*," explained Mehraji. "Then they had to subsist on whatever plants were available, so she knows how to make all kinds of tasty things out of nothing." Frugality and efficient use of resources were paramount values in Baiji's ashram. Baiji accumulated foodstuffs for thoughtful—never haphazard—distribution among the twenty to thirty people living at Rishi Ashram at any given time. In deciding what and how much to serve for meals, it seemed, she carefully planned what would be needed for an upcoming *puja* or feast and saved portions accordingly. Nothing was ever wasted. Whenever I returned from town with a box of sweets, it would inevitably disappear into one of the screened food cupboards (screened to allow air circulation but keep out rodents) and reemerge a few days later when needed for a special occasion. It was part of Baiji's duty as the head of the ashram to make sure there would be food for the next guest and *prasad* for the next *puja*. Because of careful management and Baiji's interest in cooking, food was both abundant and delicious, and, for this reason, her ritual feasts attracted large crowds of holy people.

Baiji's concern with the efficient use of resources was not a particularly renunciant characteristic, as her approach to food was very different from Anand Mata's. It was Baiji's duty as a guru with her own ashram and an emphasis on *seva* to accumulate things for appropriate distribution. In contrast, Anand Mata, as an independent, contemplative sannyasini, tried to avoid the accumulation of food, money, and material objects, as classical renunciation demands. Although her ashram provided two meals, Anand Mata kept fruit and snacks in her room for guests. Her food supply was composed of things people brought her, except for the milk that she had delivered every morning. Her *sadhana* of "total surrender" meant, in part, living for the moment without worry rather than planning for the future. One day, when a busload of unsophisticated villagers from her hometown arrived unexpectedly at her doorstep to obtain *darshan* of a saint, she told them to sit down wherever they could find a place and then disappeared into her bedroom to find something to give as *prasad*. She rapidly pulled out all her highest quality edibles—whole cardamom pods, cloves, raisins, cashews, almonds—emptied the bags onto an enormous platter, tossed it with her fingers, and handed it to me to distribute. Her reckless abandon contrasted strikingly with Baiji's careful planning. There was no management, no saving portions for future guests, no giving particular kinds of foods to particular kinds of guests. Underlying these very different styles is a shared understanding that whatever resources are obtained should (either immediately or eventually) be passed on.

The activities of food preparation provided the context for much of my research at Rishi Ashram, as I learned much in conversations carried out over the rhythmic sound of dull knives hitting wood. Many of the devotees took an interest in my research. Most considered it entirely appropriate that I should wish to write about their guru, though a few were more suspicious of my motives and sympathies. I was often asked by people I met, sadhus and householders alike, which sannyasinis I had already interviewed and, of course, the reputations of those persons shaped my own. The disciples who spent extended periods of time at the ashram often participated in both the formal interviews and informal discussions I had with Baiji. I had been at the ashram over one week when Baiji granted the first tape-recorded interview. Mehraji, Vimla Auntie, and Ved Brahmachari remained for the entire two hours, seated with me on the floor; they imbued this and subsequent interviews with spiritual value. Indeed, devotional accounts of particular saints often take the format of question-answer sessions with the guru. During the first few weeks I asked most of the questions, but they also participated by commenting, translating unfamiliar words for me, and occasionally posing their own questions.

My open-ended queries about *sadhana* or philosophy often led Baiji to offer personal anecdotes or reflections. Reluctant at first to ask for biographical information directly, I eventually realized that, as with Anand Mata, almost anything was ultimately a spiritual subject if framed as a question of morality or proper social behavior. Still, a few questions were off-limits, though I felt censored less by Baiji herself than by her disciples and my own sense of propriety. Baiji was pleased with my questions that first day and began to take my inquiry more seriously. Though she had to put other responsibilities aside for our interviews, she seemed to view them as a way to educate me and others. This, after all, was her duty as a guru.

It was after our first interview that Baiji began to refer to my previous life as a sadhu and how the *samskaras* created by habits of my past lives led me to choose this research topic. Almost all the sannyasinis I met referred to past lives in order to explain how it was that I, born in America and so recently married, had come to Haridwar to research sannyasinis. Baiji also began to remark often on how she could hardly tell I was a foreigner. Comments about my "Indianness" or my past life as a yogi were usually made in the context of an observation of how much work I did around the ashram or how well I served food. It was not so much the *amount* of work, since others did more than I, but the reversal it implied that inspired these comments. To them, I was a Westerner, a scholar, and from a wealthy, high-caste family,[5] so the humility of my labor was perhaps more significant. Once, when the kitchen was short of help and I alone served the lunch Sita Behn had cooked to a visiting family of seven, Baiji triumphantly informed the guests at the end of the meal of my true identity as a foreigner. The grandfather expressed his happy astonishment that I was from abroad and still did so much *seva*. Occasionally, Baiji explained, it happens that the experiences from some past life manifest themselves in a present life. Thus, she continued, I must have been a yogi in a previous life and was born into a family in America in order to experience (*bhog*) some karma or another, but that the influence of those past lives led me back to India to live in ashrams and listen to the wise words of Indian sadhus.

That manual work rather than spiritual knowledge or devotional fervor inspired comments about my previous life as a sadhu is consistent with the value Baiji places on social service and physical labor. In this respect, despite her orthodox reputation, she is much less "traditional" than Anand Mata, much more influenced by a morality that is both utilitarian and Protestant. In Haridwar's more orthodox ashrams, renouncers are expected to devote themselves to spiritual pursuits and workers are hired to do the dirty work but are euphemistically called "servers" (*sevaks*) rather than "servants" (*naukers*). At Gomukh Ashram, for example, a hired woman named Beena did the daily sweeping and washing of dishes. Anand Mata paid Beena extra to wash her personal utensils and clothes and had her wash mine while I was there. I had come to write a thesis, she insisted, so why waste time washing clothes and dishes. At Rishi Ashram, everyone washed their own utensils after a meal, while hired cooks washed only the pots and pans. Although devotees or cooks (never *pandits*) usually grabbed Baiji's used dishes before she could clean them, the disciples frequently remarked that Baiji washed her own clothes daily.

I was amused by the assumption that Americans would be reluctant to do physical work and the belief that my willingness to assist with chores made me not only more virtuous but more Indian. Because mundane work was so valued at Rishi Ashram and was the locus of social activity involving almost everyone (Baiji, servants, disciples, *pandits*), it offered an obvious opportunity to get involved in the ashram's social life. Regardless of our differing interpretations of my participation in ashram life, that Baiji could forget I was American clearly delighted her. Yet, in crucial ways Baiji treated me differently from her women disciples. She assigned me to my own room upstairs rather than a communal one downstairs, ostensibly because I was a student in need of quiet. Also, she gave me a lot of freedom, realizing that it was necessary for me to move around a lot, often alone, in order to complete the research for which I had come. Baiji never expressed any disapproval at my going off alone to run errands in town or to meet other sannyasinis. I once asked if she minded my going places alone. "No," she said, "because you are in the habit (*adat*) and because you know so many people here and go only to familiar places." One day when I returned from town, one of the cooks asked if my "man" would come from America to pick me up when I finished my work here. Baiji and I looked at each other and burst out laughing. "But she *is* a man!" exclaimed Baiji. I *was* like a man in the role I sometimes played vis-à-vis female disciples. When going to town I often ran errands for the women, who never ventured alone onto public transport, or was appointed escort to female visitors who wanted an excursion. Yet Baiji's comment was intended as a joke. I don't think she really viewed me, or sannyasinis who wandered fearless and alone for that matter, as masculine.

By the end of my initial ten-day visit I felt like a member of the ashram. That I was considered neither a stranger nor a nuisance by the people at Rishi Ashram made research there more fun and more fruitful. After six weeks back home in the United States my plan was to return to stay with Baiji for several months. I left with the impression that Rishi Ashram was more like a home than an ashram. And Baiji was like the lady of the house, constantly supervising servants, preparing and distributing food, welcoming guests, and treating illnesses.

When the time for my departure arrived, Baiji graciously invited me to return whenever and for however long I wanted. "There will always be room for you here. Consider this ashram to be your own home."

Sonam: Fierce Devotion

I soon returned to Rishi Ashram, arriving early one cold November morning by scooter from the train station. At breakfast, I found myself seated beside Sonam, a young woman about my age. We quickly became acquainted. She lived in Bulgaria where her husband was on a three-year government posting. There she fell ill and spent four months in the hospital, and, even after performing all sorts of tests, the medical doctors were unable to find anything wrong. Meanwhile, she had become so weak that she could not even lift her four-year-old daughter, Shivapriya. Baiji suggested that Sonam come to India with her daughter and stay in the ashram for treatment. Having diagnosed the illness as related to the spleen, Baiji prescribed a forty-day treatment that included drinking the juice of tender wheat grass, which Baiji was growing in pots especially for Sonam, and a glass of fresh cow urine (gomutra) every morning. "How did you come to know Baiji?" I asked, after we had exchanged biographical information.

"My mother-in-law was a devout follower of Baiji, and my husband and I also consider her to be our guru."

"Oh, so you only came to know Baiji after marriage?"

"Well, I myself am from Uttarkhand, where Baiji has an ashram, and I used to go with my parents to see Baiji on birthdays; we would take prasad and offer it to Bhagwan. We did not consider Baiji a guru but would visit her as one visits any saint or mahatma, to hear good words or just to be in their presence."

It was almost a week later when Sonam explained to me how Baiji was actually responsible for her marriage: "Whenever anyone used to visit Baiji's ashram in Uttarkhand, she would have my father show them around town. A boy Bharat had come with his mother to visit Baiji. Though I did not know it at the time, his parents were looking for a girl for him; they wanted a strict vegetarian girl. I was twenty, qualified to teach, and had not even thought of marriage. My father showed them around like so many others and then brought them home for tea. Within a week everything was fixed. Bharat's attitude was 'Whatever you say, Baiji. . . I only want your prasad; give me what you will.' So our marriage took place with Baiji's blessings." Sonam smiled shyly and went on to explain that her mother-in-law, who passed away a couple of years before, was Baiji's actual sister.

"Oh, that would make Baiji your masi (mother's sister)!" I exclaimed.

"Yes," she said quickly, "but we don't think of the family relationship anymore after someone has taken sannyasa. Instead, we think of her as our guru."

It appears to be common for Hindu householders to continue their relationship with a relative who has taken sannyasa, although they cease to call that person by kin terms and the nature of the relationship changes. It is not unusual for a renouncer to take on a relative as a lay or even a monastic disciple. For example, a sister or nephew may become a disciple and will be referred to as such. Usually, neither party will discuss the relationship in kin terms, although the ambiguity of the connection may be expressed in some contexts. Disciples, for instance, may take pride in their familial connection to a respected renouncer and seek to make the relationship known, though they would not do so in the presence of their guru. I once visited the cottage of an orthodox Dashnami renouncer and was surprised to find his wife there. I realized she was his wife because of prior knowledge of the family, not because of her behavior toward him. She told me that she had come from Delhi for a month to cook and serve "Swamiji." Once, when she referred to "Swamiji" during a private conversation, I asked, "Which Swami?" "My Swami," she answered, to indicate her husband. Similarly, during a conversation with an elderly sannyasini whose husband had also taken sannyasa, Baiji referred to the woman's husband as "*your* Swami." Regarding the fact that Sonam had married Baiji's nephew, Sonam's mother once remarked on the irony that, for her, coming to Baiji's ashram is like visiting her in-laws.

Sonam was very devoted to her guru and sought her advice on both spiritual and mundane matters. During her stay at Rishi Ashram, Sonam never expressed desires about what or how much she wanted to eat of any particular food. Before taking seconds of vegetables, for example, she would ask Baiji whether she should eat more. She consulted Baiji on everything from how she should discipline her child to what colors of clothing best suited her complexion. Once, Sonam obtained some cloth remnants from which she intended to sew some dresses for her daughter, but she wanted Baiji's advice on which cloth designs should be combined for aesthetic effect. It was days before Baiji had a chance to look over the cloth pieces, but Sonam waited patiently. Baiji would also discipline her daughter Shivapriya for sucking her thumb or for being obstinate, and Sonam always observed these interactions with appreciative amusement. Of all the women disciples I met, Sonam was the most resistant to making any decisions on her own when Baiji was available for consultation. If a young, married woman takes a guru she may find her devotion to the guru to be in conflict with her role as wife and mother. For Sonam, however, since her husband was equally devoted to Baiji, she could be an ideal disciple and an ideal wife simultaneously. Baiji taught her female disciples that their husband's wishes were the first priority. She never initiated any woman as a lay disciple without the permission of her husband.

Sonam and I spent many hours together at Rishi Ashram preparing raw vegetables for cooking or drying. Baiji had us chop huge amounts of leafy greens and cabbage when they were plentiful, spread them out on newspaper or straw mats, and set them in the sun to dry. The dehydrated vegetables might then be sent up to Baiji's Uttarkhand ashram where greens are unavailable in the winter or stored away for such emergencies as feeding unexpected guests. I appreciated having something productive to do rather than following Baiji around all day, but I also began to weary of chores that seemed unnecessary. My other activities included slicing fruit for *prasad* in the morning when Sonam was occupied, serving hot breads and replenishing vegetables during mealtimes, helping with accounts (the tedious rather than responsible aspects of this job), and attending the evening *prarthna*. In addition, I spent a lot of time pestering Baiji for interviews and religious discourses. Immediately following the evening prayer session, the *pandits*, disciples, and I would get up from where we were sitting to prostrate before Baiji who was usually perched on her raised wooden seat (*asan*) on one side of the room. After this, we might leave the temple or remain seated there at her feet. If Baiji was not immediately distracted by some other work and if we waited long and expectantly enough, such moments sometimes developed into an informal lecture or discussion.

Baiji as Guru: Wisdom, Spiritual Power, and Seva

One morning Baiji promised to speak with me "after Mrs. Malia's interview." Shortly after my arrival at Rishi Ashram, Baiji had begun jokingly to refer to all sorts of verbal interactions as "interviews." Mrs. Malia was a recently widowed middle-aged urbanite and longtime disciple who was visiting for a couple of weeks. She wished to discuss some personal matters with Baiji, and the two of them pulled their chairs out into the sun. Having returned an hour later to find them still deep in conversation, I sat in the courtyard with a newspaper, trying to remain unobtrusive and out of earshot but easily available should the opportunity for our interview arise. After half an hour, Baiji came to me and said that she had finished with Mrs. Malia but that the sun had made her drowsy. She insisted, however, that all she needed was something to munch on and summoned the gatekeeper to bring some white radishes from the garden. We sat down at the dining table with my tape recorder and a plate of sliced, salted radish between us.

"I slept only three hours in the night," she said.

"Baiji, please go and sleep for a while," I pleaded, to ease my guilt. "We can do the interview another time."

"What's the point? I'll only sleep five or ten minutes. . . . You must write in your thesis that sannyasinis also get sleepy." Baiji's spiritual powers, in the eyes of her disciples, were not diminished by displays of humanity such as illness, hunger, or sleepiness.

That evening, Baiji sent Sonam and myself into the temple to attend the *prarthna*, since the *pandits* were there alone, and then joined us just as the final verses were being sung. She bowed to each of the deities before taking her place on the seat and closing her eyes. After the worship was completed and the *pandits* had busied themselves cleaning the ritual utensils, Baiji asked Sonam to massage her head "because it always feels a bit strange after waking from meditation." Ved Brahmachari and I looked on silently as Sonam rubbed Baiji's head for about ten minutes. Then Baiji opened her eyes, looked at me, and asked if I wanted to do "question-answer." After about fifteen minutes of discussion, when Baiji and I were left alone for a few moments, I took the opportunity to inquire about an empty chair on one side of the room that was decorated with flower garlands. I had noticed the *pandits* making offerings to the chair during *prarthna* and Baiji herself bowing to it every day. She explained that when the *Bhagavata Purana* is being recited a chair should be available for the god Krishna in case he wants to come and listen [The *Bhagavata Purana* is a very popular devotional text detailing the incarnations Vishnu takes to restore virtue in the world. Its scenes about devotion to Lord Krishna are popular favorites.], or when any recitation (*path*) is going on there should be a chair for the god as well, "that is, if we really truly believe that these gods exist. If we take their existence as truth, we should provide a chair for them." Next I inquired about the four straw mats that one of the *pandits* had rolled out during the *puja* and decorated with flowers. She said these are spread out in case anyone from the heavenly region (*paramlok*) wants to come and join in. Thus, they are brought out before the *puja* as an invitation and are removed afterward so as to say "O.K. it's over, you can go now." With a chuckle, she waved her hand as if shooing away a pesky god who had overstayed his welcome. Regarding the chair, one of the disciples said to me later that Baiji had a vision while meditating in which Bhagwan came to her and said "Why haven't you kept a chair for me to come and sit?" One evening weeks later, in the middle of the *prarthna*, Baiji instructed a *pandit* to place an extra mat on the floor and decorate it with flowers, which he did without questioning. Apparently, Baiji had seen her disciple Bhavna's recently deceased mother enter the temple during *prarthna* and look around for a place to sit. Bhavna was moved and comforted to learn that her mother sat down for a while and was pleased with what she saw.

Baiji's spiritual power is one reason her disciples give for choosing her as their guru. Through meditation she is reputed to gain knowledge about everything from the treatment of illnesses to the whereabouts of deceased persons. Baiji is said to have cured one disciple of cancer and another of infertility, and she treats herself for various ailments. Once she was sick with a stomachache for a long time and had a vision to eat hot chili pepper on a bread roll! She was afraid of the burning it would cause, but, in an act of faith, spread a thick layer of chili pepper on a bread roll and ate it. Miraculously, she felt no burning in her mouth, eyes, lungs, or digestive tract. After three days she had a vision that she had eaten too much and should stop; then she felt the burning in her mouth, stomach, and while defecating. Red chili, she explained, like onions and garlic, kills bugs. Anyway, the stomach pains disappeared. In addition, Baiji is attributed with the ability not only to communicate with deities but to influence them as well. The most dramatic proof of this is the frequently told story of how she saved a Himalayan town from floods by performing a *puja* to Mother Ganges and asking her to retreat. Baiji's mystical powers are also expressed in everyday activities, in the knowledge, for example, of how to make tasty food "out of nothing" or how to draw up architectural plans. When I asked a disciple why something was done or how Baiji had learned something, the most common answer was "I don't know; she must have seen it in meditation."

However, Baiji's value as a guru derived as much from activities of a less glamorous nature. Her *seva* included all the mundane work of running an ashram: supervising projects, hiring and firing employees, managing the accounts, and organizing meals. One day Lakshmi Behn, Baiji, and I spent hours chopping mustard greens from the garden to be dehydrated and stored for later use. All three of us were getting tired of the work, and Lakshmi Behn was beginning to think up other chores that needed doing, hoping perhaps to find relief from the task at hand. Suddenly, Baiji began to giggle and told us an amusing story about a king whose stingy and tyrannical nature almost drove his own children to the point of murdering him. She was aware that we might think her cruel at times, but this did not fluster her. Baiji seemed to accept that the job of running an ashram necessitated strictness and that this would sometimes be seen as cruel. Scoldings or periods of hard work were often followed by expressions of consideration or love. One night, when I started nodding off at the dinner table after a day of hard work, Baiji offered to massage me; had I accepted, her massaging me would have been a dramatic reversal of normal hierarchical relations between sadhus and householders.

I gingerly mentioned to Sonam one day that I felt the cooks had too much work to do. She disagreed, stressing that we too help when necessary and that everyone has to do more work if guests arrive. I pointed out that the cooks work from early morning until late at night. "Yes," she said, "but they have no other work to do, no family to look after. . . . Besides, they sleep after lunch." I observed that afternoon naps were not the norm for them but did not pursue the matter. Sonam was clearly disturbed by my insinuations because later that day, in another context, she suddenly remarked on how much work Baiji did. "And most of it is work that only she can do. For example, she herself skims cream off the milk every day so that not a drop is wasted." It was true that Baiji herself did a lot of work around the ashram but a crucial difference, I thought, between her and the cooks was that her work was *seva*—it was a matter of choice rather than expectation and it contributed to her reputation as a true saint. The workers were simply employees and, while employment in an ashram may have a higher status than employment as a domestic servant, the work itself was no different.

Baiji's *seva* was not limited to housekeeping and food preparation. One of her charitable projects was building a hospital outside of Haridwar. While I was there, she would visit the hospital site every few days to check on the construction of a boundary wall. On these trips, one or two of the laborers might fold their hands in respectful greeting but most paid no particular attention to her. To satisfy her keen interest in the actual construction of the wall, Baiji made the foreman explain everything in detail about the depth of its foundation and how the rocky field could be leveled. One devotee had sent a planner from Delhi, and Baiji consulted him on where exactly the boundary lines were to be drawn. The original property line was at least thirty feet beyond where the wall was now going up. The man who sold the land, Baiji told me, turned around and sold that portion of it to someone else two months later and registered it in their name. Having already lost so much land, they decided to construct a boundary wall to protect the remaining property until funds were available to build the hospital. In addition to the hospital a new temple was also in the plans. Because the temple inside Rishi Ashram was inaccessible to the public, a smaller, outside one was to be built in a far corner of the field with an entrance from the street. "Since we don't allow everyone inside," said Baiji, "we'll make a small temple here where the public can come, pay their respects, and go." Making the inner temple private was not necessarily good for public relations, but it was filled with valuable things, including a few gold ornaments, that could easily be stolen. Most Haridwar ashrams are surrounded by high walls and gates and welcome only those who have some legitimate reason to enter.

In addition to running charitable projects, Baiji also supervised the ashram staff, which included two cooks, a gatekeeper, a doctor for the clinic, a man to watch and milk the four cows, and someone for odd jobs. One day, a neighborhood man named Anandji brought someone to meet Baiji in hopes that she might give him work. Anandji introduced the young man as a Brahmin qualified to work in the kitchen or with cows and who was currently working at another ashram. When Baiji asked what his duties were at the ashram and what he was paid, the young man stared at the ground in silence. "Look," she said, "just tell me. We certainly won't pay you less." He described his work and what he received in terms of pay and other benefits. Baiji said that if hired, he would receive two hundred rupees plus room and board for him, his wife, and two small children; then later, if the work was satisfactory he would get a raise.[6] She added that the ashram sometimes gives clothes as well and that whenever people come and give donations, she has them give directly to the workers rather than to the ashram. Finally, she informed him that she had just hired someone else but that if it did not work out she would contact him. When the young man left, Baiji pumped Anandji for further information about him, asking if he drank and indicating that she did not want him if he did. She also informed Anandji of her prohibition on smoking cigarettes in the ashram compound. Baiji was known to be a strict employer and supervised her staff closely.

Baiji was so involved in housekeeping, food preparation, providing hospitality to guests, and other aspects of ashram management, that she had little time for recorded interviews. Thus, most of my research took place in the snatches of conversation that broke the tedium of repetitive chores. Sometimes I would get ready in the morning and venture downstairs early, around seven, in hopes of getting a little time with Baiji before she got involved in the other tasks of the day. One such morning I found Baiji sitting in meditation in the temple, so I busied myself by cutting the morning's *prasad* of apples and bananas for distribution. By the time Baiji emerged from the temple, breakfast was ready. After breakfast a malfunction in the gas stove had to be repaired so that lunch could be cooked. After seeing that it was fixed, Baiji began gathering food to send as *prasad* to her Uttarkhand ashram because someone was traveling there the next day. In rummaging through the cupboards Baiji found three boxes of sweets that had been long forgotten. Tragically, they had begun to mold around the edges. When she suggested that we scrape off the mold, then cook them again in clarified butter, I tried to look enthusiastic and nodded affirmatively. It had to wait though because Sita Behn was alone in the kitchen that day and vegetables needed to be chopped for lunch. Once the vegetables were cleaned, chopped, and handed over to Sita Behn for cooking, there was still time left for an interview. We settled down in Baiji's room with the tape recorder, but just as she became animated in her description of the different heavenly worlds, it was time for lunch. Baiji promised to continue the interview later. After lunch we started cleaning the moldy sweets and before long Baiji began to feel sleepy and got up to lie down, saying "What's your name—Meena—I'm sorry." This was typical of my days at Rishi Ashram. While helping in mundane tasks was a way of getting to know people and participating in ashram life, I relished those "interviews" as the rare times when I had Baiji's undivided attention.

During my stay at Rishi Ashram, only one of Baiji's followers, Ved Brahmachari, lived there permanently. The householder disciples came on weekends or for longer periods when their schedules permitted. Those without the responsibilities of young children and jobs tended to come for weeks or even months at a time. Baiji also went to Delhi periodically, and even Bombay on occasion, to visit her devotees and conduct religious functions in their homes. In fact, she was planning to visit Delhi for a couple of days in late December to perform a textual reading and to be present for a special *puja* that her disciples would conduct on her birthday.[7] As usual, she would stay with the Malhotras, the family that constituted the core of her following; they had reserved a special room for her in their home. According to Dashnami rules, renouncers are not supposed to stay under the same roof as householders, although many contemporary renouncers do. The same ideal held that renouncers should wander from place to place imparting religious education to the Hindu laity, a lifestyle that would make it impossible to organize charitable projects. I had also planned to be in Delhi for that time so that I could attend the birthday celebration.

The day before I was to leave for Delhi, Baiji and I had a conversation while chopping vegetables. She had asked about my life in the United States.

"Do you do anything over there? Chanting God's name, devotional worship, and so forth?"

"No, though I have recently begun trying to do a half hour of meditation every morning."

"Which meditation are you doing?"

"*Sakshi dhyan.* The other kinds are too difficult for me."

She nodded. "In some previous life you reached quite a high state, and that is how you became interested in these things."

"I have never been very religious," I confessed, "only reflective about my life."

"I am glad you came but sorry that I have been unable to serve you (*seva karna*) . . .," she said. "When we go to Uttarkhand I will have more time to spend with you because there won't be all these ashram matters to worry about." She had invited me to accompany her to visit her Uttarkhand ashram later in February. She had a trusted man there who looked after the ashram, she said, "Otherwise, it would become like the situation here." This was the first time I heard her express any dissatisfaction, however mild, with Rishi Ashram, though she always spoke of the Uttarkhand ashram fondly as if it were the place she would prefer to be.

Ritual Purity

I went to Delhi a week before Baiji but planned to attend the birthday celebrations at the Malhotra home on the twenty-ninth. When the expected day arrived, however, I was on my period and thus prohibited from attending the rituals. I missed an event that would occur only once during my research period. Baiji's attitude toward ritual pollution at Rishi Ashram seemed inconsistent. Earlier in the month, Sonam was in a state of ritual pollution because of her grandmother's death. Baiji had told her to avoid the temple and kitchen for thirteen days and, of course, not to touch food or cooking utensils. Yet one morning when raw sugar was needed in the kitchen, Baiji sent Sonam with me to fetch it. Sonam led me to the appropriate cupboard and instructed me to pick up the sugar and carry it back to the kitchen. The next day, I noted that Sonam, on Baiji's request, went to retrieve the raw sugar herself. When Sonam was asked to make some carrot-apple juice for Baiji later that same day, I offered to operate the electric juicer. "No, this I can do," she had said. "I just cannot enter the kitchen. . . . Since Baiji is from among the saint-sadhu people, all of these things are not so important for *her.* God is in everyone." I was utterly confused. Baiji, it seemed, as a renouncer was unaffected by ritual pollution while the *pandits* and deities were. Later that day, however, when Baiji saw that I had been chopping bitter melons alone for a long time, she sent Sonam to help me. The vegetables were to be cooked and offered to the deities and then fed to the *pandits* along with everyone else.

With regard to menstrual pollution, Baiji also seemed inconsistent. When I first went to stay with her she told me that, while menstruating, women usually stayed in their rooms and she had food sent to them. One month, Sonam was prohibited from entering the kitchen but allowed to help me cut raw vegetables in the dining area. The next month, however, she had to eat in her room from a separate set of utensils that she washed in her bathroom. And, she had to keep her distance from the *pandits*. One day, Baiji and Achariji (the head *pandit*) were busy cutting bolts of cloth for waistcloths to be given in *dan*. I started helping Baiji cut the cloth, then I would take it out in the front room where Sonam was hemming them with the sewing machine. Sonam could not enter Baiji's room because Achariji was there. In addition, she could not handle food, even raw vegetables, or sit at the kitchen table with us. When I asked Sonam the reason for this sudden strictness she said, "I do what Baiji tells me. Before, Baiji had said that from drinking cow urine everything becomes pure." This month, however, things had changed. When I tried to question Baiji about the change in rules, the answer was vague. During menses, she said, the *vrittis* (inner dispositions) change and one's attention becomes focused on the body. Baiji's sentiment that menstruating women should not do mental or physical work had been echoed by Anand Mata as well. In the village where Baiji used to live, the women were not allowed to cook food during their menses, yet they were expected to fetch water from the well and do other hard work. "That is not right," she said. "They should get three days of holiday."

In Delhi I did go to the Malhotras' home after the morning festivities and found some familiar faces among the people milling about. On the wall near the front door was a framed photograph of the entire Malhotra extended family standing behind Baiji who was enthroned on a large chair in the center of the group. Mrs. Malhotra plans nothing while her guru is visiting. I found Baiji seated in a corner of the enormous, crowded dining room having lunch and discussing matchmaking and the eligibility of certain families with some disciples visiting from Bombay, to whom she introduced me simply as "our good daughter . . . married to an American." As disciples shuffled up to Baiji's chair, one-by-one, to say goodbye, she offered each a small morsel of bread with vegetables from her plate as *prasad*, which was accepted with both hands as something precious. Baiji appeared particularly poised, exuding an air of regal grace that I had not seen in Haridwar. As I was leaving she said, "I have kept the lock on your room in Rishi Ashram and will expect you back in Haridwar on the eleventh."

Ritual Activities

Arriving back in Hardiwar on the expected date, I found that Vimla Auntie had returned from Delhi with Baiji. On one of our evening walks Vimla Auntie mentioned that she was thinking of sponsoring a *Bhagavata path* for her deceased husband since it is usually performed within the first year after a person's death. Another disciple, Sarla Auntie, would be arriving in a few days to sponsor a *Bhagavata path* for her own deceased relative, and Baiji had suggested that Vimla Auntie cosponsor rather than paying for her own. "Whatever Baiji decides, I will do," she said. "If I don't do it now I'll have to come again and do it before May. My brother doesn't believe in all this stuff. I don't even consult him on these things because he thinks it is all nonsense and would tell me not to do it. I have never disobeyed my elder brother so I didn't even consult him on this. He is a staunch Arya Samaji and doesn't believe in *puja*, *path*, feeding mahatmas, and so forth. But my son is so good. He treats Baiji with respect and won't say anything in front of her. He comes to my *puja* room every morning before work, even if it is only for two minutes. On Sundays he will sit for one hour in the *puja* room."

Vimla Auntie recalled that she had come to Haridwar when she decided to make Baiji her guru but that Baiji insisted she return home to get her husband's permission first. Only when Baiji was convinced that he had no objection did she agree to initiate her. "Baiji doesn't go around making disciples just to make disciples," said Vimla Auntie. Baiji has often told her female disciples that the primary obligation for married women is to their husbands. When I asked if Baiji had ever married, Auntie replied that she didn't know, as though she'd never even thought of it before, and that she feels too embarrassed to ask such questions of her guru. For her it seemed to be irrelevant.

That evening, after the *prarthna*, Ved Brahmachari parked himself at the foot of Baiji's empty seat when she got up to pay respects (*pranam karna*) to the temple deities; soon others came and sat beside him expectantly, myself included. It was a polite way of compelling Baiji to return to her seat. Although clearly very tired, she sat down and said, "Ask." All eyes turned to me, so I asked Baiji to continue what she had been discussing earlier in the day about the *Bhagavata* being the most important of the Puranas. As she spoke the *pandits* made a lot of noise washing the brass *puja* utensils in a nearby basin, and I was annoyed at the interference with my taping. Perhaps considering the noise to be disrespectful, Ved Brahmachari also became irritated and ordered the *pandits* to stop, but Baiji, overriding his demand, calmly told them to continue their work. She never seemed bothered by interruptions or noise during her lectures or interviews. After the interruption, Vimla Auntie asked Baiji why Achariji had said a particular thing during the *path*. Baiji's response was unexpectedly sharp. "You should not ask *why*, because this implies that you know more than the other person." Thus rebuked, Vimla Auntie fell into silence. As a nondisciple, I was treated differently and my asking "why" a dozen times every day was tolerated, even appreciated.

Baiji was planning another trip to Delhi at the end of January to perform a *Bhagavata path* on the occasion of Mr. and Mrs. Malhotra's wedding anniversary. As usual the family's driver and car would be sent from Delhi to fetch Baiji and whoever else was going with her. Having missed the last big event at the

Malhotra home and now being offered a second opportunity to observe Baiji in that context, I asked if there was room for me in the car going to Delhi. "*If the car is able to come at all*," she said, "there will be room." Gasoline had been unavailable in Delhi because of the 1991 United States-Iraq War, and she was thinking of making train reservations just in case. When I noted the unlikeliness of getting first-class reservations so late, she said that ordinary class would be fine as long as we got berths in the segregated ladies' compartment.

The next morning I awoke with a flu. By the time I recovered Baiji had fallen ill with the same symptoms. I persuaded her to lie down and, since she does not drink black tea, brewed some basil (*tulsi*) tea by boiling the leaves in water with milk and sugar. I took the tea to Baiji's room where she was resting and joked about what a rare sight this was. I felt that Baiji, like the cooks, was overworked and that, while she spent a lot of time creating work (like salvaging the moldy sweets or holding three feasts in two days), the rest of us did not help with our constant demands for advice and attention. Ved Brahmachari and another disciple, Rajinder Auntie, joked that at least Baiji listened to me when I told her to rest, because she did not listen to them. After Baiji finished her tea and a snack, I argued for the curative powers of a hot salt water gargle and, when she agreed, I went to prepare one. Baiji told me to fill the glass up so that it would stay hot while she went to pay respects in the temple. I looked at her sternly, thinking of the probability of her getting involved in some work, and said impatiently, "It will get cold. Is it necessary for you to go in the *mandir?*," and then immediately wondered what had possessed me to speak to her in such a manner. She smiled and promised to be back in a minute. My nondisciple status allowed me to joke more freely with Baiji. Even though she was not feeling well, the *pandits* requested her presence for the *puja* and, of course, she obliged. Emerging from the *mandir*, Baiji said to Rajinder, "Tell Meena I've come and that I'm going to gargle right now." I was in the kitchen chopping vegetables with Sonam and Vimla Auntie when Rajinder joined us and related the message; then she pointed to Baiji's room and said to me knowingly, "This [*seva*] is the real research, isn't it?" After a pause, she wanted to know which other mahatmas I had interviewed. Without waiting for a reply, she stated that even though she has known Baiji since she was in the third grade and spends a lot of time with her, she still finds her hard to understand. "Other mahatmas are easier to understand," she said. "They may give only theoretical talks and philosophical advice, but Baiji gives practical advice. She is very 'self-dependent.' There is nothing she cannot do. She plays sitar skillfully and used to draw as well. She knows Ayurvedic medicine and construction work. Yet you can ask her about any Veda or Upanishad and she can teach you. She learned a lot from her first guru but took sannyasa from Avadhutji and considers both to be her gurujis. Avadhutji was very strict, like a lion in the jungle. He ate once a day—fruit, sweets, or whatever—and would only talk about religion. Baiji performed very difficult *tapasya*. Many people, especially mahatmas, opposed her because they did not like sannyasa being given to women. But he watched her do *sadhana* and could see that she had risen quite high. So he thought there could be no harm in giving sannyasa to such a person. He only made two disciples. Baiji did hard *tapasya*, you know . . . she used to keep silence for six months at a time."

Rajinder grew up in Himachal Pradesh where Baiji also lived with her family, and Baiji's sister (Sonam's mother-in-law) was Rajinder's primary school teacher. She said she used to visit Baiji often when she was young and liked being around her, though Baiji would discourage her from coming, telling her to go home and study. Baiji's first ashram is there; it is small but has a primary school and dispensary. Rajinder chose not to marry. Instead, she taught in the school for six years and eventually became its principal. When Baiji was young, according to Rajinder, she used to play the sitar and slip into meditation. "Her family did not accept this side of her," she said, "except her father; he believed in it." I asked how Baiji was different from other mahatmas. "Other mahatmas will have their disciples worship and serve them, but Baiji serves her disciples. She does more work than anyone else here in this ashram. Other mahatmas will give orders, but Baiji never tells anyone what to do. Instead, she'll do it herself; then we will feel that we should also do something. Also, Baiji has practical knowledge. She can do anything and she herself supervised all the work of building the Uttarkhand ashram. She even drew up the plans (*naksha*)."

"How did she learn to do this?" I asked.

"I don't know," said Rajinder, "it must have come to her in meditation."

"Baiji is always ready to learn some new thing," added Sonam. "If a laborer comes she will want to learn from him—'Learn something,' she'll say."

"Also, for Baiji all are equal," Rajinder continued. "Sannyasis are supposed to see all people as equals and Baiji really does. We may want to give an important person better *prasad* and more attention, but Baiji treats all equally. If anyone comes, whether Brahmin or Chandal, she will want to give them some good *prasad*, and no matter how sleepy she is she will want to listen to their whole story. She will satisfy them not just physically but mentally as well."

"Chandal?" I asked, seeking fuller explanation.

"A Chandal is an untouchable," Rajinder said, switching from Hindi to broken English.

Sonam added, "A Chandal is one who does any wrong things."

"Yes, Chandal is not a quality of one's birth." Rajinder corrected herself. "In Baiji's first ashram there used to be feasts constantly, and she fed the mahatmas with such love. She even used to serve those same mahatmas who opposed her in Uttarkhand and take care of them when they were sick." Taking advantage of the conversational mood, I asked whether Baiji was ever married, trying to be casual, as if the matter was not important. The enthusiastic conversation ended abruptly.

"I don't know," Rajinder finally said to break the silence.

Sonam added a gentle reprimand. "There are some things one should never ask a mahatma. Do you remember that South Indian sannyasini who told you not to ask about her previous life before sannyasa?"

"Yes," I said, reminded of my outsider status.

Rajinder skillfully changed the subject. "When I was young I used to get really disgusted with the latrine. Then one day I saw Baiji cleaning up the shit of a small child. At first I was revolted, but then I realized that if such a great mahatma was doing it then there must be nothing wrong in it." There was a chorus of praise for how hard Baiji works, especially considering that she was almost seventy and in poor health.

Baiji, meanwhile, was perched upright on her bed, eyes drooping and nose flowing like a river; instead of resting, however, she had begun a list of the necessary preparations for a *bhandara* to be held later in the week. Five hundred people were expected for the feast and no outside labor would be called in to help; it was going to be a lot of work for all of us. In response to my shock at the numbers, Baiji said that when one person hears about a *bhandara* at Rishi Ashram everyone wants to be invited (because they know it will be generous). After several minutes of scribbling and calculation she figured how many vats of each vegetable would be required and concluded that, if everything was to be ready in time, the pumpkin should be chopped and peeled tonight. Within minutes the word was out. We took our positions around the dining table, piled high with pumpkins, and hacked away at them late into the night.

The next evening several more devotees arrived, and I was relieved to see the labor force grow. As it was the eve of the great feast we were briefed of the plan. The next day was also Basant Panchami (first day of spring), which is generally celebrated with yellow food and clothing, so a rice pilaf, potatoes, and sweet dish of that color would be served, along with pumpkin, yogurt, and fried bread. The sadhus were to arrive in five batches of eighty to one hundred persons each, with the first group expected at 9 A.M. Before that, however, there would be the usual morning prayer session followed by the concluding *puja* of the ongoing *Bhagavata path* (it lasts seven days). In addition, an all-day fire sacrifice (*havan*) would be performed in the *yajnashala* simultaneously. All of these activities require participation, of the *pandits* and sponsors at the very least, which would leave fewer people to help ready and serve the food for five hundred sadhus. To have all of these events happen simultaneously seemed like an overambitious plan to me, but no one asked my opinion. Indeed, it happened frequently that, at Baiji's instigation, several ritual events would be performed concurrently, and this kept everyone on their toes.

Late that evening Baiji suddenly decided to add fruit cream to the menu; it was a favorite dish but also extremely costly and labor intensive because the fruit had to be peeled and cleaned and the milk slowly thickened over a low fire. A teenage girl and I sat down to peel pomegranates. Once we finished that job, I diced carrots for the pilaf until my hands turned to rubber from the cold. I moved toward my room long after midnight and, while passing by the kitchen door, saw two girls—someone's daughters—stirring an enormous pot of milk that was slowly thickening. They looked as tired as I was. I set my alarm for 5:30 and lay in bed thinking that when saints made programs they should consider the ordinary people who would be doing the work and who needed sleep. It was true, as Rajinder said, that Baiji never ordered people to do anything, but it would have been impossible (without a miracle, that is) to pull off the feast without everyone's help.

The next morning, I bathed and spent a couple of hours catching up on my field notes before venturing downstairs around eight, but no one noted my late arrival. Everyone was working quickly but calmly. When I asked what needed to be done, Baiji had me work on a project completely unrelated to the day's activities. The next morning she was leaving for Delhi where she would perform the seven-day *Bhagavata path* for her disciples. She wanted me to copy the underlining from her old copy of the text into the new edition that she planned to carry with her. I took the colored markers and began highlighting the significant passages, until, a short while later, Baiji decided I should dice the carrots that I had left unfinished the night before. Completing that, I joined the group of ladies in the kitchen who were rolling balls of bread flour in the palms of their hands and then flattening them with a rolling pin for frying; communal tasks were always more fun than solitary ones. In the temple, the *Bhagavata path* was proceeding as we worked. "Baiji told me that sitting in the kitchen doing work is as good as attending the *Bhagavata*," said Rajinder cheerfully. "Half of my devotion is in the kitchen and half in the temple."

Sonam came and squatted beside me, breaking off a little dough and squashing it between her palms. She looked at me and said, "The yogurt was not ready on time. Whatever goes wrong always comes out on Baiji. If the water supply stops it is Baiji's problem. If the food is not ready on time and the mahatmas must wait, it falls on Baiji's head." This was a lingering response to my earlier criticisms of the servants being overworked. "Well that's natural," I said unsympathetically. "It always falls on the manager." We continued rolling the balls of dough and, after a long silence, Sonam mused, "It's funny how things work out. It is only because of falling sick that I have been able to spend this much time with Baiji."

We were given tea and fruit, as the first batch of mahatmas was arriving. As soon as we finished, Baiji called Sonam, a younger girl, and me outside to help distribute cloth and two rupees to each of the sannyasis seated in rows in the inner courtyard. They were all men, well-groomed and respectable-looking. Ours was a ritual participation because Baiji had us each hand the *dan* to only three or four sadhus before calling someone else to take our place. As I turned to go in, I heard a woman's voice loudly reciting a Sanskrit verse on the other side of the gate. I asked Mehraji who it was and he replied that some women had also come. Hearing this, I decided to stay outside and help with the serving. There were thirteen sannyasinis in the next batch (none in any other), and they sat together segregated from the men. When I began distributing food to them, I could see that all were elderly except one. Presumably because they had few or no teeth, many asked me for especially soft fried breads. But there was one who, seeing that I was having trouble finding enough of the soft breads that everyone wanted, informed me with a smile that she liked hers hard and chewy. The sannyasinis were dressed either in ochre *saris*, or in petticoats with long tunics of the same color, and all had their heads covered.

Baiji stood among the renouncers, in the hot midday sun, supervising the amazingly efficient serving of food. That the sadhus were seated in long rows of twenty or thirty people facilitated the feeding process. The servers, carrying shining steel buckets of food in their left hands and ladles in their right, would move down the rows quickly, dumping a spoonful of vegetable or tossing some bread onto the banana leaf plate in front of each person, with the most casual attention to aim. While all the sadhus were dressed in ochre, there was great variation in the exact shade of color, type of clothing, accessories, sectarian insignia, and hairstyles. This batch, much scruffier than the previous one, was seated outside the courtyard, in what was really a driveway, rather than inside where the previous group had been seated. Were they less respected or were there simply too many of them to fit anywhere else? When I asked Ved Brahmachari why they were made to sit outside in the sun rather than in the shady courtyard, he said "Who will keep watch if someone goes inside?" Although the saints were being feasted and honored, they could not be trusted categorically, as there was sure to be riffraff among them.

The mahatmas did not eat as much as everyone predicted they would, apparently because there were four other feasts in the area that day. It took less than an hour for a group of a hundred or so people to sit, eat, and leave. As they departed en masse, the banana leaves were removed and the driveway quickly swept clean for the next batch. When all the sadhus had come and gone, there was still lots of food left, so Baiji summoned fifteen laborers who were working nearby to come eat. They were fed as the mahatmas had been.

Back inside the ashram, the *pandits* and a couple of the male servants sat down for their meal and, afterward, each of them was given a length of cloth and two rupees. Baiji told us to go ahead and eat without her because she was going to the *yajnashala* where the fire sacrifice was nearing its conclusion. It was two o'clock and the *havan* had begun around half past nine in the morning. We all followed Baiji into the *yajnashala* rather than heading toward the dining area. Sarla Auntie and her family and Vimla Auntie were seated near the sacrificial fire while Achariji officiated. At the end everyone offered flowers into the fire, then bowed to Baiji. It was over. Baiji glanced around at the group and said "Shall we go?" Achariji remarked that a few words should be said about this past week. He addressed the group in formal Hindi, expressing his hope that the activities of the last seven days would bring success to those for whom they were done; then he asked Baiji to say something. "Well, usually at this moment there is no talk." She paused, looking exhausted and waiting, no doubt, for her followers to let her go. But they continued to watch her expectantly. Finally, she closed her eyes and started speaking in a monotone voice that she only used in ritual contexts. She spoke about death and how ritual actions such as the one performed here today most certainly help our loved ones in the afterlife. She concluded by stressing that if we wish to perform certain actions to ensure a safe passage into the heavenly worlds, it is far better to do them while we are still alive. With this, the audience was satisfied and slowly began to move toward the door.

It was four o'clock when we seated ourselves around the table for lunch, and I devoured the rice, pumpkin, potatoes, and fried bread. Baiji wanted me to eat some fruit cream, a costly food, but the thought of eating it made my stomach turn. Baiji dropped a spoonful of it on my plate, and once it is on the plate it must be eaten. Attributing my reluctance to being too full rather than to taste, she suggested that I send some of it to my husband as *prasad*. "Just concentrate very hard and it will really go to him," she instructed. I closed my eyes for a moment and prayed that the stuff might disappear from my plate. I opened them again, blinked, looked at her and said "I tried, Baiji, but it is still here." Everyone exploded into laughter and Baiji explained, "It has to go from the *stomach*." As I prepared to down the little pile of fruit swimming in clotted cream, Baiji began to narrate a story about having to attend some *path* at an ashram while she was in Delhi. "The people at home [the disciples with whom she was staying] told me not to eat too much because I wasn't well. I went to the ashram and ate all the things I wasn't supposed to eat and felt fine. Then I came home and they asked if I had eaten anything, to which I responded "No." Then one of them suddenly threw up and all those things I had eaten—okra, and so forth—came out. They found out what all I had eaten because it was all right there on the floor. So, it really is true that you can send the *prasad* to your husband."

"One time I went to a *path* with another lady," Baiji continued. "Usually, this lady can hardly even eat two *rotis* (unleavened bread) but that day she ate thirteen! All the flour in the kitchen was finished and she went home feeling hungry. The hosts were dismayed because they felt they were sending their guest home hungry. I myself had only one *roti* that day and was feeling full just watching that woman eat. We went to the home where we were staying and they had warmed milk with clarified butter for me. I couldn't drink it because I wasn't feeling well, so my companion drank it. Then, still feeling hungry, she went into the kitchen and ate the servants' big, fat *rotis* as well!" Vimla Auntie turned to me and said, "These are facts that we have all experienced with Baiji."

The next day Baiji, Sonam, Shivapriya, Vimla Auntie, Mrs. Malhotra's sister Dunni Masiji, and I piled into the Malhotras' car and headed for Delhi, although the act of departing took several hours. The plan was to leave at seven in the morning. The day before, a message had come from Delhi, from the Malhotra family, that we should arrive at their place by ten in the morning, which would mean leaving at six. On hearing this Rajinder became indignant. "No one gives orders like that to Baiji!" Before departing, Baiji wanted to finish the under-lining of important passages in the *Bhagavata Purana*, perform a brief *puja* for those who had sponsored the previous week's *Bhagavata path*, and distribute *prasad* of peanuts and fruit to every person at Rishi Ashram. Dunni Masiji made concerted efforts to hurry everyone along but eventually gave up and sat quietly in a chair by the front entrance to communicate her readiness for departure. In the meantime, I began to feel menstrual cramps, and the implications of this were depressing. It meant missing Baiji's *Bhagavata path* in Delhi, my main purpose in traveling to Delhi this time. It was almost noon when our car finally rolled out of the driveway, with Sonam, Shivapriya, and Baiji in the back chanting a mantra to Ganesh—"Om namo Gana Ganapathi"— the deity of new beginnings.

The four-hour journey took six hours. We stopped at the home of Sonam's maternal uncle, who lived in a small town that fell on our route. Our hosts, who were not disciples, treated Baiji with respect rather than reverence. As we were about to leave, Sonam's grandfather arrived, and his face lit up to see Baiji. He touched her feet and they spoke for a few moments while the rest of us inched toward the door. Sonam's aunt tried to hand Baiji some cash, but Baiji exclaimed, "*He Ram!* No! This is exactly why I stopped visiting you on my way to Delhi!" The young woman persisted and finally Baiji took the money on the condition that it would be used for the medical clinic. Our hosts touched Baiji's feet as we made our way to the car, got in, and resumed our journey.

Back on the road, I pulled out my tape player and shoved in a cassette of classical vocal music that Baiji and I both loved. Within minutes, the voice of M. S. Subbalakshmi moved Dunni Masiji to serenade me with a sentimental sermon about "the depth of our Hindu culture." Squashed between her corpu-lent body and the door, I was a captive audience, and she showed no signs of pausing, until something on the road caught her attention. The beautifully dec-orated car of a wedding procession, escorting its new bride, decked in gold, to her husband's home, was followed almost immediately by a funeral car trans-porting its corpse, strewn with flowers, to Haridwar for cremation. Dunni Masiji saw in this a poignant illustration of the transience of the illusory world (*maya*) created by Bhagwan, the world of birth, marriage, death, rebirth. "You know," she told me, "when someone asked Lord Krishna what *maya* is, he responded simply: '*Maya* is the awareness of yours, mine, me (*Maya he tera, mera, men*).'"

"Once we were traveling from Uttarkhand to Delhi," she began. "We had to reach Delhi for some reason, so we asked Baiji if we should hire a taxi and she said yes. The Uttarkhand taxis could not go into the state of Uttar Pradesh, so our *taxivala* wouldn't go all the way to Delhi. Since we couldn't get a connecting taxi to Delhi, the driver offered to seat us on a bus and we agreed. We boarded a bus to Delhi and some men got up to offer us *matajis* their seats. It was so nice of them. There was a Mrs. Kumar with us and she started saying 'Look at me. I am Lady Kumar and here I am riding in a bus.' I said to her, 'Didn't you learn anything in Baiji's ashram? Here you are coming from Baiji's ashram where she considers everyone equal and you are still thinking you are Lady Kumar. No one on this bus knows who Lady Kumar is.' This is the difference, you see, between a saint and a nonsaint—the saint sees everyone as equal."

Approaching Delhi in the middle of evening rush hour, we had to first drop Sonam off at her in-laws' home on the other side of town, which gave me the opportunity to visit the home of Baiji's (deceased) sister in a middle-class suburb. Sonam's father-in-law Sharmaji and her Bhabhi (husband's brother's wife) came out to greet us, and Baiji led us into the house as if it were very familiar to her. Almost immediately they asked if they should call "Mamaji" who, I assumed, would be Baiji's brother. A phone call was made and he arrived ten minutes later with his wife and new daughter-in-law. They all touched Baiji's feet, he perfunctorily and the women more reverentially, and chatted for about twenty minutes. He wanted to give Baiji a bottle of Ayurvedic health tonic he had at home; he said he would walk home now so that we could drive by his house and pick it up on our way out. Vimla Auntie, who was in a hurry to get home, protested that Baiji was just about to leave, but he said that it takes time for important people to leave a place. On our way out we stopped at his home, a large bungalow, and Baiji sent our driver up to fetch the tonic.

When we finally arrived at the Malhotras' home, it was dark. I pulled Baiji aside and explained why I would be unable to attend the next day's *path*, upset that menstrual prohibitions would again cause me to miss an important event. "It doesn't matter," she said. "There is no harm (*dosh*) in this. . . . Just have a bath, wash your hair, and come on the fourth day." Mrs. Malhotra emerged from the house, smiling ear-to-ear, removed her sandals and fell to her knees on the stone patio, clasping Baiji's feet. I picked up my bag and walked down the street to my aunt's home. Four days later, I took my classificatory grandmother, "Granny," along to attend the *path*. The backdrop behind Baiji's seat (*asan*) was elaborately decorated with strings of yellow marigolds and religious symbols, and a framed image of Lord Krishna was propped up in front of her podium. I recognized two *pandits* from Rishi Ashram in Haridwar who were seated in a corner with their harmonium and drum. Among the audience were many familiar faces of people who had visited Rishi Ashram. Most, it seemed, were related to each other in some other way than simply as disciples of the same guru. Many had met Baiji through their relationship with the Malhotra family, whether through kinship, work, or friendship.

After a brief prayer, Baiji began reading. She would read a verse or two and then pause to explain the meaning to her eager audience. While Baiji had much knowledge of sacred texts, she did not strike me as a particularly eloquent or dynamic speaker and often fell into mumbling. Still, she was very comfortable speaking to her devotees and managed to keep the audience of thirty involved by quizzing them as a teacher quizzes her students. They enthusiastically offered answers to her questions. Whenever Baiji lost her place or for some other reason needed a few minutes to think, she had the audience sing a few lines of a devotional song with musical accompaniment provided by the *pandits*. Although Baiji began a half hour late she stopped speaking promptly at 6:00 P.M., because, I suppose, these urbanites had schedules to keep; at Rishi Ashram nothing ever finished on schedule. After performing *puja* to both Baiji and the text from which she read, everyone lined up in front of her to receive *prasad* of mango juice mixed with a little Ganges water. Granny, a tiny woman of eighty-plus, used her age and physical strength to push to the front of the line, where she touched Baiji's feet as did everyone else but then also kissed the sannyasini's hand repeatedly and playfully and touched her head so as to give *her* blessing to the saint.

The next morning Granny and I went again to the *path*. Baiji, in the midst of her textual exegesis, paused to blow her nose. Defecating, menstruating, and eating were all considered polluting while blowing one's nose in the middle of a sacred event was apparently unproblematic. Baiji's sinuses were congested and her voice hoarse, but the microphone lay unplugged in a corner of the room. Baiji had said that she wanted a microphone to lessen the strain of speaking for six hours each day but that "Bhagwan had forbid it." During the afternoon session, Baiji came to the description of Krishna's birth. To mark the joyful event, she paused for a special *puja* and the distribution of *pinjira* (a rich mixture of ghee, semolina, nuts, sugar, and so forth given to pregnant and lactating women) as *prasad*. Suddenly, Mrs. Malhotra stood up and began dancing jubilantly in celebration of Krishna's birth, while the rest of us provided accompaniment to the *pandit*'s drum by clapping. Some other ladies persuaded Mr. Malhotra to join his wife in dance. Baiji refrained from such boisterous forms of devotion herself but indulged her disciples' exuberance, waiting patiently for them to settle down before continuing. Soon after Baiji resumed, one woman interrupted with an inquiry that indirectly questioned the accuracy of something Baiji had said. Others in the room clearly disapproved and someone in the back asked loudly, "Who is that speaking in the middle?" Baiji mildly scolded the person who had asked the question. "Now the thought has been lost," she said. "If you speak in the middle I lose my train of thought so you should wait until I ask a question and only then talk."

The next day, after describing Rukmani's marriage to Krishna, Baiji said with a grin, "OK, now you folk can sing some wedding songs if you like; I don't know any of those songs." This ironic reference to Baiji's renunciation of marriage elicited laughter from the audience, and someone went to call the *pandits* from their room to sing. Soon after the *pandits* began, a disciple known for her talent in singing interrupted to ask if they had the right song, if the one they had chosen wasn't about Krishna's beloved Radha rather than his wife Rukmani. The *pandit* who had been singing said in a voice so controlled it betrayed his irritation, "Keep listening, Rukmani will come in this song; there is no need to interrupt." The woman was disgruntled by this rebuff. Thus, when another person started to question whether it was the right song, she said sullenly, "Don't bother asking; he'll just get angry." Baiji observed this exchange without intervening. The whole event must have been somewhat humiliating for the *pandits*, as they are not accorded the same elevated position that they occupy at Rishi Ashram where class differences are less pronounced. In many wealthy homes, *pandits* hovered somewhere between ritually honored priests and domestic servants. After the song Baiji continued. "So the wedding ceremony is over . . . and what happens after the wedding?" Baiji grinned and quiet snickers rippled through the audience. She spoke for an extra hour that day so that she might be able to finish the next day as planned. It was ritually imperative that the one-week *path* be completed in seven days, unless Baiji asked permission from Bhagwan to read an extra day. On the final day, Baiji did manage to finish on time.

When I arrived back at Rishi Ashram two days later Baiji had already returned from Delhi. I asked her how the final *havan* and *puja* went at the Malhotras' place. She said that seven people had eaten grains before coming (that is, ignored the rules of fasting) and that she had told them, "Why have you eaten grains and come? You have been doing *havans* since 1960, so you know you are not supposed to." I also overheard Baiji's response to Achariji's query regarding the past week and particularly regarding the scene of Rukmani's marriage. "There was a confusion as to whether it was Rukmani's or Radha's wedding," she said. "The *pandits* were lost in bliss (*anand*) while singing and did not hear when they were told." Apparently, Baiji agreed that the *pandit* had chosen the wrong song, but, in talking to Achariji, she attributed the mistake to devotional obliviousness rather than simple carelessness. Was she covering up for the *pandits'* slip and irritation at being corrected or for her devotees' arrogance?

Sonam's father-in-law Sharmaji had been looking after Rishi Ashram while Baiji was in Delhi. He was related to Baiji but never once mentioned the family connection to me. Although Arya Samaji himself, he did not take an orthodox Arya Samaji stance toward *murti puja* as a corruption of Vedic Hinduism. He was, however, keenly interested in the question of the relationship between two Hindu approaches to the divine that he labeled *nirakar* (without form) and *sakar* (with form). He talked about his own Arya Samaji approach to God through Vedic ritual, the study of texts, and meditation as *nirakar* and contrasted this with the practice of offering food, flowers, incense, and so forth to anthropomorphized deities and reading about their lives in the Puranas and epics. His contrast between *nirakar* and *sakar* paths here refers to the nineteenth century antagonism between the reformist Arya Samaj and Sanatan Dharm (literally, "eternal religion") based on disagreements over reform, belief, and ritual. The early Arya Samaj (although led by Brahmins) attacked other Brahmins and the structures of priesthood for corrupting original Vedic religion, and the Sanatan

Dharm movement emerged to defend Brahmin and caste orthodoxy and to challenge this modernizing ideology (Bhatt 2001:18,85). Devotional practices, or *puja-path*, which were vociferously criticized by the Arya Samaj, are also associated with Sanatan Dharm in this context. Today, Hindu nationalists often use the term Sanatan Dharm to refer to Hinduism itself.

One afternoon, Sharmaji asked me if I had interviewed any *nirakar* sannyasinis in addition to the *sakar* type like Baiji. The day before I had learned about a sannyasini named Vidya Mata who had left the Arya Samaj to follow a path of Krishna worship. Sharmaji suggested that I ask both Vidya Mata and Baiji why we have these two paths of *sakar* and *nirakar*. "Why not just choose one path? Which is the better of the two? Then, you should compare the answers of both. You can ask Vidya Mata how she got into *puja-path* and whether women are more suited to one path or another." He elaborated the difference between these two forms of worship: "The Arya Samaj emphasizes knowledge (*jnana*) . . . thinking and being convinced about certain beliefs. Sanatanis [that is, followers of Sanatan Dharm] emphasize faith (*shraddha*) and devotion (*bhakti*). If you do whatever Baiji tells you without questioning or doubting it, then that is devotion. Knowledge eventually leads to devotion and you must have both. Both together will give you bliss (*anand*)." Here again, religious paths that are opposed at the level of practice and doctrine, are said to merge at a higher level. "There is no mention of Hindu gods and goddesses in the Vedas," he continued, "and the stories describing their lives developed later. Arya Samajis do not do *path*. Now they have started doing it, though they do not see Ram as a god, only as a perfect individual." He seemed a bit concerned that Baiji might not like the fact that he was filling my head with all these questions. His friend Nanda Sahab, who had joined us in the middle of the conversation, had met Baiji four years earlier through Sharmaji.

"Is there any difference in having a female guru?," I asked.

"Women have more confidence and faith," said Nanda Sahab. "Men, on the other hand, will always criticize."

Sharmaji was about to sit down with his breakfast of fried bread when Baiji summoned him into the temple for a special *puja*. He jumped up and said, "Oh! I'll get a scolding from Baiji; I was supposed to sit in the *puja*." Those participating in the *puja* were prohibited from eating grains beforehand. Later in the afternoon, he returned to the earlier topic. "You know, I have heard Arya Samajis criticize idol worshiping Hindus, but I have never heard Sanatanis criticize those who do not worship idols." He himself attends Arya Samaj events and then also comes here and does whatever *puja* Baiji tells him to do. "So what?" he said. "Do both."

The next morning when I inquired of Baiji about the possibilities of an interview, she suggested that I visit the Vidya Mata I had been wanting to meet and that she would have finished her accounting work by the time I returned. I asked Sharmaji if he would like to come along and he said "How can I when Baiji has given me this bank work to do? I must ask her permission to go." While leaving, I came across his friend Nanda Sahab who was standing in the sun reading the newspaper. In response to my invitation, he hesitated for a moment, then put down his paper and said "Let's go."

Vidya Mata was seated outside in her courtyard, next to a space demarcated for performing fire sacrifice, when we arrived at her home. She greeted us warmly and, when I explained my desire for an interview, disappeared to install her dentures so that her voice would be clearer on the tape. When she returned, she told us first to have *darshan* and then led us to her shrine with an image of a youthful Krishna playing the flute. After the interview, she invited me to stay with her for a few days so that she could teach me "the practical along with the theoretical." She said that she could teach me yogic breathing (*pranayama*) in two or three days. "I won't tell you what result you will get from doing it but will let you see from your own experience."

On the way back to Rishi Ashram I mentioned to Nanda Sahab that Baiji might not like my staying with Vidya Mata, especially since I sensed that she did not think highly of her, although she rarely criticized another renouncer directly. He agreed. "Though I came along with you, I was worried that Baiji might come to know and might not like it." As we approached he quickly ate the orange she had given him as *prasad* and instructed me to hide mine in my bag (so that Baiji would not see it). I told him that Baiji knew I had gone to meet Vidya but also realized that his visiting another sannyasini had a different meaning than my doing so. He was a disciple who was supposed to have full faith in his guru, while I was merely a researcher who had come to interview sannyasinis without promising faith or devotion to any guru. When we reached the gate, Nanda Sahab asked the gatekeeper if anyone had asked about him. The man smiled and said, teasing, "Who would ask about *you?*"

Later in the afternoon, Sharmaji, who was still working on the bank accounts, clarified the distinction between my visiting other sannyasinis and his doing so. He said that his friend was very impressed with Vidya Mata and that he too wanted to hear the tape of our interview. "Nanda Sahab was raving about it, saying that she spoke *very* well." I told him that she had invited me to stay with her and I felt Baiji might not like it. More than being concerned about Baiji's disapproval, I wanted to know whether he shared his friend's opinion. "She won't mind because you have come with a mission," he explained. "We always get attracted to that which is far away. Like when I come here Baiji tells me to do some *sadhana*, to learn something from her, but I have not reached that stage yet. Think about what you can get from her and see if you cannot get that here. . . . One thing is true—Baiji is very busy. Perhaps the reason that I do not learn from her is that her knowledge is there for the asking. It is in my pocket. That is why I didn't go with you to Vidya Mata, because Baiji might feel that I am going to someone else because I don't think I can obtain that same thing from her. Baiji wouldn't tell me not to go, but I myself would feel my conscience bite. Here you have freedom to go wherever you want; Baiji won't mind. She also gives us freedom to go where we want. I do my *havan* morning and evening and Baiji doesn't say anything. One of my sons follows Radhasoami and Baiji doesn't mind."

Vidya Mata, who so impressed Nanda Sahab, was devoted to the god Krishna. Bhakti constitutes the single most important value system in popular Hinduism today, and, historically, every Hindu school of thought has placed a high value on devotion. Even Shankara's monistic philosophy and elitist monastic institutions, as discussed in the previous chapter, had a place for devotion. For Shankara the various deities represented one monistic divinity, so initiates into sannyasa who worship a personal god will usually venerate others as well. By contrast, followers of other schools of thought often worship one particular deity exclusively (Embree 1988:322–23). All the sannyasinis I met during the period of my field research seemed to be influenced by bhakti, in different ways and to different degrees. For example, devotion can be directed toward a personal deity or to a formless Brahman. Anand Mata emphasized emotion over scholasticism, but her bhakti was not directed toward a personal deity (in this respect *her* renunciation is more "orthodox" than Baiji's). Baiji worshiped gods and goddesses in anthropomorphic forms, although she did not focus on one exclusively. Vidya, by contrast, was devoted to Krishna. All the independent sannyasinis I met incorporated bhakti in one of its many forms.

Baiji Reflects on Her Gurudom

One evening, after I had been pestering Baiji for an interview all day, she told me to come into her room with her and she would talk to me while she worked. She and Achariji were busy cutting bolts of cloth for waistcloths and preparing other things to be given in *dan*. Baiji was to carry all these things to Uttarkhand with her. When Achariji started to light a candle to use for sealing a plastic bag, Baiji instructed him not to use a candle by reciting a verse.

> *Agni, jal, sadhu, aur raja*
> *In charon me bharosa nahin rakh sakte hen.*
> Fire, water, sadhu, and king
> In these four we cannot trust.

As Achariji laughed, Baiji insisted, "It's true. With a flame, if a little wind comes along then it is all over. And a sadhu? Well, they might just get up and leave at any moment (*chal parna*)."

The next day we started on a what turned out to be a two-day project: chopping vegetables and measuring spices for making Baiji's much-loved cauliflower and radish pickle. On the second day, as Baiji and I sat together to finish chopping the last heads of cauliflower, she asked me, "You'll write this in your thesis? Sadhus do what sort of work? Householders' work." We laughed. The moment seemed right to pose a question that had been on my mind since she recited the verse about how one cannot assume that a sadhu will stick around or stick to a plan.

"Baiji, have you ever felt like leaving this ashram and running off to Uttarkhand?" She always spoke of the place so fondly and often said that there she had no headaches or work.

"Yes," she responded quietly while glancing at her surroundings wistfully; "I used to think of that a lot, but now I try to calm my mind and tell myself that if it is God's wish, then . . ."

That evening a *pandit* who was visiting from Panjab joined the prayer session. He used to be one of the young *pandits* of Rishi Ashram but now worked as a priest elsewhere. After the ceremonies he and I both sat at Baiji's feet. He first reported on what all he had done that day and his plan to return home the next day. Soon, it became clear that he wanted Baiji's advice. Someone had suggested that he get a bachelor's degree in education and he was seriously considering it. Baiji encouraged him to go for the degree. She told me earlier that she thought very highly of him—that he was very knowledgeable (*vidvan*). By then Achariji had also joined us. The *pandit* mentioned to Baiji that Achariji advised him not to go for the degree and felt that this religious field was the best one. Baiji, however, was more pragmatic. Now in Delhi, she said, there are about four hundred priests who are not of Brahmin birth (*pujaris*), but they are performing *pujas* because they are educated with Ph.D.s, and so forth and because educated *pandits* are not available. "And they are demanding a lot of money, too," she added. She offered the young man further advice about performing *puja-path* for householders.

"You must look at your own experience," she continued. "The hardest thing is not to get stuck in the egotism (*ahamkar*) of I am, I am doing, and so forth. A person may give five thousand rupees one time and nothing the next, but you must remember that it is the same person. Then he may give five hundred rupees the third time. It should make no difference to you. Another person may give nothing, but at least he's taken out the time to *come*. And you must not wonder why someone who gave money the last time is not giving any this time. After all, it was not *you* who took that first five thousand rupees. . . . The money was not for *you*. He gives it for himself. Whatever is given is not given to you but to God, so if you take it for yourself then you are stealing. You must not accumulate it or it becomes filth. The one who does not see any difference between those who give money and those who don't, the one who is unaffected by what people give, whether praise or criticism, that person is the real saint. It is very difficult to save yourself from egotism. If you can, then your life will be successful; otherwise you will go on being reborn. Paramatma is simple (*saral*), but this

worldly business (*vyavahar*) is not. It is very difficult to be in this worldly business and not be touched by it, but there are still some great saints around. There
was one very great saint called Narayana who lived in Uttarkhand. He used to
be a judge. He only took alms in a small bowl from one house once every three
days, and in between he did not even drink water. He spoke little and very quietly. If someone offered him money he neither looked at it nor touched it. He
was very beautiful, with long black, matted locks."

Was Baiji speaking about her own life when she emphasized the difficulty in
being involved in the world without being affected by it? She was familiar with
the dangers and pitfalls of the path of *seva*, which demanded that she live in the
midst of householders and worldly concerns. At times Baiji would reflect on the
pitfalls and temptations faced by a sadhu who devotes herself to serving the society of householders: the temptations to think of the donations as personal possessions rather than things held in trust (to be redistributed to the needy), the
desire to run away from all the hassles for a quieter life, and, most of all, the ego
produced by reverence. Yet Baiji seemed confident that she had chosen the right
path, even if it was, in her estimation, more difficult than the path of contemplation and ascetic isolation.

Sannyasa as Service

If there is any single quality of Baiji's *sadhana* that colors most of her activities and teachings, it is an emphasis on action or karma, both ritual and charitable. Originally karma referred to the proper fulfillment of the ritual duties of a
householder, so it represented a path renouncers had rejected. The *Bhagavadgita*,
which is part of the great epic *Mahabharata* and probably the single most influential text in India today, assumes an active way of life and speaks in terms of
yoga (application of self-discipline) rather than *moksha* (Embree 1988:278).
However, the *Bhagavadgita* also addresses the problem of how one can attain liberation while continuing to act in the world, and, thus, incorporates elements of
renunciation. Thus, Lord Krishna advises Arjuna that one should perform an
action without any concern for or interest in the results. Action that is free from
attachment and self-interest is thus better than inaction. This ideal of acting
with detachment legitimizes the work of actively engaged renouncers. Baiji had
committed the *Bhagavadgita* to memory, referred to it often and considered it to
be a distillation of all the Upanishads.

While the notion of renouncing the fruits of one's actions goes back to the
Bhagavadgita, the interpretation of karma as charitable social service is relatively new. The valorization of selfless action in the *Bhagavadgita* has been
widely interpreted by modern renouncers as a call to work for the uplifting of
India's poor. Ursula King has argued that modern Hinduism, shaped in part by

increased interaction with Europe, has reinterpreted the *Bhagavadgita* so as to give individual initiative and action a new legitimacy. The notion of karma, which originally referred specifically to Vedic ritual activity, later came to mean human action in a much wider sense. One implication of this change was a relatively new evaluation of physical work and social service, partly brought about by Christian missionaries who explicitly equated karma with service rather than ritual activity. King has noted that the Hindu social ethic of *karmayoga* (the yoga of good works), even if introduced by Christian influence, can be grounded either in the absolute monism of sannyasa or in the belief in a personal god (King 1980:42–48). Thus, in its insistence on breaking down the boundaries between one person and another, Advaita Vedanta provides a philosophical justification for spontaneous service motivated by compassion for the pain of others. Alternatively, all good works can be interpreted as an offering to a personal god. Dazey has discussed the way in which new monastic institutions ("committed organizations") have incorporated a broad range of social services including medical aid, famine relief, literacy campaigns, and village development through complementarity and hierarchy of spiritual disciplines (1990:311–13). In accordance with this, Baiji, like all renouncers I met, held that one cannot reach liberation through service alone; good works must be combined with austerities (*tapasya*) and knowledge (*jnana*). It was also clear that she did not view the classical and modern meanings of karma (ritual activity and social service) as mutually exclusive since both are an important part of religious life at Rishi Ashram.

This modern reinterpretation of sannyasa occurred during a period of enormous social change. During the eighteenth and nineteenth centuries, British colonial officials and missionaries targeted sadhus, along with ritualism, untouchability, child marriage, and Sati as evidence that India was mired in irrational spiritualism and regressive social values and in need of Britain's help; the sadhu was thus perceived as a drain on India's meager resources—even as a *reason* for its poverty (Narayan 1993b). Partly as a response to this onslaught of criticism both educated Indians and ascetics themselves began to envision a new socially "relevant" form of Hindu renunciation. Swami Vivekananda, a disciple of Ramakrishna, was a key figure in this reinterpretation of sannyasa.[8] Vivekananda represented Hinduism at the 1893 World's Parliament of Religions in Chicago, after which he toured the United States for several years, established the Vedanta Society, and even initiated Western disciples. Vivekananda promoted the Orientalist opposition between the Materialist West and Spiritual East (Chatterjee 1986). More importantly, he believed that renouncers could help in a national effort to uplift the poor rural masses and promoted a new vision of the ideal renouncer committed to India's cultural, material, and spiritual renewal (Sinclair-Brull 1997:32). While Baiji's approach is informed by an ethos of charitable service, some contemporary renouncers, most notably Swami

Agnivesh, have combined renunciation with a social justice agenda that addresses the underlying structural causes of poverty and social inequality (see Hatley and Inayatullah 1999).

During the last century, then, sannyasa has come to emphasize active involvement in society in the form of social service activities. This new emphasis on social service and reform has not come to replace the focus on disengagement from worldly life. On the contrary, many contemporary renouncers still consider activism to be a distraction from the goals of true renunciation and most think it impossible to attain liberation through social service alone. These critics are skeptical that social service can ever be truly disinterested and that a renouncer can maintain his or her detachment and egolessness while being intimate with householders. While some renouncers may choose one or the other of these competing ideals, many attempt to balance them. The values of detachment and social involvement are held in tension, and individual renouncers hold varied opinions on the relative importance of each. The tension can be resolved by combining active involvement in social service with an internal attitude of detachment, though this is considered to be a very difficult balancing act to maintain.

Seva was the one word that Baiji's disciples consistently used to describe their guru's religious path, and she would inevitably begin our interviews by asking how she could serve me. That this is an inversion of classical ideas of the relationship between guru and householders or disciples, according to which the guru is the recipient rather than the giver of *seva*, was frequently pointed out by Baiji's disciples as one quality that distinguished her from other, more ordinary gurus. My conversations with Baiji and my observations about the details of ashram life illustrate the tensions that arise for a renouncer committed to the service of householders. According to her devotees, Baiji's spiritual knowledge and power enable her to consult deities directly, guide disciples, treat illnesses, administer charitable projects, and perform the humble work of running an ashram, and this capacity for *seva* is taken as a sign of her saintliness and power as a guru. At the same time, for Baiji, the very act of being a guru creates tensions between the goals of service (*seva*), detachment (*vairagya*), and the destruction of ego (*ahamkar*). Egotism, most renouncers agree, is the most tenacious obstacle in spiritual progress, especially for those who take on the role of guru. Baiji herself acknowledged this from time to time; it would be much easier, she once said, to live a quiet life of solitude and contemplation and at times it seemed she longed for such a life.[9]

Chapter Four

(Ir?)reconcilable Tensions: Individual Existence as Spiritual Journey

The chapters on Anand Mata and Baiji demonstrated that sannyasa not only embraces both social engagement and detached transcendence, but also that it is eclectic in drawing from various religious traditions considered distinct from, if not contradictory to, renunciation. The coexistence of worldly and otherworldly values is an analytical frame for understanding the shifts in sannyasinis' practices and commentaries, but these terms evoke a set of Hindu frames of reference (*laukik* and *alaukik*, for example) that require distinct modes of reasoning. Baiji, Anand Mata, and the householders who visit them do not view their engagement with one another as corruptions of an otherworldly renunciant ideal, although they do have to negotiate contradictions that these alternative values create in their lives. I argue here that this dialogue is *internal* to sannyasa and that the resulting tensions are not just philosophical or logical, but social and emotional as well. This chapter explores a central metaphor through which I believe the tension is understood and, to some extent, resolved.

The tension between worldly and otherworldly values within renunciation is at least as old as the Dashnami Order, although the specific motivating factors that have led renouncers from forests and caves into greater proximity with worldly life have varied over the centuries. Whether it is militaristic defense, nationalism, love, or teaching that pulls renouncers back into society, these forces are always balanced by the image of the lone wanderer, with ultimate status reserved for the latter (although this, again, would depend on the particular frame of reference).[1] How do renouncers deal with these competing demands in their own lives and explain the religious eclecticism within their ranks? One way is through a dynamic metaphor of journeys. Sannyasa, and individual existence itself, is commonly referred to as a path (*marg*) and described by metaphors of place and movement that locate the person in a specific context.[2] Sannyasa itself is one path among many and, within sannyasa, there are many paths or styles of religious thought and practice. Persons move in and out of these renunciant styles, as when a sadhu leaves her disciples for periods of isolation, emerges from meditative isolation to begin lecture tours, or changes her guru thrice during a lifetime. The limits as to what can be defined as renunciation will be explored in the next chapter. To marry, beget children, or take up paid employment is clearly to give up one's renunciant status, but within these parameters there is a wide range of legitimate beliefs and practices.

Places of Transcendence and Places of Activity

Baiji's two ashrams in Haridwar and Uttarkhand were very different. As described in the previous chapter, Baiji's Haridwar ashram revolved around Vedic and devotional ritual, rules of purity and pollution, social service projects, and the activities of householders. Sometimes everyone was treated the same, consistent with the rhetoric of Advaita. At other times, distinctions were made between influential disciples, *pandits*, servants, and guests, and even between high-status mahatmas and ordinary sadhus, in terms of where they sat for meals and how they were treated. Here I describe my visit to Baiji's Himalayan ashram and contrast it with Rishi Ashram. Baiji had invited me to accompany her to her Uttarkhand ashram in late February. Since my aunt, who had met Baiji once through me, was also interested in going for a couple of days, it was decided that she and I would travel together a few days after Baiji and her entourage (composed of Nanda Sahab, Sonam, and her daughter Shivapriya), but that I would stay on longer and return to Haridwar with Baiji. My aunt arrived at Rishi Ashram one evening with her car and driver, and we set off early the next morning for the ten-hour ascent into the mountains. The day was cold and rainy, and darkness had fallen by the time we reached Gangotri Ashram, a rose-colored building that was small and nondescript compared to its Haridwar counterpart. Inside, the damp cement walls and floors of the ashram only intensified the February chill permeating our bodies.

As I tried to absorb as much heat as possible from the cup of tea cradled in my palms, I could hear the evening worship being performed by two young *pan-*

dits in a temple at the end of the hall, though no one made any moves to attend. It was only a hot meal, served around seven, that succeeded in warming us. Baiji sat on a stool not more than a foot high with her plate on a slightly higher stool in front of her. The rest of us sat on cushions to shield us from the cold as there was only a thin rug covering the cement floor. Meals were much simpler affairs here than at Rishi Ashram. Everyone ate together and ate the same food. I was shocked to see that the cook, after serving us, retired to the kitchen to consume his own meal. At Rishi Ashram eating was considered a polluting act and there-fore never done in the kitchen. The Rishi Ashram cooks could neither taste a dish while preparing it nor bring a *jutha* utensil (one polluted by contact with saliva) into the kitchen without polluting all the food therein. Although Gangotri Ashram was far "cleaner" (in a hygienic sense) than Rishi Ashram, where the cooking area was coated in grime, it was not governed by strict rules of purity. I had expected that ritual purity would be even more strictly guarded here, since Baiji and her disciples always described this place with such rever-ence, as the ideal place for *sadhana*, but in fact the opposite was true.

Since the meal was finished by eight and the only warm place was in bed under a heavy quilt, we all retired to our rooms around nine. After I had a good night's sleep the ashram seemed a more cheery place. It was built on the steep banks of the Ganges River, and even though the sun had not yet risen the out-lines of snow-capped mountains were clearly visible. The crisp morning air was silent and still. It was about five-thirty and, since the wood-burning kitchen stove had just been fired up, it would be some time before we would each get our allotted half-bucket of hot water for bathing. The bathing and toilet areas were at one end of the ashram and the temple at the other end, with a kitchen and six private bedrooms in between. Each tiny room was sparingly furnished with a single bed, a small bedside table, some shelving, and a clothesline. As is appro-priate for a place intended for meditation and *sadhana*, each room had one single bed. Rishi Ashram, by contrast, had not only single rooms but also a few rooms with double beds for couples and some large, communal rooms with four or five beds. The rooms at Gangotri Ashram were connected by a ten-foot wide corridor that had once been an open balcony and was later enclosed. The corri-dor was flanked by bedrooms on one side and windows facing the Ganges on the other. It was the only common area of the ashram for socializing and eating.

Accustomed as I was to the Rishi Ashram rule of no one entering the kitchen before bathing, it was a welcome surprise to be offered a steaming glass of tea as I sat huddled in my shawl. A woolen shawl protected my hands from the scalding metal glass, as I perched myself on a cushion across from Baiji and said, "Omji," the all-purpose greeting preferred at Rishi Ashram. I did not, how-ever, touch Baiji's feet since I was as yet unbathed and therefore polluted. She was warming her own hands on a glass of *gomutra* (cow urine), so fresh that steam gently rose from it. "Baiji? Is a male cow considered as pure as a female one?" I asked sleepily. "Yes," she smiled, beaming. "And its urine is just as good for the health." Baiji, I had noticed ever since arriving here, seemed to exude an air of calm relaxation—even radiance—that I had rarely seen in Haridwar.

It was Shivaratri (Night of Shiva), and Baiji's plan for the morning was to make a round of the local temples, distributing some of the fifty packets of *prasad* that we had assembled the previous night. "Before," she said, "I used to go to all the temples personally and give *prasad*, but now I only go to a few because I no longer have the energy." After bathing, Baiji, my aunt, and I performed *puja* at the four little shrines on the ashram premises. From there we made our way across a garden plot to a little cottage where three sannyasinis lived. All three fell to the ground and clasped Baiji's feet in full *pranam*, then got up to show her around the cottage and point out areas in need of repair since, even though Baiji had been there several days, it was the first time she had visited the cottage. It was built about thirty years ago specifically for housing women; male guests were expected to stay at the main ashram. Baiji allowed the three women to live in the cottage on a permanent basis and gave each thirty-five rupees per month as stipend, which was apparently enough to provide essential food when supplemented with donations. Baiji insisted the three women eat in the main ashram with the rest of us as long as she was in town. Ordinarily, they would cook their own food in the daytime and eat at a nearby ashram in the evening. When Baiji came to visit she also made sure that the women had enough clothing to last until the next year.

As Baiji toured the cottage, they followed her through the rooms with the enthusiasm of puppies, all talking at once and pawing at her arms affectionately. The youngest was Subhadra, an Assamese woman whose somber facial expression and chattiness made an odd combination. The second, a South Indian whom Baiji called "Madrasivali" (One from Madras), spoke broken Hindi but communicated much through her cheery smile and easy laugh. The quietest of the three was very old and bent, her estimated age ninety-one. Baiji treated the elderly one with some deference, telling me to ask her any question and see what good answers I would get. She said that years ago "Mai" (an intimate term for "mother") used to read the *Bhagavata Purana* and was always asking Baiji to explain the meaning of certain passages. It was clear that even though this sannyasini was literate and older than Baiji, the two women agreed on who was the more knowledgeable. She originally came to Uttarkhand thirty-five years ago with her husband, and the two of them lived as an ascetic couple (as *vanprasthis*) in another ashram until he died. Every year on his death anniversary, she would hold a *bhandara* for as many sannyasis as she could afford to feed: four or five. When she left home, said the sannyasini, her daughter was crying. But she left everything behind—house, land, cows, and family—to come here. In typical renunciant style, she dismissed my question regarding how many children she had with a wave of the hand and a statement that she had only Bhagwan. Then, gesturing toward Baiji, she said "This is also Bhagwan."

Of the three, Madrasivali seemed to be the most friendly with Baiji and only she remained with us as we headed back to the ashram. As we walked, Baiji explained which parts of the ashram were built first and which were later additions. While passing the cowshed Baiji indicated with animated gestures how, during the year of torrential floods, the water had almost reached its door and drowned the poor cows. "There were helicopters flying around and many government jeeps!" she exclaimed. "There were buses for evacuating the people who were being told to go higher up into the mountains. I refused to leave my cottage. Even the government people were trying to convince me to leave, but I refused. There were lots of buses in the city, ready to evacuate people. . . . Then I did a *puja* and the waters really, truly started going down."

Baiji seemed to be enjoying this tour and clearly loved being here; she had none of the constant demands and problems of the other ashram. The caretaker Prem Singh took care of the meals himself, from planning the menu to cooking the food. Since most of the year he managed the ashram alone, Baiji trusted him to do everything. Uttarkhand was also the place where she had lived in proximity to her guru Avadhutji and performed her intense *sadhana*. Her reputation here was that of a real *tapasvini*, a performer of austerities, and a saint who saved the town from ruin. In short, she was associated with otherworldly activities. Rishi Ashram was built by her disciples; her primary role there was that of a guru engaged in worldly activities.

In response to my expressed interest, Baiji decided to take us to Shanti Kutir, the cottage where she lived during her period of *sadhana* in the early 1950s, before Gangotri Ashram was built. The next day we took the road to Shanti Kutir, parked the car where the road ended, and started walking up a hill. Though a few homes were now scattered along the hillside, the area was very isolated at the time when Baiji lived there. On the path we passed a woman who lived in one of the nearby homes; she neither knew Baiji nor showed her any deference. The deserted cottage where Baiji had once lived was peaceful and lovely, bathed in a gentle sunlight filtering through the large trees. There was no road leading up to the hill in the days when Baiji lived there, only footpaths, and no running water at all. Baiji's guru Avadhutji had had a pipe installed to bring water from a creek higher up, but if cows dislodged or blocked it then they would get no water. Baiji recalled with a smile how simple her life was then. She never carried money and of course there were no cars in the town at all.

Baiji pointed out the remnants of a tiny one-room building where Avadhutji had lived; someone, the caretaker Baiji thought, had placed a *lingam* in the empty room.[3] Avadhutji, she said, used to go to the Ganges River at night and meditate while standing in waist-deep icy cold water. She lived in the larger building beside Avadhutji's cottage, sometimes alone and sometimes with one or two other women (householders, not sannyasinis) who would come to do *sadhana*. Shanti Kutir was built for Avadhutji by a group of followers. "Muslims,

Sikhs, and Hindus would bow before him," said Baiji, "all thinking that he is one of us. When he expressed his desire to perform *sadhana* in Uttarkhand his devotees got together and built Shanti Kutir. So it was built specifically for the purpose of *sadhana*." Avadhutji, like Baiji, was from an Arya Samaj background, "from a good Brahmin family." There was a lot of money left for him by his family and most of it was spent to establish a school after Avadhutji's death.

On our third morning in Uttarkhand my aunt departed for Delhi, leaving only Baiji, Nanda Sahab, and myself, apart from the caretaker Prem Singh, in the ashram. Sonam had also been given a room, but this was her hometown and she spent the nights at her parents' house. She had wanted to stay at the ashram with Baiji, she confided to me, but Baiji insisted that she stay with her parents so as not to hurt their feelings. Still, Sonam spent her days at the ashram. That morning, soon after Baiji and I had begun a round of the shrines on the ashram compound, Sonam caught up with us, having just arrived from her parents' home. Baiji sent the two of us up to have breakfast while she completed her rounds. She would have only *phalahari* food without grains, because she was holding an annual feast to mark Avadhutji's death anniversary and fasting was required for this.

The *bhandara* took place at another ashram that had large cooking facilities and space to seat the large crowd. After the meal Baiji had the sadhus walk to Gangotri Ashram to collect their alms of two rupees, fried sweets, peanuts, sesame candy, and clothing. The sadhus who came referred to themselves as "icon" (*murti*) rather than "person" or "man." Since some had come to collect the *dan* for themselves as well as someone else too old or disinclined to make the trek themselves, Baiji would ask each "One *murti* or two?" She made sure that each person wrote his or her name in a book before receiving *dan* and asked a few, with a note of skepticism, which ashram they were from. One elderly sadhu pushed his chest out and threw his head back proudly in the face of Baiji's query. "I am a sadhu," he said. "Why should I tell a lie?" Unperturbed by his challenge, she handed him the gifts. Another sannyasi claimed to be collecting alms for seven people in his ashram who had not come themselves, but the list he presented Baiji contained only six names. Baiji questioned him repeatedly, insisting that he should have come with all seven names written down, but ultimately she gave him the seven packets. Some sadhus greeted Baiji with "Om namah Shivaya" and others with simply "Om." After accepting the offering, many simply turned and left while others touched the packet of *dan* to their forehead. One said "Thank you" (in English) to Baiji and another very elderly sannyasi maneuvered himself around the table piled with goods to put his hand on Baiji's head in blessing, though she did not acknowledge the gesture in any way. Of the few women who came, most were quite old and all looked destitute. A couple touched Baiji's feet and one exclaimed "Mataji, we are getting your *darshan* after a long time!" Baiji, in her dramatic, saffron-colored woolen cloak with large round collar, looked not only dignified but healthy and well-groomed in comparison to most of the sadhus who came for alms, and they seemed grateful to Baiji in the same way that the poor express appreciation for the generosity of the rich in secular contexts. Among saints, as among Hindu householders, prestige comes from giving wealth rather than accumulating it.

Later that afternoon Nanda Sahab and I sat outside in the sun and lis-tened to one of Baiji's interview tapes; he wanted to hear each of them in turn. He suggested that I ask Baiji *how* the turning point came in her life and how she came to know the Malhotra family. "You see, I cannot ask these ques-tions myself."

"Yes," I nodded. "I have so many questions to ask Baiji, but whenever we plan to sit and talk, something or another comes up. And here she has much more free time than in Haridwar; I only have three more days with her, since I must leave as soon as we return to Haridwar."

"The only way to get your interviews is to be aggressive, " he insisted. "You must *demand* them from Baiji! Catch hold of her feet (in an act of humility and supplication) and tell her she *must* give you one hour daily. She is too busy and spends a lot of time in unnecessary things."

Though other Indians, always men, had told me that I must be more aggressive if I wanted to get information from the sannyasinis I interviewed, I ignored their advice. Nanda Sahab's comments suggested, however, that an overt act of supplication could also be aggressive and demanding. Certainly Baiji's devotees made constant demands on her, the respectful demands that inferiors make of superiors. I knew that Baiji wanted to help me in my research, but it was precisely because of her accessibility—she rarely refused anyone who demanded her attention for whatever reason—that there was much competi-tion for her time. Since I was less aggressive, it tended to be my interviews that got postponed for the concerns of other, more insistent, people. Acutely aware of the fact that my time with Baiji was running out, I decided that Nanda Sahab was right. I marched into the building determined to throw myself at Baiji's feet and plead aggressively for more interview time. My sense of melo-drama deflated immediately when I found her deep in conversation with a local man. I waited for her to finish. As soon as the man left, Baiji turned to me, smiled, and said that she was sleepy. I looked at her droopy eyelids. Just then, Subhadra Mata came strolling in with a handful of papers and requested Baiji's help. Baiji said she would be back in a minute to talk with her and went off to the bathroom.

While we were alone I tried to get Subhadra Mata to talk about herself. She had been in this ashram for ten years at that point and considered Baiji to be her guru. Born in Assam, she had come to Uttarkhand on a pilgrimage once long ago with a female companion; they traveled on foot to several Himalayan holy sites and stayed with a family here for a while before returning to Assam. Eventually, she migrated to this area to live. "I have no family," she said, "except Bhagwan. Even before sannyasa I had no family." The youngest of five sisters, she was orphaned during infancy and raised by her paternal grandmother. When she was about to leave her natal village for Uttarkhand, her "Guru Mata" realized that if she went wearing white clothes she would not get alms anywhere, so she performed a fire sacrifice (*havan*) and presented her with ochre robes and a mantra. This was her initiation into sannyasa. "People used to say, and some still say, that sannyasa should not be given to women," I remarked.

"Yes, even now they say it."

"Why do they say that?" I pushed.

"Who knows?"

As soon as Baiji returned Subhadra Mata handed her some bank papers that, being nonliterate, she could not read. They included two savings certificates, one for two thousand rupees and another for a thousand. She wanted to know which one was coming due. Baiji studied the papers and then offered pragmatic financial advice on how to manage this money. It was Baiji who had originally advised the sannyasini to put her money into savings certificates. "After a sadhu dies," Baiji explained to me, "a *bhandara* is given in their name; one of these certificates is for that purpose." Subhadra Mata wanted to close her post office account, but Baiji insisted that she keep that account because it served as her only form of identification. "These village post offices really harass people," said Baiji, addressing me. "They refuse to give people their own money back without a bribe." I wondered what Subhadra's life would be like without Baiji's support. Would she have a safe place to live? Would she have enough food? After completing the work, Baiji got up to take a nap. Realizing that it was now or never, I quickly made my plea, though not as dramatically as initially intended. I reminded her that there were only a few days left and asked that she allow some time for me. She promised me an interview after her nap. Subhadra Mata followed her into the bedroom to massage her legs in an act of reciprocity and deference.

While Baiji napped, I dared not leave the vicinity of her room, in case she might wake and, not seeing me around, get involved in some other task. When she finally emerged from her room, I went to fetch the warm milk she generally takes in the afternoon in lieu of tea. She ate a few nuts and dried fruits, *prasad* from Rishi Ashram, and gave the rest to Prem Singh to distribute with the late afternoon tea. Baiji trusted him to distribute something so costly and valued as dried fruits, a task she would never trust her Haridwar cooks to perform. Also, perhaps simply because there were fewer people, food seemed to be more equally distributed here. In the time that Baiji took to drink her milk no one came to her for help or conversation and, as a result, we had our "*satsang*" in the temple as planned. During that interview I gingerly asked if a person could progress spiritually without *puja-path*. Her answer was nothing short of revelatory.

"Yes, with meditation." She went on to explain that in the beginning she did not have any of these *murtis* or photos for worshiping. She only had a single photo of the sage Bhrigu, especially important in the Arya Samaj, and since the frame she had was a double one she added an Om symbol to the other side. Then Avadhutji gave her a picture of Shiva and instructed her to replace Bhrigu's image with that of Shiva, the patron deity of Dashnami renouncers. "See how straight he sits?" he had told her. "You should sit just like that." Baiji pointed to the photo and said, "So that photo of Shivji was also placed in the temple. Then one Mataji who was staying here asked me for a calendar—I had brought many of these calendars with me to give away—so I gave one to her. She had the picture framed and then asked me if she could keep it in the *mandir*." Baiji told her that it did not matter to her whether she kept that picture in the temple, so the woman placed the photo in the *mandir* and began worshiping it every day. Then, with a sweep of the hand, Baiji indicated that the rest of the photos had been added by the elderly Mrs. Malhotra, the matriarch of the Malhotra family. She and her husband, who are now deceased, had been lay disciples of Avadhutji, and their descendants now comprised the core of Baiji's following. Baiji continued. "It doesn't matter whether one does *puja* or not. Like after cutting the hair, some people throw it in the Ganges and others throw it down the toilet. One gets no merit from throwing it in the Ganges and there is also no harm (*dosh*) in throwing it in the toilet. Similarly, there is no harm in not doing *puja*."

These comments downplaying the spiritual importance of performing devotional worship came as a surprise to me and to Baiji's two disciples, as all of us were aware of the care with which the elaborate *pujas* were performed at Rishi Ashram. All four of us expressed our pleasure with the *satsang* and we decided to do it again early the next morning before bathing. Baiji said she used to bathe and sit in the *mandir* for three hours. "But now I must pay attention to the body. If we neglect the body for other things it suffers and vice versa." These days she drinks cow urine, which as a product of the cow is a purifying substance, and then waits to clear her system before bathing. This means, she said, that she bathes later than usual here. "My eyes automatically open at 3 A.M.," she said. "Then I do everything lying down."

In response to my question about why the local Kashi Visvanath temple, where we had gone on Shivaratri, was called "Kashi," Baiji answered, "No one knows who put that *lingam* there in the temple. It is believed to have sprung up all by itself." Having been raised as an Arya Samaji, said Baiji, she used to criticize the worship of *lingams*, but an experience involving visions of gods and goddesses led her to stop criticizing it and start believing it. "One day," she began, "while planning a *bhandara* of giving raw sugar and tea to mahatmas, I was calculating how much would be needed. I was staying in the building where the school is now. Then Shiva appeared to me in the form of light and asked, 'You mean you are not offering any to me?' I saw a bright stream of light going from where I was to the Shiva temple. After that, I included in my calculations five kilos of sugar for Shiva, five kilos for the Devi, and five for the Hanuman temple. When we went down to where people were counting the chunks of sugar, they told me that there would not be enough if we offered so much to the temples. But whenever I looked at the figures it seemed as if there would be enough. One fellow was very angry with me and said, 'There is not enough to go to all the mahatmas and still you want to give so much to the temple first?' I insisted on first offering the allotted amounts to the temple and assured him that there would be enough. Ultimately, there was more than enough sugar and it seemed as if our supply went on increasing!"

Because of her Arya Samaji upbringing, Baiji used to criticize sharply those who worshiped deities by telling them that there can be no incarnation of Paramatma. She would even say this to senior Brahmin priests while she was still quite young. But when she was worried about something she would get a vision; sometimes it was a figure with four arms, wearing a crown (*mukut*). Upon hearing this, her father asked her if she had ever seen a picture of Devi. She had not. In their home they only had pictures of Lakshmi and Ganesh, which were accepted by everyone but not worshiped. "My father listened and must have understood what his daughter was seeing; I did not understand. In one vision there was an ocean and a man in the middle of snakes. And at that point in my life I had never seen an image of Vishnuji or Shivji. . . . Now tell me, this is the fruit of *sadhana* from some life, is it not? Anyone who becomes engaged in doing *sadhana* in this life is always involved in the *sadhana* of several lifetimes, not just of their present life."

The next morning at half past five, I was standing outside Baiji's room with tape recorder in hand; it was still dark. There were no signs of life in the ashram except a sliver of light that escaped the curtain on Baiji's window. When the door opened I greeted her by folding my hands together and bowing my head forward rather than touching her feet in unbathed status. "Omji" I said cheerfully and she returned the greeting, both of us giggling slightly at the craziness of having an interview at this hour.

"We can sit in the *mandir*," she said.

"Without bathing?" I asked without disguising my surprise.

"Well," she explained, "I usually sprinkle a few drops of Ganges water on myself and sit, but we can sit in my room." As we settled down on her bed she remarked that Nanda Sahab and Sonam would want to join us and that there was no place for them to sit in the tiny room.

"Well, it *would* be nice to sit in the *mandir*," I remarked quietly.

"So then let's sit there," she said decisively, and we both stood up.

In the hallway I met Sonam who had spent the night at the ashram so that she could attend our early morning *satsang*. When I told her where we planned to meet she looked a bit surprised, until I added, "Baiji said so." Then she simply nodded and followed me to the temple. The four of us gathered at the entrance to the *mandir* where Baiji sprinkled a few drops of purifying Ganges water on each of us and had us ingest a little before entering. Considering the negotiation that had gone on that morning regarding the suspension of purity rules, it is telling that during the interview, in the midst of a discussion about menstrual taboos, Baiji launched into the following story.

"One time you know what happened?" she began. "Bhagwan Ram told Lakshmanji to go find their Guruji and escort him back to Ayodhya. Vashisht Guruji was in Uttarkhand at that time. Vashishtji's wife, her name was Vasundara. . . . No, what was it? Arundhati. Yes. So Vashishtji and Arundhati had come here to Uttarkhand. Vashishtji did not bathe some days. You haven't seen how cold the water of the Ganges is these days. Here at least one can take baths. Further up in Gangotri, one cannot even bathe, and in Gomukh it is hard even to put one's hand in the water! How cold it must have been at that time. In those days there weren't even many people around; here and there some *rishi* would be performing austerities.

"So that was the situation in which Vashisht Guruji was performing his austerities. So when Lakshman gets there what does he see? Guruji tells him, 'Have a seat. I'll talk with you in a few minutes.' He noticed that Arundhati Ma was a *rajasvali* (a menstruating woman) and that she was making food with her own hands. And Guruji was eating it! Guruji was *mast* (carefree and radiant with joy); otherwise he did generally bathe. He was *mast* in the current of knowledge (*jnanadhara*). 'Guruji, I have come to fetch you,' said Lakshman. 'O.K., we'll go.' Guruji got up from his meal just like that and, without even bathing or washing, started off. When they reached the northern region of Haridwar he told Lakshman to stop for a moment. Lakshmanji watched as he bathed in the Ganges and transformed his appearance to that of a *pandit*. He wore a waistcloth, put a rosary around his neck, and even applied the appropriate ritual marks to his forehead, then resumed his journey. Lakshmanji said to himself, 'Look, now he has done all of this just to show others that he is a *rajaguru*. What is this? There didn't used to be this affectation in him, so why has he become this way now?' But he said nothing to Guruji. Finally, when they arrived at their destination, he described everything to Ram. Ram smiled and said, 'Lakshman, you are asking me; why not ask Guruji directly?' Lakshman said that he didn't have the courage. 'O.K., let's go,' said Ram. 'Ask him in front of me.' So they went to Guruji and Lakshman asked, 'Guruji, there's one thing I don't understand. Over there in Uttarkhand, Mata Arundhati was a *rajasvali* and you were eating food cooked by her hand. But then when we approached Haridwar you bathed, put a rosary around your neck, wore a waistcloth and did everything. It was not until then that you assumed this form, while up there you did not even care about what was good (*accha*) or dirty (*ganda*).'

"Guruji started to laugh. 'Brother,' he said, 'this is the land of activity (*karmabhumi*), understand? That was the land of knowledge (*jnanabhumi*), the land of austerities (*tapobhumi*). Within the land of austerities, who is female and who is male? Who is menstruating (*rajasvala*) and who is pure (*shuddha*)? Over there only the current of knowledge (*jnanadhara*) was flowing, the current of the

Ganges. The current of the Ganges is so full of knowledge that in Uttarkhand all this is unnecessary. The necessity exists wherever one must teach the performance of action (*karma*) so that the system continues. It only became necessary there in Haridwar, and so that is where I took on that form. Wherever knowledge predominates karma is not necessary.' So for this reason, where knowledge predominates all the rules that exist regarding the performance of action are not needed. And where activity predominates knowledge cannot remain. So that is why, in such a place, one must make karma supreme (*pradhan*). What characterizes the lower regions? Perform action, perform action, perform action (*karma karo*).

"Once we were traveling upward into the hills and discovered that those same customs still exist. People used to make a set of warm clothes once a year, and would keep wearing them on their bodies. Some would bathe only after a year or so, and others once a month. When we arrived we saw some people wearing torn and crusty clothing, and then we found out that they bathe only once a month. And when we went further up we found out that people bathe once a year. But they were carefree (*mast*) . . . peaceful (*shant*). You won't find anyone depressed because there is no grain in the house. You know the scorpion plant of the woods, the one that stung you yesterday? The people would cut some of that, grind it with wood or whatever, and if no one had a pot then they'd put it in a canister—or a clay pot if that were available. They would put water in it and boil it. They would sweep the ground clean. Then they would eat it without even salt, and everyone would be satisfied. Today, to the degree that desires (*vasnas*) and happiness (*sukh*) have increased, to that degree disquiet (*ashanti*) has also increased. Today there is no one in the mountains who doesn't have money; whether less or more, everyone has it. But there is no peace (*shanti*). Those who lived in dirtiness, let's say, or in poverty, had a peace that does not exist today. So this is why that was the land of knowledge and this is the land of activity below. The two cannot meet. With knowledge there can be no devotional or ritual activity (*karmkand*). And if we combine knowledge with *karmkand* then only the latter will come into prominence."

Although I cannot explore these issues here, storytelling is central to religious teaching imparted by Hindu gurus (Narayan 1989:231–47) and in this story Baiji articulated her philosophy regarding the relationship between renunciation and ritual: each was understood as appropriate for particular social contexts. Sonam and Nanda Sahab appeared to be as surprised as I was by Baiji's comments on ritual activity. We had all participated in the elaborate *pujas* at Rishi Ashram: changing and ironing the deities' clothes twice a month, laying out their bedding at night so they might sleep comfortably, singing their praise for an hour and a half each morning and again in the evening, and so forth. Shortcuts were never taken in matters of worship even when there were many other events going on and people were busy. If a *path* was in progress, then two *pandits* would get up at the usual time and simultaneously perform the prayer session in entirety. Although Baiji herself participated to varying degrees in these ritual activities, she clearly orchestrated them. I had even heard Baiji scolding the *pandits* at times for performing the *puja* without inspiration. And now she was saying that it did not matter whether one did worship or not, even implying that such worship was a lower or elementary form of religious discipline! Sonam, who performed *puja* and *jap* regularly, suddenly expressed an interest in learning meditation. "Baiji, do you think that I could do it?" she asked.

"You can do a little, not too much, and you should start with yogic breathing." Then I asked if one could progress spiritually without meditation. "No," said Baiji. "One will not get yogic powers (*siddhis*)." The epiphany of this *satsang* left us all feeling excited. We all agreed that the early morning time, devoid of disturbances, was so conducive to religious discussion that we should gather again the next morning. Sonam decided that she would bathe first and join us a few minutes late. This time Baiji did not even bother to purify Nanda Sahab and myself with a sprinkling of Ganges water before we entered the temple.

This visit to the Himalayas taught me much about Baiji. I realized how much she loved her simple ashram and lifestyle in Uttarkhand. She did not concern herself with meals, leaving the planning and actual work to her capable and trusted man Prem Singh, who produced food that was simple but good—and the same for everyone. In Uttarkhand, the rituals were abbreviated and the rules of purity and pollution all but ignored, which suggested that the elaborate worship services and rules of purity that governed daily life at Rishi Ashram were done self-consciously and with some intent. Indeed, I had often noted that Baiji was more an organizer and instigator of ritual activity at Rishi Ashram than a participant. The purpose of these activities, I believe, had more to do with the perceived needs of the *pandits* and disciples than with Baiji's own spiritual needs; it had to do with appropriateness. And, of course, all this had to do with the fact that Rishi Ashram is in Haridwar which, for Baiji, represents the world of householders and Brahmin priests.

Haridwar, for Baiji, constitutes a physical, social, and symbolic space. The sacredness of a particular space is defined relatively. For example, just as Haridwar is the land of the otherworldly *rishis* and *munis* for those who reside in Delhi, it is quite worldly relative to holy sites higher up in the mountains. For Baiji, Uttarkhand was the land of knowledge because it was the place where she performed her intense *sadhana*, while Haridwar was the land of activity because, for her, it revolved around her circle of lay disciples. Since Baiji had experienced a reclusive period of intense *sadhana* in Uttarkhand before becoming involved in the lives of householders, she explained the differences between her two religious lifestyles primarily in terms of place. There was a particular photograph of Baiji that was worshiped by all her devotees; in it, she was very young, with radiant skin and beautiful, luminous eyes. All Baiji's devotees had enlarged and framed this black and white photograph for worship in Rishi Ashram and in their small shrines at home. Taken when Baiji was performing her *sadhana* in Uttarkhand, the photo signified her spiritual power and knowledge.

Anand Mata, like Baiji, had experienced both social activism and a more contemplative lifestyle, but she pursued the two in reverse order. For Anand Mata, Haridwar was "the land of the *rishis* and *munis*" because it was the place where she performed her years of intense *sadhana*. When she abandoned her life of social activism, she went to her guru's metropolitan ashram. Eventually, she left this place for Haridwar. Most sannyasinis I knew believed that only if a sadhu has already passed through a period of *tapasya* (often associated with a particular place) and been transformed by it can they proceed to get involved in society without becoming *of* society. In other words, a renouncer must first leave society in order to reenter it as a different person, with a different outlook. Moreover, "leaving society" is symbolically constructed in terms of place and time. Just as particular places are good for *sadhana* because they contain the effects of all the saints who practiced austerities there in the past, other places, specifically urban ones, are particularly bad for *sadhana* because they contain all the desire, attachment, and pain of their inhabitants.

Anand Mata once elaborated on the importance of place in a story about Ram and Lakshman. When I was staying with her, I wandered down to the kitchen one sultry afternoon to return some utensils to their proper place. The kitchen was empty so I stood a moment taking it all in, my bare feet relishing the coolness of the cement floor. The smell of burnt wood pervaded the large and empty room. My eyes scanned the darkness, emphasized by the unpainted cement walls, and fell on a corner piled high with wood. In the center of the floor was a pit intended for cooking with wood; it looked as if it had not been used in a while. I peeked behind a cement counterlike structure, where I knew that most of the cooking was done, expecting to find a gas stove. Instead, there was another pit that was full of ash and half-burnt logs. Staring at the huge stack of wood, I imagined the dwindling forests and the women who had to travel further and further to harvest what they could from the impoverished trees to use for cooking or to sell. I decided to purchase a gas stove for the ashram.

An hour or so later I sat reading when Anand Mata returned from a meeting. She greeted me cheerfully and asked about my morning visit with a neighborhood sannyasini. She sat down next to me, removing her head scarf, letting her waist-length hair hang down, and resting her feet on the table.

"Oh, by the way," she said, "you remember the money you wanted to donate to the ashram? Well, I had been thinking it would be better to give the money for some specific purpose rather than just as cash. That way we know it will actually be used for the ashram. So today I told Swamiji that you wanted to buy a new stove for the kitchen because it is something we need." I stared at her in disbelief for a moment and then related to her what I had been thinking an hour before.

"Oh?" Her eyebrows went up.

"What time was it when you told Swamiji about the stove?" I asked.

"The exact time is unimportant," she declared and then proceeded to tell a story.

"Look," she began. "Lakshman, as you know, loved Ram so much that he left his wife behind in order to go to the forest to protect Ram and Sita. He would remain awake all night to guard them as they slept. One evening Lakshman was sitting alone at their camp while Ram searched for his lost wife, when the surprising feeling came to him that he should leave Ram and Sita and go home. 'Why am I wasting my life here in the forest,' he asked himself, 'when I can go home to my wife and palace? Tomorrow I will leave quietly when they are not paying attention.' They did not find Sita that night. The next morning the two brothers set off on their search again, and Lakshman began to have second thoughts about deserting them. He felt pity for Ram and decided that he would leave the following day instead. That day their search carried them into a new forest and the surroundings changed. As they walked, Lakshman began to feel great remorse and was unable to understand how he could have even thought about leaving Ram whom he loved so much. That night as he sat massaging Ram's legs, he began to weep.

"'Don't worry,' Ram consoled him, 'we will find your Sister-in-Law.'

"'You do not understand,' corrected Lakshman. 'I have committed a great sin and cannot believe that I have done it.'

"'Lakshman, you are not capable of sin,' insisted Ram. Lakshman confessed.

"'Last night when you were out looking for Sister-in-Law I had planned to desert you here in the forest and return to the kingdom. I don't know how I could have even thought of doing such a thing.'

"Ram smiled and said, 'Did you know that one thousand years ago in that very place where we camped last night two brothers fought? They had a boon that each could only be killed by the other and no one else. Since they loved each other so much, they felt secure that they would never fight and therefore never die. One day, a very beautiful girl named Mohini came into their presence. Since both of the brothers wanted to marry her, it was decided that they would fight and the winner would marry Mohini. They fought for eight hundred and eight days until they finally killed each other. . . . And to think that Mohini was only an illusion (*maya*) anyway!' Lakshman was filled with wonder as he heard the story. Ram continued: 'Since that fight took place at that very same place one thousand years ago, its effect is still there. That is why you became angry at me and thought of leaving.'"

This is a tale about the threat women pose to patrilineal solidarity, but it also comments on the moral power of physical places. Baiji's story about Vashisht Guruji suggested that morality is relative to spatial contexts. Anand Mata's narrative contains a different but related lesson—physical places absorb and exude the moral and spiritual qualities of all those who have been there. Daniel (1984) has described in detail the *substantial* influence of places on persons and events in Tamil culture. That places are seen, in South Asia, to have moral qualities and that these moral qualities may seep into anything in their proximity is established in the ethnographic record. In understanding renunciant notions of place, however, we should be wary of overemphasizing the material and gross (*sthul*) relationships between persons, events, and places, as renouncers themselves would highlight the subtle (*sukshma*) connections. In this sense, radio waves may be a more apt metaphor than fluids.

Writing on the locative aspects of Hindu piety, Diana Eck (1981) demonstrates that ritual traditions are linked primarily to place, hence the importance of pilgrimage. A *tirtha* ("crossing place") is a place for crossing both over and upward (combining metaphors of both bridge and ladder), such that "[t]he act of crossing in the Upanishads is a spiritual transition and transformation from this world to what is called the world of Brahman, the world illumined by the light of knowledge" (Eck 1981:331). Forests and mountains, particularly the Himalayan mountains, are the *tirthas* most consistently associated with sages and renouncers. In both ancient literary and contemporary understandings, then, the power of the place itself is so extraordinary that austerities performed in such places result much more quickly in spiritual transformation and transcendence. As Lutgendorf elaborates, the dense forest is invoked as a contrasting landscape to that of the royal court and city-state in the *Mahabharata* and *Ramayana* as well as in the narrative tradition of the Sanskrit and vernacular Puranas (2000:270). While kings enter the forest in exile or for recreational hunting, sages *choose* to live in the dense forest rather than in the city, for it is here "that transcendence of human limitations becomes possible and that communication occurs between heaven and earth; it is here that gods most often descend to communicate with human beings, and that the latter ascend to heaven, and it is here that superhuman beings and demigods are most often encountered" (Lutgendorf 2000:280). In addition to forests and mountains, the Ganges River has the power to bring about spiritual transformation. In his analysis of the degradation of the sacred Yamuna River as it enters Delhi and absorbs the city's industrial waste, Haberman observes that environmental damage also results in cultural damage (2000:351). In an age of industrial pollution the Ganges River, especially high up near its source, remains a most appropriate place for austerities and still offers the possibility of transcendence.[4] Indeed, the further up one goes toward the source of the Ganges, the greater the power, so Haridwar is better than Delhi, but Uttarkhand is better than Haridwar. Advaita Vedanta associates liberation with the transcendence of social distinctions and inequalities. Similarly, Eck points out that the ideal in the Dharmashastra tradition is that the way of the *tirtha* is open to all, particularly to those who were excluded from brahmanical rites: Shudras, outcastes, and women, for in a *tirtha*, all bathe in the same waters (1981:338–39).

Time and Life-Stage

The stories of Vashisht traveling from Uttarkhand to Haridwar and of Lakshman traveling through the forest are not only about place but also about movement. Just as particular places are good for *sadhana* so are particular times, including times of the day, periods of the year, and stages of life. Life-stages can be understood as a conjunction of time (*kal*) and the individual actor or vessel (*patra*). Ramanujan has made a lasting contribution to the study of Indian culture in his insight that some cultures have a tendency to idealize, and think in terms of, context-sensitive kinds of rules (1989a:47). "Even space and time," he writes, "the universal contexts, the Kantian imperatives, are in India not uniform and neutral, but have properties, varying specific densities, that effect those who dwell in them" (1989a:51).

One implication of the metaphor of journeys is that any particular lifestyle or religious practice can be a spiritual tool for one person and an obstacle for another, depending on the path they have chosen. Thus, any particular action, even something so outrageous as the consumption of liquor by a Dashnami renouncer, can be rendered meaningful with reference to this metaphor of individual journeys. Furthermore, since a person's perspective and spiritual needs are assumed to change as they travel along their path, what is a tool at one stage in a person's life may become an obstacle at a later stage, either in the same life or the next. As Anand Mata once put it, "If you take a plane somewhere, then you must know to get *off* the plane when you have reached your destination. Otherwise, you'll just remain seated in the plane without reaching your goal." When Anand Mata reached the point where her own vow of silence had fulfilled its purpose of turning her focus inward, she began speaking again. Similarly, reflecting on her own experiences, she insisted that it is important to have a guru but also to know when to leave the guru. *Sadhana*, according to Baiji, is nothing but a means of moving forward. Thus, a person interested in action can read the *Bhagavadgita* and progress through *karmayoga*; others may prefer *bhakti* or *jnana*.

What is deemed appropriate religious behavior, therefore, is relative to a person's spatial and temporal position on a particular path. But this personal journey is not one that begins at birth and ends at death; rather, it spans countless lifetimes. A person (*atma* combined with all the trappings of a particular birth), then, is a spiritual being progressing, quickly or slowly, on a journey of self-transformation. I found that individual personalities and eccentricities, crisis situations and miraculous events were typically explained with reference to the *samskaras* of previous lives. Uma Bharati is from a poor, rural, but religious family. At the age of six, with little formal schooling, she suddenly began reciting scriptures and, once, corrected the mistake of a visiting Brahmin scholar. She said to me in an interview that her miraculous display of knowledge was explained by some as memories from a previous life. The reason everyone is different, said Baiji, is that they must begin from the point they reached at the end of their previous life. Thus, she explained, someone who was a *karmayogi* in his last life, and reached the very peak of *karmayoga*, is positioned at the beginning of Vedanta. Renouncers are constantly moving—spiritually if not literally—in the sense that they are expected to continually progress beyond what they have done. Even the guru or sannyasa itself, the two most powerful vehicles for liberation, may eventually become obstacles in the search for liberation, particularly if a renouncer develops dependency on the guru or pride in the ochre robes. Recall the story of King Sikhidhvaja and Queen Chudala from Venkatesananda's translation of the *Yoga-Vasistha* presented in chapter 1. When the king finally, after many years of forest living, abandoned the trappings of renunciation and achieved enlightenment, Chudala asked him what he wished to do next. He responded that he will follow whatever she considers appropriate. Accordingly, they returned to rule the kingdom and enjoy, without attachment, the pleasures of the world for ten thousand years, after which they attained liberation (Venkatesananda 1984:333–34). Because religious practice depends not only on the path one chooses but also on where one stands on that path at any given moment, what is a tool at one point in a person's life (a particular guru, a discipline of silence, even sannyasa itself) may become an obstacle for that same person at a later stage.

If renunciation is a journey, then the path is strewn with obstacles. Baiji spoke about the obstacles she faced in her renunciation. She first went to Uttarkhand in 1952, and "since it was the land of the *rishis* and *munis*" she liked it there and stayed. When she next descended to the plains and met her first guru again, he was happy with her progress. "Now you are independent," he said, "and if someone comes to you for learning then you must teach them." When Baiji wondered how she could teach others when she herself did not know, he said, "No, now I have told you this and have given you the freedom to teach others." She began advising householders while still wearing white clothing. Although she found herself guiding people who had trouble understanding sacred texts or practicing yogic breathing, she still had unanswered spiritual questions of her own. When she returned to Uttarkhand, she memorized several scriptures and then began to ponder the questions "Who am I?" and "What is that power that is running everything?" She already knew the answer from reading texts but became determined to experience it clearly in the way that the *atma* sees the world. It was then that Baiji vowed not to leave Uttarkhand until she experienced this, even if it meant dying there.

Baiji had spoken often about her days of living in the mountains. She talked about how when she looked in her diary and saw that the experiences recorded in the diary were consistent with Advaita Vedanta, she felt encouraged to memorize more texts. She was so engrossed in memorizing Upanishads that even while brushing her teeth or running errands she would memorize passages. She did this because she had very little time, as she had to serve her guru and meditate from midnight until two thirty or three in the morning. After finishing the meditation she would attend to the ashram work. She was able to accomplish all this, she says, because she was young. Not only was there power in her blood but also the enthusiasm of youth. Baiji went on to describe how Bhagwan tested her while she was living in Uttarkhand by putting obstacles in her path, which related primarily to her 1954 initiation into sannyasa and the illness that followed.

Until 1954 she had been wearing the white clothing of celibate studentship. While still in white she had had a dream in which Avadhutji initiated her into sannyasa, but when, upon waking, she asked him about the possibility of initiation he responded simply that he does not give sannyasa—that he had taken a vow not to initiate anyone. He offered instead to have an old, "very good swami" initiate her. She told him that she had seen herself taking sannyasa from *him* in a dream and that if he would not give her sannyasa then she was not ready to be initiated by anyone else. She and Avadhutji went on "fighting" about this for two or three months in the sense that neither of them raised the subject for discussion. Then the elder Mrs. Malhotra, Avadhutji's devotee, visited Uttarkhand, and the young Baiji asked her advice. "Let me ask you one thing," said the older woman. "If you have so much faith in him, then what harm is there in going along with him on this one thing? Whoever he gets to give you sannyasa, you can just pretend that he himself is giving it." Baiji was not convinced. "But Mataji," she said, "this would mean that my dream did not come true. If the dream is not true then it means that it was only a figment of my imagination (*mere dimag ki kalpna*). It should happen just as I saw it in the dream." Baiji refused to take sannyasa "from her imagination" and Avadhutji refused to initiate her.

The question of whether a woman of such young age should be initiated led to a debate among the local sadhus. "Avadhutji," said Baiji, "was also a *dandi* swami [those who carry a staff] of the Dashnami Order, and *dandi* sannyasis did not initiate women into sannyasa, so how could he initiate me? All the good saints felt that Avadhutji should not initiate me and that he should have me initiated by someone of the Giri or Puri Order, since those particular orders did admit women. Avadhutji was prepared to have sannyasa given to me by someone else, and the other swami was also willing to give it. I had decided to do it but told myself to understand that 'since this is not your dream, it means it was a figment of your imagination.' This thought kept going through my mind. For two days a *havan*, and so forth was going on, but my mind kept thinking that I was only doing this for show, that it was a mistake because if my dream was not coming true then sannyasa would not sit properly. If the dream was not true then sannyasa was also not right.

"Meanwhile, what happened? There erupted such a controversy among the saints that one disciple of Ganganandaji's went to Avadhutji and said, 'Swami

Tapovanji, Ganganandaji and all the important saints request that you not give sannyasa to the one whom you are planning to initiate tomorrow. Please don't do it because the scriptures are opposed to this initiation [of a woman].' So now the dream was about to come true, Oh Bhagwan! Hearing this, Avadhutji became angry and said, 'OK, tell them that I was not going to initiate her, but now that the issue of scripture is being raised, I myself will give her sannyasa. And anyone who wants to debate the meaning of the scriptures with me can come to the edge of the Ganges and do it there [at the initiation site].'" Baiji was thrilled to hear this. In the morning, however, someone told the other swami that he would be giving her sannyasa, so he was also ready. Baiji was standing in her cottage confused, wondering whether Avadhutji had changed his mind about giving her sannyasa after all. "The only thing on my mind was that this has become my imagination and the dream is not true. Just then Avadhutji called me: 'Bitti!' They used to call me 'Bitti' (Girl Child). I went out. 'Let's go to the banks of the Ganges,' he said in a stern voice. I saw that the other swami was with him. When I reached the river he explained, 'Now a dispute has arisen among the saints, and the issue of what the texts say has come up. For this reason, I myself am going to give you sannyasa, not he.' As he spoke, I felt as if consciousness had suddenly come back into my body." Avadhutji did perform the ceremony. But since he could not touch a woman, Baiji had to perform the tonsure on herself and, being unskilled in using a razor, cut her own scalp badly. After reciting some more mantras, Avadhutji said, "These are your clothes, Bitti. Bathe and then put them on. After that, call us back down." After Baiji bathed in the river, the two men returned from the riverbanks above. A special mantra was given to her and a sermon. He did all this, then told her to go and pay her respects at the Shiva temple and then return. When she arrived at the temple, she ran into the disciple of a saint who had opposed her initiation. Though she knew that he opposed her initiation, she still felt no hatred toward him; instead, she touched his feet and a sincere blessing slipped out of his mouth. He wished that she should fulfill whatever purpose had led her to do so much renunciation (tyaga) in her life.

The second major obstacle she faced while undergoing intense sadhana was illness. The very day of her initiation, she caught a fever from standing so long in the cold on the banks of the Ganges. And in the midst of all the conflict about her initiation, Baiji's eyes went bad. She developed glaucoma "from being in all that cold, though no one knew it was glaucoma." A few months later, the elder Mrs. Malhotra arrived, two days after they had put some medicine in Baiji's eyes that had the effect of making her unable to see any kind of light at all. "It felt like fire in my eyes," she says. Mrs. Malhotra told her to come up with her own medicine through meditation. The first medicine that came to Baiji's mind was unavailable in the area. Then some natural medicine appeared to her through meditation, and, after she used it, her eyes improved somewhat. "The next time the military doctor came, he folded his hands [in supplication] and said he would give me some medicine if I would accept it. I told him that I had a vision that suggested the condition would get worse if I took medicine, but who listens? They gave me some pills the next morning, and within one minute of taking the pills there was smoke and I thought my hands and feet would die. I became crippled and couldn't go anywhere, not even to the bathroom or down the hill. At that time there were no bathrooms in the cottage." Then Baiji's first guru arrived in town for his winter *sadhana*. He told her to go down to the plains immediately, but she kept refusing to go. Suddenly, she says, he looked at her with such sternness that she knew she had no choice. They used sticks to immobilize her limbs, bandaged her eyes, sat her on a donkey, and covered her body with blankets for the journey. "No hands, no feet. Like that I went. In those days, motors still did not come up as far as Uttarkhand. It was very difficult." After a long time, they arrived in the plains and there, with the application of her own treatment, her eyes gradually recovered.

Metaphors of place, time, and movement are ubiquitous in renouncers' comments about their own lives and about sannyasa in general. Anand Mata once described sannyasa as a "jumping board" that gives you a push toward your final destination. According to Baiji, "sannyasa is like traveling by jet plane rather than by foot." Renunciation is perceived as a shortcut, difficult and full of obstacles, but faster than the long route. Such obstacles can cause the traveler to stumble, even fall, but if her determination is strong she will pick herself up and keep moving forward. And, the one who has reached the final destination of liberation is referred to simply as "having arrived" (*pahanche hue*). The longer routes will take one to the same place but slowly, after many lives. For Anand Mata, a vow of silence was a way to intensify and speed up her effort to turn inward. Sannyasa is the "fast track" to liberation. All beings are moving toward the same destination, although along different paths and at different speeds.

Otherworldly withdrawal and worldly involvement are seen by sannyasinis themselves not as mutually exclusive paths but as two orientations appropriate to different moments in a person's spiritual journey. The renouncers I met indicated that it is possible to have intimate contact with householders, conduct monetary transactions and supervise employees with detachment only if one balances such involvement with otherworldly spiritual practices. Lay Hindus also seemed to distinguish socially involved saints from ordinary people devoted to good works on the basis of whether or not they combine their involvement with otherworldly renunciation. The *ashrama* system reserves renunciation to the final stage of life after one's children are married and one's debts paid, but even within the renunciant life, periods of activity that drain spiritual power may be alternated with periods of austerities, meditation, and withdrawal. Anand Mata and Baiji did not reject social involvement, since it was required by the *renunciant* values of compassion and service. Social involvement motivated by compassion or selfless service cannot in itself lead to liberation; indeed, it can be a challenge to the goal of liberation since it creates opportunities for emotional attachments. Renouncers must first withdraw from society in order to transform themselves through a period of intense *sadhana*, and then, once transformed, they may become involved in society but with a different attitude, withdrawing periodically for spiritual renewal and returning with powers intact. Sadhus move in and out of society. They are just as likely to suddenly walk away from an ashram, guru, or commitment, as they are to emerge from isolation to take on disciples or projects.

Conclusion

Sannyasa, and human existence more generally, is seen by renouncers as a movement toward liberation. While one's spiritual journey may be long and twisted, full of falls, wrong turns and temporary setbacks, it is never cyclical. Within the spiritual journey are shorter cycles of birth, death, and rebirth, but the larger journey is a gradual and linear movement toward liberation. These cycles provide different frames of reference, dialogues within dialogues, for renouncers' comments about many things, including the importance of *puja-path* and the relevance of gender. Once someone "has arrived" they cannot regress; they may reenter social or even political life, but with an attitude of detachment.

Implied in this metaphor is the notion that spiritual paths are defined individually. As Anand Mata put it, "Each person has a different path. The guru is within every person, and as a person advances on his spiritual path he begins to communicate with his inner guru. The guru's instructions are compatible with the disciple's inner nature. When the outer guru realizes that the dormant inner guru of the disciple has been awakened, then the outer guru renounces the disciple and tells him or her to follow the voice of the inner guru." According to Anand Mata, no two persons can have the same path, but the goal and the intention are identical for everyone. In order to progress spiritually, one must choose an appropriate path, and appropriateness involves attention to place (*sthan*), time (*kal*), and individual actor or vessel (*patra*). The conception of individual existence as a journey along a particular path provides Hindus with a way of understanding individual variation in religious life and engenders a context-sensitive view of the world. These concepts underlie Baiji's shifting statements and practices; they varied depending not only on time and place but also on intended recipient of the message (Sonam and I, for example, received different messages).

A second implication of this metaphor is epistemological in that it contains a certain attitude toward ambiguity in general and hiddenness in particular, themes which will be developed in the next chapter. Integral to this metaphor of journey is the assumption that Truth, the final destination of every journey, is elusive and hidden. The reason spiritual discipline must be subjectively defined is that Truth looks different depending on the path one takes and where one stands on that path at any given moment (Trawick 1988). My description of Baiji's style of renunciation, for example, is inextricably tied up with the fact that I entered her life at a certain juncture of both place (Rishi Ashram rather than Uttarkhand) and life-stage (after she had become a guru). If I had met her at a different time I would have known a different Baiji, or perhaps not gotten to know her at all if she were too aloof to take any interest in me or my project. Traube (1986) and Trawick (1988) have both described what they see as indigenous conceptions of wholeness and truth (not to be confused with the extensively critiqued anthropologists' holism). Given the eclecticism of renunciation, I believe that this notion of journeys is also a renunciant vision of wholeness, completeness, and truth.

A third implication is that it is difficult to judge the authenticity of particular sadhus simply by observing their actions because genuine sadhus can behave in all sorts of ways. What one really needs to know is the attitude behind the actions. Is Baiji guiding disciples with detachment or for the purpose of self-aggrandizement? Does she ignore rules of purity at Gangotri Ashram because she has transcended such worldly distinctions or because it is easier? Did Anand Mata not study scriptures because she had already absorbed the spirit of their teachings into her every word and action or because she lacked knowledge? The next chapter will show that there is no clear and consistent set of criteria for establishing the "saintliness" or "legitimacy" of Hindu renouncers. It is possible to render almost any particular lifestyle, action, or statement meaningful with reference to metaphors of journey.

Chapter Five

The Genuine and The Fake: What's Attitude Got to Do with It?

Many lay Hindus, when describing their guru, comment on the qualities that make their guru special, different, not like the rest. Despite stereotypes of spiritually inclined Hindus who venerate anyone and anything touched with divinity, the material already presented demonstrates that Hindus treat holy persons with a combination of cynicism, indifference, and reverence. During my conversations with and about sannyasinis, the question of legitimacy (both asserted and doubted) came up frequently. Here I argue that there are no objective criteria for making such evaluations. At the same time, discernible patterns suggest that the process of distinguishing real saints from the riffraff is complex and related to various frames of reference, including worldly and otherworldly, internal attitudes and external expressions, the eternal and unseen *atma* and the living person (*jiva*) who embodies it.

The issue of saintly legitimacy is complicated by three characteristics of sannyasa. First, the social world of Hindu renunciation operates on a "free market" model with little in the way of institutional constraints defining who can call herself a sadhu or wear the ochre robes, at least with regard to independent renouncers. Outside of monastic institutions, then, it is left up to spiritual seekers and other observers to decide who is and who is not a genuine saint. Second, sannyasa both upholds social distinctions such as caste and gender and claims to transcend them. Thus, the final state of liberation is defined as a transcendence of the very social conventions and distinctions (regarding, for example, ritual purity) that characterize much of renunciant social life. Third, Hindu cultural evaluations regarding saintly authenticity are further complicated by epistemological assumptions about the nature of religious Truth. Truth is the final destination of a journey spanning countless lifetimes and is assumed to look different depending on one's chosen path and where one stands on that path at any given moment. But, Truth is also elusive and hidden, only available to those capable of perceiving it (Trawick 1988; D. Gold 1988:24). There is a parallel assumption that the best sadhus are also hidden, either literally in that they live in some remote place, conventionally identified as a cave or jungle, or metaphorically in that they appear before us in some unrecognizable form: an ordinary beggar, an animal, or even a thief. Not only can frauds masquerade as saints then, but genuine saints may pose as frauds in order to avoid the demands made upon those who are spiritually elevated.[1]

There exists a tension, in Hindus' approach to holy persons, between the values of faith (shraddha) and discrimination (vivek).[2] The necessity of approaching holy persons with a healthy dose of skepticism is taken as self-evident, and various methods of reasoning are used to discriminate between asli (genuine) and nakli (false) sadhus. Spiritual seekers compare sadhus; many pumped me for information about how a particular sannyasini compared to others I had interviewed. In addition to shopping around for a guru, spiritual seekers also tested sadhus in various ways and considered their social background, including their biography, circumstances of their renunciation, and reputation of their guru. Observers also examine the exterior attributes and lifestyle of a sadhu for their general "fit" with expectations of physical poise, emotional indifference, appropriate speech, and general austerity of lifestyle.

Ultimately, however, saintly authenticity in sannyasa is a question of inner attitude. Renouncers may become involved in social relationships, engage in social service, or even blow up in anger, as long as their external actions are accompanied by an inner attitude of vairagya. Renouncing family can be motivated by detachment or by frustration, just as a vow of silence can be a method of focusing inward or a convenient way of avoiding certain people or situations. Thus, genuine renunciation is a matter of attitude. Since inner attitudes can be concealed by deceptive exteriors and ordinary people cannot really know the interior of a holy person, what is important is that they have faith. Once a sadhu attains the status of genuine, liberated saint in the eyes of a particular person, then everything else (such as their external actions or biography) may be attributed to some divine purpose. Their behavior ceases to become the object of critical evaluation. As one young man, a devotee of Baiji's, said, "it doesn't matter if one takes a thief for a guru as long as one's faith is strong enough."

The contradictory values of faith and discrimination are two ways to ascertain the inner states of sadhus. Most people do not commit to one strategy; rather, they emphasize one or the other in different contexts. One of these contexts has to do with the person's relationship to the sadhu, as either uncommitted observer or as disciple. Someone may have unshakable faith in their own guru yet assume that most others are fakes. Similarly, with regard to any particular sadhu there is a multiplicity of competing interpretations. This makes it impossible to talk about the legitimacy of female renouncers in general, as we must always ask the question "According to whom?"

A series of ethnographic vignettes illustrates how particular sannyasinis are represented by nondisciples, disciples, and by themselves. The first two vignettes show that the *asli* and *nakli* are neither dichotomous categories nor, without further elaboration, are they sufficient to identify a given sadhu. For example, the *nakli* variety includes both ordinary, harmless frauds who possess neither sincerity nor power and the really dangerous ones who have gained spiritual power but use it to satisfy their lust and greed. Similarly, among the *asli* sadhus, there are those who are sincerely, if imperfectly, treading the path of spiritual discipline and those who have already arrived at the final goal of liberation.

Ordinary Frauds or Dangerous Witches?

During the seven months my husband was with me in Haridwar we lived not in an ashram but in a private home; it was the ancestral property of my great aunt and had been vacant for years prior to our arrival. A family across the street enthusiastically befriended us. Within a few days of our arrival, their teenage daughter Rashmi took me to meet three sannyasinis who lived in a house just around the corner. The eldest was called "Babaji" and the younger two "Behnji;" all were disciples of a female guru, a Sanatani who lived in her main ashram several hours' bus ride from Haridwar. The two Behnjis were young, in their early twenties, and deferred to Babaji who appeared to be in her forties. Of the younger two, one was very quiet and the other, referred to here descriptively as "the Fair One" (as she was called by my neighbors), was exceedingly friendly and warm. My conversations with her felt more like chats with a girlfriend than conversations with a sannyasini; we spoke more about clothes, family, and life in America than about religious matters. And the older Babaji promised interviews that were never forthcoming. During the next couple of weeks, I visited the women repeatedly and accompanied them one day to a wedding celebration where they had been invited to sing devotional songs.

Meanwhile, my neighbor Rashmi had also taken me to an ordinary-looking house nearby that was actually the temple of a (deceased) female saint called "Sita Behn." Sita Mandir is where she lived when alive and where her *samadhi* (saint's tomb) was now located. Men, and even the male children of worshipers, were not allowed inside the building. There I met two devotees of Sita Behn, the unmarried female caretaker who lived upstairs and a vivacious householder, Usha, who was visiting from Bombay. The former was very old and sickly; the latter was a trustee of the temple and a niece of the enshrined saint Sita Behn. At the time I knew nothing of the hostilities that were brewing between Sita Mandir and Babaji's ashram. Sita Mandir's board of trustees, it seems, had made Babaji a trustee but was now trying to have her legally removed from the board. The members had accused her not only of embezzlement but also of contributing, by deliberate neglect, to the elderly caretaker's ill health.

Hostilities had become so intense that there was even talk of spies. The Fair One must have discovered that I had been visiting Sita Mandir, because she sent her servant girl to call me over one afternoon and, almost immediately and unprovoked, began to warn me about how sly (*chalak*) Usha was and that she was telling everyone in the neighborhood that Babaji was no good. According to the Fair One, an older devotee who died years ago had given Sita Mandir to Babaji, with love, as *dan*, but now the current caretaker wanted to take it for herself. "Babaji has no greed," she said. "We have performed so much service for that place, and lovingly." She then instructed me to tell Usha that they wanted nothing more to do with Sita Mandir. When the elderly caretaker's poor health declined even further and led to her death a few days later, Babaji's culpability was insinuated. Babaji had intentionally neglected the frail woman, it was felt, so that her health would deteriorate. Usha was convinced of Babaji's ambitions to take over the property and was determined to prevent it. Saving the shrine was, for her, a matter of both devotion to a female saint and loyalty to an ancestor. One day Usha, distressed to the point of tears, cautioned me to keep a safe distance from the three sannyasinis lest they try to brainwash me. "They'll take you to meet their guru," she warned in English. "She will put a string around your neck and say some mantras. Eventually, you'll be totally brainwashed. Then they will want your property, and so forth. They have done a lot of *tapasya* and get some power from that. Just as Parvati did *tapasya* to get Shiva, they can get people to come to them in the same way.[3] They use mantras and say the rosary backward. They have a big outfit—lots of wealth—and ashrams in every city because they get people to give *dan*. They persuade virgin girls to join, girls who should be happily married in their own homes; they must have some feelings after all, and these have been suppressed. They recruit them and then send them out to earn money by singing devotional songs." One reason for Usha's harsh judgment was the ashram's wealth, which always raises suspicions about a particular renunciant order or saint. Another reason was the prevalence of young women (whom Usha referred to as "small children") among their ranks. She evoked the *ashrama* system to stress that people should marry first, before renouncing worldly life. "If family life is not good," she said, "*then* think of sannyasa, but otherwise wait until age fifty. There are always exceptions, and for them anything goes, but they are rare."

Her warnings reflected more than a concern that I might be deluded into following the women's guru or tricked into giving them my possessions. One day Usha came to my home and implored me *never* to take my husband to their place because Babaji would try to use magic (*jadu*) to create a rift between us. "Before you know it," she said as she clasped my shoulders intensely, "your husband will be telling you that you are crazy and that Babaji is the greatest person in the world." Upon hearing this my elderly neighbor Amrita, who had happened upon our conversation, suddenly burst into tears as she began to tell Usha how much she worried about me lately, about my visiting the three sannyasinis, since I was so naive. Amrita warned that her own guru had told her long ago that this Babaji was dangerous. "You see," said Usha, "everyone knows about them but no one says anything."

In order to better understand the meaning that accusations of witchcraft have when applied to renouncers, I had consulted Anand Mata the previous week. Without offering much detail, I mentioned Usha's warnings and the fact that Babaji had asked for my tape recorder. She had remarked that it would be best to avoid Babaji if possible but was not overly concerned. "Yes," she had said, "perhaps the neighbors are spreading vicious rumors because of some petty grudge or jealousy. Who knows? But then perhaps they know these women well and know that they merely wish to take advantage of you." She paused a moment and said, "Right now you are very receptive." "Receptivity" was a good thing if it helped one absorb the guru's teachings, but it could also render one vulnerable to malevolent forces.

The next time Mehraji and I visited Anand Mata I related in more detail the concerned warnings of Usha and Amrita as well as the Fair One's persistent invitations for me to come over, just to keep her company. I mentioned too that I was often invited there for a meal. Once, when I declined by saying that I was busy, the Fair One *insisted* that I come for a meal, even if only for breakfast. When I told Anand Mata and Mehraji that the Fair One had even sent *prasad* to my house twice when I did not show up, both became very serious and replied in unison, "Don't take any food from them!"

"Then I should give their *prasad* to some other person to eat, or to an animal?" I asked. They looked at each other and concurred. "An animal."

"The neighbors have been very alarmist," I remarked, "warning me that I should never take Peter there to meet them. And it's strange . . . but the Fair One has specifically asked several times when I will bring my husband to meet them. . . . I think she just wants to meet a foreigner."

"These people have ways of causing a rift between husband and wife," Mehraji said ominously.

Anand Mata added, "It is best to avoid such people."

I had promised to go there for breakfast the next day and wondered aloud whether I should just send a note through someone saying I was not well. "Do not send a note," ordered Anand Mata. "You can send a message through

someone, but do not send anything written." She had become visibly agitated; I
had never seen her like that before.

"I do not understand."

She muttered something about people who can gain power over others by
acquiring a scrap of their handwriting, but elaborated no further. Mehraji
nodded in agreement and added, "You should also be very careful not to leave
behind any belonging at their place, not even a hair."

"You cannot understand these things," said Anand Mata. "If your grandmother were still alive, she would never have allowed you to stay here in
Haridwar for so long because she would have understood the dangers involved.
Even your aunts do not really understand the world as she did. You should avoid
these people lest you get caught in some mess (*chakkar*) that you do not understand. . . . Paramatma is in everyone, but in some he is sleeping." I said that it
might be necessary to go just once more to give some explanation. Anand Mata
instructed Mehraji to go there with me next time and check everything out,
either because she did not believe me or because she simply wanted to let Babaji
know that I had people looking out for me.

A few days later Mehraji and I went to meet the three women and, as usual,
the Fair One deferred to her senior guru-sister for an interview, which she stu-
diously evaded. Her furrowed eyebrows, lack of poise, and inability or unwillingness to participate in religious discussion indicated to Mehraji that she had no
spiritual power and, therefore, was not particularly dangerous. And he detected
no signs of magical tantric practice, such as lemon or chili peppers hanging in
doorways. The following week, he reported back to Anand Mata. "This Babaji,"
he said, "is just an ordinary commercialized type of sadhu."

"Then they are not dangerous? Meena can go for interviews?"

"Yes, but she won't gain any knowledge from them." Anand Mata dismissed
this comment with a wave of the hand and told me that I could go to them for
the purpose of research. The experiences of those two weeks taught me that
within the category of false sadhus, there was an unstated distinction between
the ordinary variety and the really dangerous ones. Most religious frauds are
thought to be without spiritual knowledge or power; they masquerade as sadhus
to make an easy living, to satisfy sensual desires, to evade family obligations or
even to escape criminal justice. Such people are the relatively harmless *nakli*
sadhus. In contrast, those who have gained spiritual power through austerities
but use those powers for evil ends are fewer but far more dangerous because they
are able to manipulate other persons, the gods, and the material world. Their
power to inflict suffering on others is immense. What distinguishes them from
genuine sadhus then is not spiritual power or austerities, but their lack of
vairagya. Their powers are the servants of desire.

Magicians (*jadudars*) may be either tantrics or ordinary renouncers who
have gained powers (*siddhis*) through legitimate, right-handed *sadhana*, then use

these powers to gain control over others. If some forms of bhakti ignore orthodox traditions regarding ritual purity and its concern with gender and caste,
Tantrism involves a symmetric inversion of those traditions and, thus, is more
extreme in its heterodoxy.[4] In addition to subverting brahmanic ritual prescrip-
tions followed by orthodox renouncers, Tantrism also admits all without concern
for caste or gender, on the condition that they have been initiated. Both
Shankara and Ramanuja are said to have criticized the "left-handed" practices
of particular tantric sects (Briggs 1973:220–24). Conventional Hindus often suspect tantrics of practicing magic, but they seem to be less suspicious of those following the Dashnami model of sannyasa. Firmly positioned within the realm of
the right-handed religiosity sanctioned by brahmanical Hinduism, they tend to
emphasize purity and celibacy. Intersectarian evaluations of genuine and false
sadhus are complex, as there are many varieties of ascetics. For example, some of
the more orthodox Dashnami sannyasis still refuse to recognize the possibility
that a woman could be a genuine renouncer. Similarly, bhakti ecstatics may feel
that sannyasis have philosophical, scholastic knowledge but lack true devotion.
Tantric ascetics may view Dashnamis as pure but powerless. Here I am concerned with interpersonal commentaries about authenticity and cannot address
these intersectarian discourses.

Although there are no self-identified tantric practitioners (*yogi; yogini*) featured in this account, I did find a range of attitudes toward Tantrism. For example, while one sannyasini spoke to me of awakening the *kundalini* through yoga,
another turned up her nose in distaste at "that *kundalini* stuff" and also held a
low opinion of the aforementioned sannyasini.[5] Baiji, as an "orthodox" sannyasini, viewed Tantrism as a lower spiritual path and when I asked her about it
she responded flatly that she didn't know anything about it. Anand Mata
seemed more sympathetic to tantric ideas. She felt it was possible to achieve
anand or bliss through sexual intercourse because it creates an unbroken, powerful cycle. As an analogue, she also spoke of the energy cycle created when a guru
places his hand on a disciple's head at the same time that the disciple touches
the guru's feet. "Not all gurus understand this," she said. Tantric practitioners, in
popular imagination, are reputed to have supernatural powers obtained through
yogic practice and healing skills obtained through the use of exorcism, magic,
and charms.[6]

When I told a local man about Mehraji's assurances that Babaji was not a
magician, he warned me that the practice of magic need not be accompanied by
the presence of ritual objects and that Mehraji may not be spiritually advanced
enough himself to pick up the cues. "*Jadudars* may look like ordinary people," he
said. "It is also a type of *sadhana*, but the lowest kind of all. *Jadudars* always end
up with miserable lives." Mehraji, however, had been confident that he could
ascertain Babaji's interior state by various external signs. The following vignette
suggests that there is not only a distinction between ordinary frauds and the

really dangerous ones, but also one between ordinary genuine saints, who are sincerely treading the path of spiritual discipline, and those who have already arrived at the final goal of liberation.

The Cave-Dwelling Firangi Mata

One morning Mehraji accompanied me to meet a *firangi* (foreign) san-nyasini who had migrated from Germany and now lived in a cave on the out-skirts of Haridwar. I had heard good things about her from some people in town, that she was a foreigner who had become a real Hindu sadhu. Comments spoken with reverence usually pointed to her lengthy *tapasya* of living in a cave for some thirty years or to her skill in singing devotional songs. That morning, after our climb to her cave, though, it was clear that Mehraji was not impressed. In describing our meeting with "the Firangi Mata" to Anand Mata later that day, he expressed his disdain and certainty about her fraudulent character. "Meena will have nothing to gain from visiting her again," he told Anand Mata, "since it was obvious that she has no real knowledge."

Mehraji had been put off, I think, by the Firangi Mata's agitated and cynical mood as it signified that she had not achieved the detachment and emotional steadiness expected of renouncers. The very morning of our visit, a boy who helped carry supplies from town and whom she was putting through school in return had run off with all her money, and this was apparently not the first time it had happened. Under government pressure to move from her cave to make way for a public facility, she had recently given a man two thousand rupees for a piece of land, but he disappeared with the money. "I am only a body for exploita-tion," she had muttered in English. Her cave dwelling was guarded by two huge, well-fed, European-born Alsatian dogs whose ferocious appearance was enhanced by the large spiked collars that ostensibly protected them from tigers. The dogs had terrified Mehraji and me as we approached the cave. To him, their presence signified the Firangi Mata's fear and hostility, hardly qualities appropri-ate for a holy person. The dogs aside, she was hospitable and ushered us into her cave in the center of which a sacrificial *dhuni* fire smoldered. Searching the smoky darkness, I found two fierce, amber tiger eyes staring back at me. The tiger was beautifully sculpted from cement, by the Firangi Mata herself, and had glass marbles for eyes. Once inside the cave she continued to vent her cynicism, insisting that I use my book to warn others that it is very difficult for a woman to live alone in India unless she has food, shelter, clothing, someone to help with chores, and her own bank account! Her brother and sister back home used to send her money every month but then stopped because they felt she was "ruin-ing her life" in India. She emphasized that a woman should not renounce every-thing: "If everything belongs to God, then why must we leave it all? If a woman gives up everything then she'll be dependent on someone or another, and this is not good. In foreign countries a woman can live alone, but in India it is very difficult." For Mehraji, such bitterness regarding the obstacles facing independent women was unworthy of compassion and devoid of wisdom, since a true saint would rise above these problems. The fact that two young European men, tourists on a hiking expedition, were temporarily living in the cave next to hers did not help; Mehraji could not have looked favorably on the arrangement of a single woman living alone with young men. The combination of her cynicism, her dogs, and her lifestyle left him feeling certain about her fraudulent character and he clearly held her responsible for her own degradation.

Later when Anand Mata and I were alone I defended the Firangi Mata by relating stories I had heard about how she was once attacked and beaten by an intruder wielding a steel rod and, after that, acquired the guard dogs. These were stories that Mehraji too had heard. My sympathies sprung from an awareness of her prior sufferings and an acute sensitivity to the problems that single women, especially white women, face when living alone in North India. Anand Mata also perceived a heroic quality in the fact that the Firangi Mata was a woman living alone in a cave "as the *rishis* and *munis* had done." And having once lived in a cosmopolitan ashram herself, she was probably more likely to understand the different expectations that a European woman might have regarding independent living and the disappointment to which such expectations might lead. For Anand Mata and for me, the guard dogs symbolized not simply her failure, as they did for Mehraji, but also her endurance, her determination to continue doing *sadhana* in the face of extreme adversity.

But Anand Mata refused to romanticize this woman's life; she compared her to another sadhu we both knew who, accepting her limitations as a young woman, sensibly settled into a cottage with her spiritually-inclined father to practice *sadhana*. Anand Mata felt too that these limitations were practical rather than spiritual in nature, suggesting that compromises made to a patriarchal social order should not be obstacles for sannyasa. More importantly though, according to Anand Mata, if one wants to perform intense *sadhana* while living in a cave one must have faith that whatever suffering one encounters is sent by Paramatma. "Then there is no question of becoming upset when faced with suffering." Rather than becoming resentful or anxious, the Firangi Mata should have responded to the theft either by reflecting on her attachment to material belongings and financial security or by moving to a safer dwelling. Yet, at the same time, she had endured many obstacles and still persisted with her *sadhana* rather than simply giving up; that counted for something. Anand Mata, without having met her, accepted the possibility that this woman was a genuine sadhu not in the sense of being liberated but in sense that she would eventually overcome this crisis of both finances and faith, and continue her *sadhana*. Anand Mata refused to see saints and frauds as dichotomous categories. Mehraji, by contrast, was confident in his ability to "read" her interior disposition from her external actions and words. The following vignette, also revolving around the

Firangi Mata, further illustrates the discriminating tendencies of nondisciples and addresses the issue of how sadhus represent themselves.

The Breaking of Renunciant Conventions

My second encounter with the Firangi Mata, at Rishi Ashram, occurred under very different circumstances. Three carloads of Baiji's disciples, all related to each other, had gathered there for several days of religious events. When a young man suggested that I should meet his uncle "Mamaji" (Mother's Brother), who was expected to arrive that day, he was quickly silenced by his sister and aunt. His aunt shook her head vehemently and pulled him aside, out of my earshot. For the remainder of the afternoon, there was a debate going on in hushed tones about whether I should meet Mamaji or not. When I asked the young man privately why no one wanted me to meet his uncle, he said vaguely, "Because he's a little 'off' and hard to get along with." Later, his aunt, who was the estranged wife of Mamaji, said, "I asked Baiji and she said that you should stay away from him. He's not good. He doesn't have good intentions. And that sannyasini he is bringing with him—she's not good either. She takes whiskey in everything. What *sadhana* can you do with *tamasic* (ignorant; dark) habits? I am only telling you this about her and then it is for you to decide." In the afternoon, when we women gathered in Baiji's room to cut lengths of cloth, Baiji spoke to me directly about Mamaji. "You know the man who arrived this afternoon? You are not to get close to him, understand? He'll start getting 'loose' with you. And that sannyasini he's brought with him—she stayed alone with a man for a whole month!" The sannyasini she spoke of was the Firangi Mata, though Baiji did not know that I had already met her.

Mamaji's elderly sister "Masiji" recently had her own room built at Rishi Ashram, where she would pass her final years. She had arrived at the ashram the day before and was having a *havan* performed to sanctify the new space. It was this auspicious occasion that had brought her brother to Haridwar. Masiji, who had not been privy to any of the conversations regarding her brother, made a special point of inviting me to the *havan* so that I might meet the sannyasini who was coming with him. "In fact, he has gone to fetch her now; she lives in a cave up in the hills," said Masiji with awe as if that were enough to establish her authenticity. I told her I would try to attend but had no intention of disregarding Baiji's explicit instructions to stay away from these guests. When the time came someone appeared at my door with a message from Mehraji. "You should come now so you can meet the Firangi Mata because she is about to leave." Mehraji was unaware of Baiji's warnings and did not realize that his invitation put me in an awkward position; he must have told the Firangi Mata that I was in the ashram.

The Firangi Mata smiled as a look of recognition animated her face. I folded my hands in greeting and sat down next to the *havan*, across from a large, middle-aged man I assumed to be Mamaji. The Firangi Mata recited Sanskrit verses along with the priest. As soon as he finished the *havan* and went to call Baiji for the final blessing, Mamaji started talking to the sannyasini. His loud voice and exaggerated gestures suddenly made me realize that people tend to speak softly in ashrams and especially during rituals. His eyes, which continually strayed to the door, betrayed his impatience for Baiji to come and bless the room so they could depart. If they did not leave soon, he kept repeating, his companion would have to make the dangerous climb up to her cave in the dark. The lions in those hills had even eaten one of her goats, he said. While the Firangi Mata herself remained silent, staring into the fire, he resumed his monologue by addressing the side of her head. "Next time, I will take you up to Mussoorie for the night. What are you doing tomorrow? Perhaps I could come there and spend the night in your cave, huh?" She did not respond. Both the tone and content of his words, as well as his body posture (he was leaning very close to her) violated every cultural rule about how to interact with a sadhu, especially one of the opposite gender. He proceeded to announce all the places he planned to take her: mountain pilgrimage sites, a Madras temple, and other tourist spots. The flush of her cheeks could have been attributed to embarrassment or to the fire on which her eyes were fixated. She wore pink toenail polish and a colorful pink scarf, hippie-style, tied around the head. A man's watch hung loosely on her wrist, and she glanced at it now. "I have another battery for that in the car," Mamaji remarked. Then he turned to me and asked where I was doing my thesis, in the United States or India, and what level of education I had completed. Upon learning about my project, he aimed his thumb toward the sannyasini seated next to him and declared, "You should take *her* interview."

"I have already taken one of hers." I said, as she and I exchanged warm smiles.

"One won't be enough for her."

"Yes, but it's difficult you know, going up into those hills alone and all that. . . ."

"But *she* goes up alone," he insisted.

When Baiji finally arrived, she and the Firangi Mata gracefully exchanged bows. Baiji asked how long she had been in the area, but Mamaji interrupted, "You should see, Baiji, she makes such great *murtis!*"

"Where did you learn to do that?" asked Baiji.

"I worked as a sculptor in my country," she spoke for the first time, with a combination of warmth and respect.

Mamaji informed Baiji, "You can speak to her in Sanskrit, Hindi, or English. She knows all these languages." Baiji gave the younger woman *prasad* and she prostrated fully in return, touching her forehead to the ground and reciting "Om Mataji, Om namah Shivaya" three times. When the Firangi Mata got up to leave, everyone stood. Masiji and another of Baiji's disciples touched her feet and the former shoved a cash donation into her palm. As soon as they were gone Baiji quickly bestowed her blessings on the room and the ritual was concluded. Later that evening, Baiji brought up the subject of the Firangi Mata again. Rumor had it that she went to stay at Mamaji's house in Delhi where she drank liquor and ate meat. The servant there boldly told her that sannyasinis should not consume these things, and she responded that once one has reached a high state one can take anything. Baiji remarked that it is people like her who give sannyasinis a bad name, though she reserved some blame for Mamaji as well. "He's got sex running through his blood," she said with a look of utter disgust. "But now why does he have to corrupt (bhrasht karna) foreigners?"

Weeks later, a wandering sannyasini of the same order as the Firangi Mata visited Baiji's ashram briefly on her journey north. Baiji informed me that she was "good" and that I should interview her. When I mentioned to her, during a casual conversation, that I had met her guru-sister, she was full of praise. "Oh what a beautiful soul she is!" Very gingerly, I indicated that I was a little concerned for her because she had been associating with a disreputable man who did not seem to treat her well. The sannyasini dismissed my concern with a wave of the hand, indicating that the Firangi Mata was mature and knowledgeable and could most certainly take care of herself.

The Firangi Mata elicited strong responses, both positive and negative. Some emphasized her devotional activities, the austerity (tapasya) of her life, the virtue of renouncing the wealth of a foreign country to live in a cave. Anand Mata saw her as a sincere sadhu but one whose current spiritual crisis indicated that she had not yet reached the highest stages. After all, she reasoned, all renouncers experience setbacks on their path and the sincere, determined ones who persist will eventually succeed. For Mehraji, the Firangi Mata was not dangerous as such, but was without dignity or knowledge. For Baiji and her disciples, the Firangi Mata's association with Mamaji and reports of her breaking renunciant conventions by living with a man, drinking liquor, and eating meat, were enough to cast her as a fake.[7] Outrageous behavior is occasionally tolerated in sadhus, if they possess such traits that place them unambiguously in the category of jivanmukt (one who attains liberation while still in the body). If they are thought to be liberated then anything they say or do, even drinking liquor, is simply a confirmation of an elevated spiritual status. If such a person eats meat it is not because she desires it; rather, it is because she sees no distinction between meat and any other food. Similarly, if a jivanmukt drinks liquor it is not to become intoxicated but to prove that she has indeed transcended any distinction between ordinary and intoxicated states.[8] The Firangi Mata's (rumored) attempt to justify her behavior to a servant by implying that she was beyond all rules obviously fell flat; she was not perceived as having reached that level. Why? One reason is that by making an open claim to jivanmukt status she was actually proving that she had not attained it. Also, however, by staying overnight alone with a male householder (and a disreputable one at that), she crossed the boundaries of what a female renouncer, at least in

respectable circles, can get away with. Clearly, *asli* and *nakli* are not dichotomous categories, but, rather, ends of a spectrum. Most sadhus fall somewhere
in between the two extremes.

Treating Everyone Equally

It is felt that saints should treat everyone equally, for treating everyone
equally signifies that they have attained the knowledge that the *atma* which
resides within themselves and the *atma* which is in everyone else is one and the
same. A Dashnami sannyasini named Guru Mata, with whom I spent one week,
inherited from her male guru a small ashram and a handful of lay disciples. Like
Baiji's Rishi Ashram, her ashram housed a temple and two priests who looked
after it, although there were no social service activities. Still, the ashram did
provide rooms and hospitality to guests traveling on pilgrimage. Guru Mata's disciples were unfailing in their conviction that everyone was treated equally at the
ashram. I examine the distribution of food and chores, juxtaposing the disciples'
interpretations of behavior and events with those of ashram employees and
other nondisciples.

While everyone, except short-term "guests" who were visiting for the first or
second time, contributed to the work of running Guru Mata's ashram, it is
unthinkable that I or Guru Mata's middle-class disciples would have ever been
asked to get down on our hands and knees to wipe the floor. As with most other
ashrams I visited, including Rishi Ashram, there were unspoken distinctions not
only between various sorts of manual labor but also between administrative and
manual tasks. In both places, some disciples who had age, education, and class
status in their favor, clearly avoided certain types of work, and hired employees
performed the lowliest chores. When there were guests at Guru Mata's ashram
the kitchen was in a flurry of activity during much of the day. Although Guru
Mata herself, her disciples, and the two middle-aged *pandits* assisted in the
preparation of food, the bulk of the hard work fell upon the shoulders of the two
women employees, who were called (descriptively) "Fat Amma" and "Small
Amma." They received room, board, and a small salary for their labors. The two
women worked hard, especially Small Amma. Fat Amma was not only bolder
and more energetic, but was also an expert at decreasing her workload by dele-
gating and taking shortcuts wherever she thought they might go unnoticed.
Small Amma's work was slow, punctuated with heavy sighs and full of anxiety
about making mistakes. Not only were both women friendly to me, but they also
felt comfortable complaining to me about Guru Mata, who, it was noted, made
Fat Amma sweep the room one day even though she had a fever. Similarly,
Small Amma was sick one day and had just taken a break to rest in the sun,
when Guru Mata asked why she was lying down and told her to come in and
work. Small Amma was clearly dissatisfied with her job and with her employer.

Insinuating that a sadhu lacked compassion was far more serious than the same complaint levied against an ordinary employer, as it called into question her very authenticity as a saint.

The issue of equality also arose in the distribution of food, and this was not peculiar to Guru Mata's ashram. At one ashram, the two female heads took their meals together just outside their bedrooms rather than in the main dining hall with everyone else. The obvious reason was that arthritis prevented them from sitting comfortably on the floor, though one resident was convinced that the women ate separately to camouflage the fact that they were served better food than the rest of us. He sarcastically referred to our own food as "the people's plates" (janta thalis) and made it clear that my decision about where to sit for a meal was a political one.

Guru Mata employed two women for cooking and other chores but strictly controlled the distribution of food. Her explicit ideology of equality did not always correlate with actual behavior. Sometimes, special foods were in fact distributed evenly so that every single person in the ashram, including servants, received an equal amount, even if it was only a tiny portion such as half a walnut or a single almond. At other times, however, the food was distributed among Guru Mata's special guests, after others had eaten. Guru Mata, like so many other sannyasinis I visited, was very aggressive about feeding me, and I often found myself on the receiving end of highly desirable foods, such as fresh apples or oranges. Mr. Gupta, who was a frequent guest and donor but not an initiated disciple, saw Guru Mata's ashram as very egalitarian. But one day when he and I overheard Guru Mata inform Small Amma that she had taken out two cups of basmati rice for the guests and herself and the remainder ordinary rice, he acknowledged the discrepancy between his perception of the ashram and what went on in the kitchen where he never ventured. He cut his eyes to me and said under his breath that this is what goes on in all ashrams.

When something was being distributed as prasad rather than as ordinary food, it was especially crucial that everyone eat some, if the rhetoric of equality was to be convincing. One evening dry, black chickpeas were served with dinner as Hanuman's prasad, because they are the type of "energy-food" that the monkey warrior-god Hanuman required to maintain his strength. Each person sat cross-legged on the floor with their plate (thali) on a small table in front of them. Small Amma had placed a bowlful next to Guru Mata's thali, more than she gave anyone else. Guru Mata spooned a bit onto her thali rather than taking the entire bowl and then set the bowl down on an empty table next to hers. We had finished our meal and Small Amma was about to sit down with hers when Guru Mata noticed that there were no chickpeas on her thali. After confirming that none was left in the kitchen, she told Amma to take the bowl from the table, stressing that it was not jutha (contaminated by saliva).

"Doesn't matter," Small Amma responded wearily. "Everything is *prasad* here."
Guru Mata insisted. "Everyone should eat some of everything that is made
in the ashram whether they get a lot of it or only a little." Small Amma showed
no enthusiasm, but Guru Mata did not give up. "These chickpeas are *prasad* so
you *must* take some." Finally the tired woman held her *thali* out to accept it
indifferently. The night before Guru Mata never offered Small Amma the sweets
consumed by the guests and perhaps her words now about equality sounded
hollow to Amma. The indifference with which Small Amma accepted the *prasad*
was an insult couched in an overt act of deference and subtly but powerfully
called into question the public display of equality that helped define Guru
Mata's reputation as a genuine saint.

One evening Guru Mata and I were chopping lemons to make pickle when I
came across one fruit that was large and greenish, unlike a lemon. "Look," I said,
"it looks like a *masumbi* (sweet lime)!"

"Go ahead and eat it," said Guru Mata.

"No please, I really don't feel like having it."

She took it, chopped it into six tiny pieces, one for each of us present and
pronounced, "Now it's *prasad*. Take one for yourself and give one piece to each
of the Ammas." Now that it was *prasad* I could no longer refuse to eat it.

I walked to the kitchen where the women were cleaning, holding one slice
of fruit in each hand. Small Amma took one unenthusiastically. Fat Amma
shook her head vehemently that she did not want it. "But it's *prasad*," I pleaded
quietly. Mercifully, she relented. "O.K., give it here. It's Mataji's *prasad*," she said
with a heavy sigh. I quickly set it on a plate for her to eat later because I heard
Guru Mata urgently calling me. I went out to find her laughing hysterically with
her face all puckered up. "It *is* lemon!" she said. I ran back to the kitchen.
"Ammaji! Don't eat it! It's a mistake; it's actually sour lemon!" As Guru Mata
and I laughed, Fat Amma shot her deadliest look our way. When Guru Mata
does give us something special, that look seemed to say, it turns out to be sour
lemon! While disciples often pointed to Guru Mata's treating everyone equally
as a sign of her saintliness, discriminating nondisciples (in this case employees)
clearly disagreed. And, through what Scott (1990) has called a "hidden tran-
script" they expressed their own opinion about their employer's saintly status.

Being without Passions

Sannyasa teaches a person indifference to various emotions such as pain
and pleasure, insult and praise. A renouncer should be emotionally poised,
which is an internal disposition. Disciples and nondisciples have different ways
of interpreting a sadhu's external displays of emotion. The following incident

illustrates how Guru Mata's external expression of anger has multiple and contradictory meanings for different observers.

When Fat Amma went on leave for a couple of days, I helped in the kitchen by cooking and serving the food. One night at dinner I began to serve the two *pandits* their food. They requested seconds on the vegetables so I brought half of what was in the pot, leaving a generous amount untouched. I had already filled the plastic thermal dishes with hot food for the guests who would eat later with Guru Mata. The *pandits* requested thirds, which polished off what was left of the vegetables in the pot. I did not feel that it was my place to tell the *pandits* that they had eaten enough, and Small Amma did not protest when I announced that they wanted more food. There was still food left in the thermal dishes, but when Guru Mata entered the kitchen and saw the empty pot, she addressed her irritation to me. "Did you give out all the vegetables?"

"They kept requesting more, so what could I do?"

"Then you give them something else instead, or add a little water," she scolded. "Or you just say that there is not enough of this. Think about the others coming afterward too; there should be something for them." Guru Mata turned and left and there was no time to dwell on the matter because Guptaji and Kapoorji (a disciple visiting with his wife and grown daughter Pinky) had seated themselves on the floor for dinner. Kapoorji had already been served one *roti* and needed another when Pinky came rushing up to the kitchen door (she was menstruating and could not enter the kitchen) and told us to make one quickly for Guru Mata who had just sat down for dinner.

"Your father also needs one and he has already started eating," I snapped.

She insisted that Guru Mata's should be made first, but Small Amma was not in the habit of moving fast and I was not skilled in making *rotis*. Mrs. Kapoor had just arrived and started cooking Guru Mata's *roti* when Guru Mata herself came in complaining angrily that her vegetables had become cold as ice because the *roti* was taking so long. She stood there while the dough finished cooking and, as soon as her *roti* was ready, she took it in her hand and left in a huff. Small Amma looked at me pointedly and said, "You have seen this." Mrs. Kapoor tried to diffuse the tension with cheery commentary about how much Guru Mata liked me.

In a few moments Guru Mata wanted a little more, less than half a *roti*. Meanwhile, another visitor had sat down and needed *rotis*, but (as lower-class rather than middle-class visitor) he was having the thick, precooked ones that the *pandits* and employees ate, and those still had to be reheated. And, of course, Guptaji's *rotis* were also being made to his taste. It seemed unreasonable, to me and to Small Amma, to demand that so many different styles of *roti* be served to different people, all hot and on demand, with only two barely functioning gas flames. But none of the disciples, even those who helped in the kitchen, ever expressed even the slightest discontent with the situation.

The chaos of the feeding process could be heard in the frenzied clap of wooden sandals, mostly mine, rushing between the dining area and kitchen. I took Guru Mata's second *roti* out to her and, momentarily distracted by my irritation at what seemed to be an unfair reprimand, dropped it in her plate. As soon as I did this, I realized my mistake. Mataji only wanted half of it, and she hated to waste anything. But it was too late because the *roti* was now *jutha*. She looked at me with a flash of anger and I thought I'd had it; then her face softened. "It doesn't matter." When I returned a few moments later, she smiled sweetly and began to narrate a humorous story about falling short of food during a feast.

While I wanted Guru Mata to act in a predictable and "reasonable" manner, the disciples held no such expectations of their guru (see Potter 1991). To them her status as a genuine saint meant that she would inevitably act in ways that expressed her wisdom but were beyond our comprehension. This was evident with Baiji as well. One evening at Rishi Ashram, I was chopping vegetables with Vimla Auntie and her daughter Pallavi (who was visiting from Agra). The mood was festive since a special *puja* had just been successfully completed, and we talked and laughed as we worked. Pallavi remarked that they always have a good time when they come to Baiji's ashram. However, she and I wrinkled our noses when we saw that only the cabbage remained to be chopped, and its leaves were rotted and full of worms. After we removed the wormy leaves only the core was left in each head. We knew without discussing it that Baiji would expect us to salvage whatever edible stuff was left in those leaves. Baiji, like Guru Mata, does not waste food. Finally, at Pallavi's instigation and to my great relief, we decided to throw the leaves away. "Quickly," she said, "throw them out before Baiji returns. . . . Anyway, taking a scolding from Baiji is better than cleaning those wormy leaves." Sure enough, Baiji came to survey our piles of vegetables and expressed her surprise that we ended up with so little cabbage. Pallavi confessed immediately: "So much of it was insect-ridden, Baiji, that we put it in the cow's pail." Baiji was indeed angry, but not for the reason we expected.

"Did you wash it first, or did you put it in the pail just like that?" she asked.

"Just like that," answered Pallavi, "without washing."

Baiji exploded. "The cow is Ma and you give her *that* to eat?! Well, in *your* next life as a cow you'll get insect-ridden cabbage to eat! Go take it out of the pail and wash it for the cows." Vimla Auntie got up first to retrieve the foul stuff from the rubbish pail while Pallavi and I looked appropriately remorseful. As soon as Baiji left the room we all looked at each other and started giggling. "Oh, there's Baiji for you," said Pallavi cheerfully. "We only think that we'll give this to the cows, but she remembers that the cow is Ma."

If sannyasinis, as teachers, consider it necessary to scold those who are making mistakes or straying from a path of virtue, they also, as renouncers, emphasize that the anger expressed at such moments should never be felt inside. It is like scolding a small child, explained Anand Mata. To teach young children not to touch something hot, you must admonish them sternly in a harsh voice even though you feel no anger inside. As one of Baiji's disciples once said, "Baiji's anger is like a balloon, it builds and then just goes *phuuus* [the sound of a balloon deflating]. She does not get mad, but she must scold us sometimes or how will we know if we've made a mistake?" A saint, it seems, can express anger only if it is assumed *not* to reflect an inner feeling of anger. The anger is assumed to have a didactic purpose rather than being the uncontrolled bursting forth of some inner emotion. Disciples faithfully assume the presence of an interior state of detachment that can be expressed in unpredictable and contradictory ways.

Ordinary Sleep or Meditative Trance?

The incidents described below illustrate how a single act, specifically Baiji's habit of nodding off in the middle of conversations, was represented by nondisciples, by disciples, and by Baiji herself. As indicated in chapters 3 and 4, my research with Baiji consisted of both interviews and casual conversations, interviews defined by the presence of a tape recorder. It was not easy to get time for interviews, because the activities of running an ashram demanded Baiji's attention most of the day and late into the night. Helping offered me a way to participate in the life of the ashram and to be near Baiji, but I sought "interviews" with the hope of eliciting extended and focused narratives that could not be squeezed into the free moments between chores. One day Baiji promised me an interview in the morning and it actually happened. About ten minutes into our discussion about the seven heavenly worlds, she began nodding off. On her request, Sonam brought fried chickpeas for her to munch on to help her stay awake, but this did not seem to help. Periodically, she would tell me to turn off the tape recorder because she was falling asleep (*neend ati*), then she would wake with a start and continue whatever she had been saying as I scrambled to hit the record button. "Have you ever met a mahatma as crazy as me, who falls asleep in the middle of doing things?" she asked.

During those long moments when Baiji was out cold, Sonam and I patiently and respectfully waited for her to wake up again. We watched with suspense as her head slowly rose and then dropped again. In the midst of one such moment, Achariji entered the room and I whispered by way of explanation, "I turned off the tape recorder because Baiji has fallen asleep (*so gai*)." Sonam corrected me. "Baiji doesn't fall asleep, she goes into meditation (*dhyan*)." Baiji eventually opened her eyes and looked at me sheepishly through droopy lids. "When you go back home and listen to this tape you will laugh, because you'll remember that in the middle of the interview I was munching on chickpeas and falling asleep." This went on for several weeks. Baiji would say she was falling asleep while Sonam insisted that Baiji falls uncontrollably into meditation (*dhyan*) or a meditative trance (*samadhi*). Although Sonam often said this in Baiji's presence, Baiji neither confirmed nor contradicted her interpretation.

One evening Baiji entered the temple during the worship service, settled into the lotus position on her seat (*asan*), and promptly nodded off. After the worship a priest always carried the platter around to those present so they could touch the flame to absorb its auspiciousness. Thus, a priest named Vishnu offered Baiji the flame but she did not open her eyes. He was shy by nature and stood there quietly, platter in hand, looking somewhat embarrassed. Another priest, Krishna, then took the platter, held it firmly in front of Baiji's face and called her name softly until she woke with a start and reached out to touch the flame. Since Baiji had often stressed the danger of disturbing someone who is in *samadhi*, Krishna would not have dared to disturb her if he thought she was meditating.

One day, Sonam and her mother joined us for an interview. Baiji spoke for about a half hour and then started feeling sleepy. She would have me turn off the machine when she started to fade and, upon resuming her lecture, would have me go back and erase the parts where sentences became inaudible or were left unfinished. While she dozed, Sonam's mother remarked matter-of-factly to me, "This is her weakness." Baiji lifted her head and said, "No, it is because of illness (*rog*) on the side of my face." She pointed to the side of her face and indicated that a blocked sinus caused pain in her face and right ear. The cold air, she said, was making her fall asleep. "Perhaps it will help if I sit outside in the sun for a while and then continue the interview." On second thought, she decided to have us get out the electric room heater instead. I fetched a chair and Sonam retrieved the dusty box from on top of the cupboards. As Sonam set up the heater, I brought some peanuts for Baiji to snack on; the interview continued until she was called to meet someone.

That was the first time Baiji had ever addressed the question directly, and the next time she nodded off during an interview Sonam told me to turn off the tape recorder because Baiji was "*feeling sleepy.*" A few days later, when I was talking to Sonam's mother about saints and the meaning of the phrase "having arrived" (*pahanche hue*), I asked whether Baiji had "arrived." After a moment of silence, she said, "Yes, I think so." In response to my question about whether Baiji had always fallen asleep the way she does now or if it was something recent, she said she did not know and became thoughtful. "In a way, it is also a kind of *samadhi* for Baiji, although to us it seems like sleep." She said that once she told Baiji, "You get very sleepy during *prarthna*," the kind of thing her daughter would never have said to her guru. Baiji explained to her that she also tends to lapse into meditation, whenever her mind is on God. Obviously, there were no verifiable explanations for what Baiji actually experienced when she closed her eyes. It was our relationship to and knowledge about Baiji that determined our interpretation. Sonam was a devoted follower who knew that Baiji did in fact have visions and did experience states of *samadhi*; Baiji had spoken explicitly about these on other occasions. Sonam's mother, also a disciple but less devoted than Sonam, attributed Baiji's habit to physical weakness but did not feel that illness lessened Baiji's status as a saint. I was a nondisciple who took Baiji's statement about "falling asleep" literally. I knew that Baiji slept little and worked a lot. Moreover, while I accepted the possibility that she did experience trance states, that this might happen in the context of our interviews seemed unlikely to me. The priest who interpreted Baiji's nodding off as sleep also appeared to do so matter-of-factly rather than seeing it as a form of deception.

The comments of another sannyasini were less generous: "Hypocrisy is very common and I have even seen it in prominent mahatmas. They'll be sitting on a stage with other mahatmas and will start falling asleep. Then they'll suddenly wake up and yell the name of god. . . . 'Ram, Ram!' or 'Hari Om!' as if they were in *samadhi*. Most of these mahatmas sleep, especially during worship services. It is all a big lie." This suggests that had Baiji unambiguously represented her nodding off as *samadhi* then she would have opened herself up to accusations of trying to deceive people into thinking she was in *samadhi* while actually sleeping. Instead, she always said she was "sleeping," which could be interpreted either literally as a straightforward statement of fact or as a concealment of actual *samadhi*. This is an example of what Trawick (1988) has called "intentional ambiguity" where meaning lies in the ambiguity itself. Neither Sonam nor her mother seemed perturbed by the inconsistency in Baiji's explanations or interested in ascertaining whether her habit of nodding off was "actually" a lapsing into meditation, ordinary sleepiness, or a response to a sinus problem. Saints cannot assert their own authenticity, at least not directly. For this reason, as has been noted by McDaniel, a disciple often serves as the guru's spokesperson, publicizing their powers and spiritual experiences, while the guru remains aloof (1989:246).

Vivek and Shraddha

Due to the lack of institutional constraints there is ample room for deception in the social life of sannyasa. McKean's (1996) analysis of the political economy of gurus and ashrams presents a picture of power-grabbing gurus and a gullible public but does not acknowledge the skepticism central to indigenous discourses regarding holy persons. As one Haridwar resident commented to me, "The wealthy bring their black money to Haridwar to make it white in the eyes of god." That the theme of false sadhus permeates Hindu literature, folklore, and popular culture has been well-documented (Bloomfield 1924; O'Flaherty 1971; Siegel 1987; Narayan 1989; McDaniel 1989). Siegel (1987) has traced India's comic tradition from early Sanskrit literature to modern times. In satire that parodies serious literature and religion the false ascetic is a key character. "Yogis," writes Siegel, "are simultaneously respected and suspected, respected for taking the most arduous path, suspected for taking the easiest one. The distinctions between the holy man and the bum are subtle. The fraudulent ascetic, the freeloader who passes for the holy man, a stock satirical figure in ancient and modern Indian literature, expresses the cultural ambivalence toward the renouncer" (1987:229).

Since the stereotypical ascetic is also male, these parodies take on a gendered perspective. One of the amusing examples provided by Siegel suggests that the yogi (who hides his lust) is really a whore underneath, while the whore (who feigns her lust) is really a detached holy mendicant (1987:230–31)! Tarabai Shinde, a social critic writing more than a century ago, expressed what must have been a fairly common perception about sadhus, although the intent of her satire was to suggest that deceitfulness was generally a *male* quality.

> You smear your body with the so-called holy ash, grow your hair long into a mass of matted locks, proclaim that you have renounced the world, and roam all over cheating and deceiving people with your beguiling tricks. "Who's this?" "Ramgirkarbuwa." "Who's that?" "Shastribuwa." "And this?" "The great sage, Ganpatbuwa Phaltankar, a mahasadhu!" "That one there?" "A follower of Nanaka." Somebody just has to say "Look at his virtues! They defy any description! He's wonderful. Besides, he is free from all worldly desires. He has great magical powers," and so on. That is enough of an introduction for a credulous public! Then the fake sadhu goes on prolonging his stay, putting on grander and grander pretensions. He gorges himself with rich, sweet food like a fat tomcat, and then begins his "worship." That is, reposing in a corner, he closely eyes all the women who come for an audience with him, and selects a few beautiful ones whose names he reiterates on his rosary. That's the end! All gods are forgotten promptly and forever. And these "goddesses," in the form of beautiful women, occupy that place. In his eyes, their lovely, smiling faces and in his heart a burning desire for money. Torn between these two cravings, the sadhu hovers between the worlds of sanity and madness. . . . (Schinde 1882, trans. Pandit 1991:229–30)

Tales of power-hungry, greedy, and lecherous male sadhus are a frequent subject of casual conversation among sannyasinis. However, the suspicion with which lay Hindus regard male sadhus applies as well to their female counterparts (Bloomfield 1924). Indeed, the following chapter will suggest that female sadhus must be even more circumspect in their behavior in order to maintain respectability in the eyes of householders and other sadhus. McDaniel (1989) attempts to analyze *how* Hindus actually distinguish between sacred and secular states of madness or, more generally, between genuine and false saints. Her work, based on biography and scripture, offers a microlevel understanding of the topic. While McDaniel's concern is specifically with Vaishnava and Shakta ecstatics, much of what she says resonates with what I have learned about renouncers. There are also important differences between ecstatic and renunciant religiosity. Most importantly, ecstatic religiosity does not necessarily require the celibacy so crucial to sannyasa. In addition, moodiness may be tolerated, even expected, in ecstatic saints, while renouncers are expected to overcome moodiness, fear and anxiety, joy and pain, always maintaining a state of emotional equipoise.

It was generally assumed by most people I met that, while the vast majority of sadhus are frauds, genuine saints do exist, and discrimination is required to distinguish between them. Using one's faculty of discrimination means not only comparing one sadhu with another or "shopping around," but also testing them. Once while I was sitting with Baiji and her disciple, Mrs. Malhotra, the sannyasini narrated a story about an *avadhut* to illustrate the close relationship between spiritual progress and indifference toward distinctions. "An *avadhut*," she explained, "is someone so spiritually advanced as to be without consciousness (*behosh*) of the external world. There was one such holy man who spent much of his time meditating. One day, while seated in mediation, he decided that he should not eat anything with his own hand. Instead, he would eat only if someone came and put food in his mouth; otherwise he would go hungry. So a man used to come every day and feed kidney beans to this *avadhut*. He was so *behosh* that he defecated right there where he was sitting. One day the man decided to feed the *avadhut* some of his own feces. When he did this, the holy man spit it out and exclaimed, 'Yuck!' You see," said Baiji, "if he was really unconscious he would not even have known that he was eating feces. But obviously difference (*bhed*) still existed for him. This was a test." As Baiji and I chuckled, Mrs. Malhotra murmured somberly, "These are very high thoughts." Less crude forms of testing a sadhu include discerning whether he or she can cure an illness, display some special insight into a person's past or future, or, the method preferred by more erudite persons, express some knowledge of the truths contained in sacred texts, whether obtained through scholastic learning or religious experience.

In addition to comparing and testing sadhus, a third form of discrimination is to consider the saint's social background or biography, although this may be difficult since renouncers are supposed to be "dead" to their previous lives. Nevertheless, the personal background of a sadhu can be known through hagiography (for well-known renouncers) or, more commonly, though informal conversation or gossip. Baiji's followers saw her current involvement with householders as saintly because of her past period of austerities and withdrawal. They viewed her activities as extraordinary because they assumed them to be motivated by an attitude of detachment; the primary proof of this was the difficult *tapasya* that Baiji had performed years ago under the tutelage of a genuine *jivanmukt* and the powers that she demonstrated to them.

Among the factors of greatest concern to those who observed renouncers were the legitimacy of the sadhus' gurus, their family background, and the circumstances of their renunciation. Was the saint married? If so, did they irresponsibly abandon a family with young children, or did they ensure that their children were settled before taking sannyasa? If it is known that a female renouncer was married it may be assumed that she was "running away" from family problems, and this raises questions about her sincerity as a renouncer. Women who have left married life are more likely to see their religious aspirations as a *cause* of family problems rather than their result. Alternatively, some say that the suffering they faced at home was a divine gift intended to make them realize the meaninglessness of worldly life. While men are also accused of "running away" from family problems, this criticism is used more consistently for women. Aware of these negative stereotypes, sannyasinis may be reluctant to disclose information about a previous marriage. In general, if a person had much to give up in the first place, in the way of wealth, a good job, family prestige, or children, their renunciation has more meaning. By the same token, the presence of sophisticated philosophical knowledge in an unschooled girl is more meaningful, even miraculous, than its presence in a Brahmin man. Even though many famous renouncers, including Shankara, had humble origins, previous social status, as I will discuss below, often persists into renunciant life as that which is renounced.

The circumstances under which a person took sannyasa are also examined. However, just because it is agreed that someone has taken sannyasa in a moment of sincere detachment, this does not immunize them against corruption later in their ascetic careers, especially if they become powerful gurus with large followings. The path of sannyasa is understood to be long and full of obstacles. Even good, sincere renouncers can stumble and fall or take a wrong turn by succumbing to sexual attraction, egotism, or greed. Indeed, one paradox central to renunciation is that spiritual success only invites more challenges to that success in the form of adoration, gifts of service and material goods, and demands on the guru's attention and powers. It is in recognition of this risk that some renouncers eschew any kind of social involvement, even the teaching of disciples.

A fourth form of discrimination is to examine the saint's exterior attributes and current lifestyle. In terms of everyday interaction with householders, saints may be warm and affable but should not show much interest in developing relationships with people. One point all agree on is that detachment to the fruits of actions is the very essence of renunciation (Potter 1991:38–39). A saint's demeanor should include a calm facial expression, steady gaze, and physical poise, which indicate a dispassionate and disinterested interior. This is not to say they must always be serious; on the contrary, humor is appreciated as a sign of spiritual contentment and carefree disposition (*masti*). They are expected to speak primarily about religious matters, or, when discussing mundane, worldly topics, to do so selfconsciously and with didactic purpose. They should avoid gossip and frivolous topics. People also look for simplicity of lifestyle, compassion, and the practice of some form of austerities, whether meditation, yoga, silence, and so forth. A saint is also expected to show some evidence of spiritual power, which may include such varied things as the ability to heal, special insight into mundane problems, or even physical beauty or "radiance." As noted, Baiji's youthful appearance and radiant skin signified spiritual discipline and power to her disciples (see Alter 1997:284).

One sannyasini I occasionally interviewed was considered by most of her peers to be something of a joke. Among the reasons for this harsh evaluation was that she talked about her accomplishments—how many books she had published and the success of her latest lecture tour—too frequently and without provocation. And, it was felt, she was too quick to accept gifts. She was also obese. Sadhus are not expected to be skeletal; on the contrary, a healthy body is considered by many to be necessary for performing any kind of spiritual discipline. I have never heard a sadhu criticized for being plump or "healthy," but this particular sannyasini was so fat that walking had become difficult. Not only was her weight considered physically problematic but it was also a sign that she still felt attachment to food. During the course of my fieldwork, she obtained a refrigerator, which in Haridwar in 1990 was a luxury not even found in wealthy ashrams or middle-class homes. Without prompting, she explained its presence by first offering me an ice cream and then stating that she obtained the appliance so that she could offer cold water and ice cream to her guests. Her peers did not accept her claim that obtaining the appliance was motivated by a desire to offer better hospitality to her guests. One reason her refrigerator did not go over very well was that she had a history of obtaining luxury goods that her peers in the ashram did without. For example, she had a telephone in her room, which she said she needed so that her followers could contact her easily when they wanted to invite her for lecture tours. Eventually, she confided to me, she gave up the telephone because everyone else in the ashram was always asking to use it.

A saint is expected to live simply, to approach householders with benevolent detachment, and to give religious discourses when called upon to do so. This, of course, is advantageous for an ethnographer, as recording the (formal) words of saints is a culturally appropriate thing to do. Even so, some sannyasinis had ways of resisting my prying questions that could be read as saintly. For example, one expressed disdain for my project of trying to elicit lofty spiritual truths for the trivial purpose of a thesis, and another humbly insisted that she had no knowledge that would be of use to a research scholar. However, the sannyasini with the refrigerator had developed a habit of falling into an unscheduled silence just as I appeared for a scheduled visit. This was not readily legitimated behavior, as most renouncers who took vows of silence did so periodically for a specified number of hours, days, or weeks. In this way, nondisciples used various methods of reasoning to interpret observable signs for what they indicated about interior states.

Status, Power, and Saintliness

Do sadhus give up politico-economic power in order to acquire spiritual power? Or prestige? Or does the status they gain through sannyasa actually give them power over others? Ortner argues that one must always look at *both* cultural ideology of "prestige" and on-the-ground practices of "power" in order to examine the historical dynamics of a given case over time—not in order to apply static and dualistic structural classifications such as status and power, or cultural values and the "hard" facts of economic or political domination (1996:143, 172). Here I consider the ways in which politico-economic power transforms into saintly prestige and vice versa by examining renouncers' life trajectories.

Schooling and wealth play an important role in the prestige of particular renouncers, even though this is part of what they are supposed to have renounced. Of course, material wealth may contribute to a *nakli* reputation if it is hoarded or displayed in the form of luxury items like fancy jewelry or (ochre-colored!) cars. I once watched Uma Bharati mercilessly tease an older, politically prominent sadhu for his "*herovali*" Rolex watch; it was the first time I had seen him at a loss for words, for what could he say in response? Indeed, in Haridwar people often pointed to particular sadhus as fakes because of the wealth that they had accumulated. After one sadhu's death gossip circulated about the wads of cash found under his mattress and expensive shawls stacked in his cupboard. It is common practice for householders to give renouncers cash and goods for distribution, which should prompt us to revise our idealized image of sadhus as mendicant-consumers rather than as redistributors of wealth. If wealth is used to help the poor, sponsor rituals, or support sadhus with food and clothing, then it contributes to the sadhu's prestige.

Baiji's ashram was large and her disciples wealthy, and she was often praised locally for her generosity. Local sadhus enjoyed the quality food and other items distributed during her feasts, and the poorer households in the neighborhood made use of the free dispensary and sewing school. Baiji's disciples emphasized that whatever wealth Baiji receives in *dan* is used for charitable purposes. They frequently point to the fact that she owns only two or three changes of clothing at any one time and that she wears them until they are in absolute tatters. Indeed, she darned and patched her clothing until there was nothing left to mend. Some took this as a sign of Baiji's simplicity and saintliness. Baiji had access to money and *could* wear the highest quality ochre robes if she chose to. Thus, her refusal to do so took on an exaggerated significance and legitimated her access to wealth in the eyes of her disciples. "She does not spend the money on herself," they constantly reminded me.

Hierarchies among sadhus resemble "class" in that they are linked to education and other cultural capital (including knowledge of Sanskrit and/or English) as well as the control of wealth. In chapter 3, I described the feast that Baiji held to honor some five hundred sadhus. Certain respected sadhus were invited to come an hour before the general feast would begin so that they could be fed and sent home before the mass feasting. They arrived in a slow and dignified fashion, were seated in the shaded inner courtyard and fed with steel plates and cups. Once they left, sadhus of uncertain character arrived en masse and were directed to sit in the driveway under the midday sun. They were fed the same food, but with banana leaf plates and disposable clay cups. When I asked an ashram resident why they weren't being fed in the shaded courtyard, he said,

"Oh, we wouldn't let them inside—what if something was stolen!" An ashram member stood in front of each doorway, "guarding" the ashram from the people being honored outside. Such distinctions were less pronounced but also evident at Baiji's Himalayan ashram. After an annual *bhandara* and distribution of *dan* had been successfully completed, a Bengali swami of the Ramakrishna Order came to visit and partake of the *bhandara* food. He was fed the same food as everyone else but individually. The three sannyasinis who lived in the cottage arrived at the same time. All three fell to the floor and touched the feet of both Baiji and the Bengali swami. Baiji's ability and willingness to help others meant safe shelter and a decent life for the three women she supported. Baiji was popular and respected in Uttarkhand and Haridwar for her efforts to increase the rural poor's access to education and medicine as well as for her generosity in the offerings of food, cash, and cloth to sadhus that she makes herself and instructs her householder devotees to make. The Bengali swami was also respected locally for the medical expertise and homeopathic medicines that he dispensed free of charge. Differences in social standing among sadhus may, to various degrees, be related to their wealth, education, previous profession or family name, status and number of disciples, titles and offices, reputed spiritual powers, lifestyle and, least of all I think, caste (although caste does, of course, determine access to education and other resources).

This trading of wealth for prestige is the most obvious way in which material and economic power can be transformed into saintly prestige, but not the only way. If renunciation entails the giving up of wealth, material comforts, and social status, then the more a particular person had to give up the more significant their renunciation. Followers who thought very highly of Anand Mata, who accorded her the status of a "real saint," noted not only her spiritual achievements since taking sannyasa but also the fact that she was from a "good" family and that she left a happy marriage, a good career, and a promising future in politics to lead a quiet life of solitude and austerity. Clearly, her renunciation meant much more than that of someone who had little to renounce in the first place. Although renouncers do not generally talk openly about their previous life before sannyasa, if they came from a prominent or wealthy family, this is usually public knowledge that is deemed relevant to their current status as a saint. This, of course, brings to mind historical cases of princes, such as Mahavir and Buddha, who became exemplary renouncers; their politico-economic power was transformed into saintly status by the act of renunciation.

If the ways in which politico-economic power can transform into saintly prestige are clear, the reverse process is not. Baiji is from a Brahmin but not a wealthy background. Partly through her connection to a reclusive and highly revered male guru, Baiji has acquired wealthy and well-connected urban disciples. Because of this she has gained influence over them and their wealth, and power over servants and young priests who live in her ashram. Uma Bharati's origins are poor and rural. Because of several miraculous events in her childhood, she gradually acquired an international network of disciples (even travel-ing abroad as a child-saint) and was eventually elected to Parliament. She con-tinues to pursue a successful political career while wearing the ochre robes.

Stories about the abuse of power by prominent gurus are often told from the point of view of current, potential, or past disciples. Looking at the interaction *between* gurus and disciples suggests the kinds of influence that disciples exert over their gurus. For example, Baiji's group of core disciples were middle- and upper-class, English-educated urbanites, though Baiji herself was from a respectable Brahmin family of modest means. Baiji had a religious education in the Arya Samaj tradition rather than a secular schooling; thus, she knew Sanskrit but not English. When I went to live with her, it was in her new ashram, recently built with the funds of her urban disciples who wanted a com-fortable place to stay when they visited their guru. As already noted, each of the upstairs bedrooms had an attached bathroom, with a Western-style toilet. Baiji told me that she had wanted common latrines at one end of the building, but her devotees insisted that they needed private bathrooms—so these were added at the last minute. It was *seva* that motivated disciples who underwrote the building of temples, schools, and hospitals, but it also gave them influence. Furthermore, their association with a prestigious guru enhanced their own status. In the "falling asleep" incident, each time Baiji said that she "felt sleepy" her devotee Sonam insisted instead that she was slipping into a trance. Is Baiji, as a guru and renouncer, not allowed to feel sleepy? Baiji attempts to respond to every small demand made of her and appears to sleep less than four hours per night. Baiji may feel that her sleep is never ordinary or that the distinction between ordinary sleep and meditation is irrelevant. Then again, she may be expressing her desire to sleep like an ordinary human, a need her disciples do not recognize. This recalls Satyajit Ray's classic film *Devi* which comments on the constraints facing those who are made into an object of worship.

Anand Mata had no disciples and actively sought to limit the assistance she accepted from householders because of the threat that this posed to her inde-pendence. Initially, after leaving her home and family to take sannyasa, her hus-band tried to send money every month so that she might live comfortably. She refused what she felt to be a sincere offer of support because of the attachment it would have implied. Some of her "well-wishers" wanted to combine their resources and build a small ashram for her to live in peace. She refused because it would have obligated her. As adamant as Anand Mata was about maintaining her independence, whenever people came to visit her (including me) she felt obligated to sit and talk with them. One well-intentioned visitor aggressively insisted on massaging Anand Mata's legs to express her deference, even though Anand Mata said repeatedly that she did not want this service and tried to pull her legs away from the woman. Another man arrived at her door one day with his wife and proudly presented her with a chair, a throne really, with a shiny sil-very frame and red velvet cushion. He and his wife had had it custom made for

Anand Mata to express their high regard for her; indeed, she was very fond of this family. As the husband enthusiastically instructed her to try it out, Anand Mata oohed and aahed over the shiny chair (just as she once did over a radio I gave her!), extolling its beauty and comfort. It looked out of place in the austerity of her otherwise plain hall furnished only with a few folding lawn chairs and a wooden table. For the remainder of their visit, she sat on her throne like a queen while the rest of us sat on the rug. She told the man that she would keep it in her small private bedroom because she spends most of her time there and would use it more often. In fact, it became clear after the couple left and we dragged the massive piece of furniture into her tiny room, that she wanted it there so no one would see it. It would embarrass her to be seen sitting in that chair, she said, tossing a worn, ochre-colored bedsheet over it. Offerings such as this were more of a burden than anything else, but she felt obligated to accept it since it was given with sincerity and love. It would be much worse, she said, if she allowed her admirers to build an ashram for her; then she would have to give in to all their needs. These examples suggest we ought to pay more attention not only to the powers exerted by sadhus but also to ways in which devotees control their gurus. There is an acute awareness among renouncers of the paradoxes in their relationships with householders. Spiritual achievements may propel renouncers into positions of reverence, which may lead to the acquisition of ashrams and disciples—the very things that can cause their downfall.

The Mutuality of Gurus and Disciples

Since there are no objective criteria for judging the authenticity of sadhus, any attempt to determine the reputation of a particular sadhu must always examine the question from the position of particular observers. The guru-disciple relationship is central to Hindu asceticism, though it is less important in the Shaiva tradition of sannyasa than among Vaishnavas. The potential for abuse in this relationship is part of a vast folk tradition, and tales of corruption generally emphasize the power wielded by a tyrannical guru. McDaniel says of ecstatic saints, "Even one disciple radically changes the status of the ecstatic, as one child changes the status of a woman from wife to mother. . . . Once there is a disciple, there is respectability. As one informant pointed out, madmen and drunkards do not have disciples—only gurus do" (McDaniel 1989:246). Similarly, Ghurye notes that sadhus may desire disciples as intensely as householders desire sons (1964:171). Stories about abusive gurus are grounded no doubt in the reality of the abuse of spiritual authority. However, sadhus become *nakli* not only for using their power to control people or the material world, but also, and somewhat less malevolently, for misrepresenting their internal activities or states.

One sannyasini in her mid-thirties described how a sannyasi, who offered her guidance and shelter, grew to be very possessive. He did not like the fact that people sent her money because it meant she could leave his ashram when-ever she wished. He even requested that she forbid people to send her money, but she refused. She indicated as well that his attitude toward the householder disciples who supported him was not very saintly. Apparently, he never scolded those who showed him a lot of respect and did their *puja* properly. But if he dis-liked someone because they failed to touch his feet or if he didn't need anything from them, then he would scold just to enjoy the torture. "At the ashram where I used to stay," she narrated, "I used to wake up at five thirty, have tea and then attend the *arati* at six. One day Swamiji, the head of that ashram, called me into his room and inquired as to when I bathe. He said rumors had been circulating among his lay disciples that I would enter the temple without bathing. I told him it was true that I bathe after the *arati* because I wake up at five thirty and cannot bathe in cold water. I asked him if I should stop attending. He said, 'No, just lie to them. What does it matter to these people?' You see, he never came out of his room before nine or ten. A thermos of tea was left in his room at night. When people asked, he would say that he rises at three o'clock and sits in *samadhi*, but I knew that he never woke up before eight. In the morning, people in the ashram would speak in whispers, saying, 'Shhhh . . . keep quiet. Swamiji is in *samadhi*.' It was really funny. My own guru was good; he was honest about his physical needs." The sannyasini who narrated this story seemed to deny this sadhus' sincerity. However, we have also seen in other contexts (Baiji's narrative about Guru Vashisht and Lakshman, for example, which was actually a com-mentary on her own mixed messages) that what might *seem* like hypocrisy to ordinary people may in some cases be a matter of sadhus responding appropri-ately to different audiences in different contexts. In other cases, it may be simple hypocrisy or deceit.

Sometimes, saints may be praised specifically for their honesty. There are at least three possible internal attitudes that might accompany a guru's attempt to deceive disciples or visitors. Simple lying is when a guru misrepresents his inter-nal experiences for self-interested reasons, as the swami who lied about waking at three was doing. There are also many contexts in which gurus might conceal certain information for "appropriate" reasons, to bring themselves down to the disciple's level, so to speak. For example, a sannyasini may actively conceal or simply fail to mention the fact that she was married before renouncing for fear that it will be incorrectly interpreted as a sign that her renunciation was insin-cere, that it was simply an escape from a bad marriage, when she herself may feel that her prior ascetic leanings were the *cause* of the marital troubles. A third possibility is when a guru conceals true saintliness for the sake of humility. The ambiguity surrounding Baiji's habit of nodding off at odd moments could be read either as a sign of weakness or, because she would explicitly say she was "falling asleep," it could be read as a humble concealment of genuine spiritual experi-ences. Hiding genuine internal experiences is not perceived as a lie but an attempt to conceal one's true, genuine nature for reasons of humility. When sadhus talk about authenticity and hypocrisy it is with a nuanced understanding that renouncers may by necessity communicate different messages to lay disciples and to peers.

Stories about the hypocrisy, greed, anger, and lust of powerful gurus are often told from the perspective of current, potential, or past disciples. But what about the guru's perspective? As Anand Mata once said, "Hundreds of people may come to a guru and say, 'This is our question, please answer it.' Perhaps he cannot answer it but gives a discourse and, after hearing it, all those people decide that he is their guru. Perhaps he knows inside that he is not their guru and they are not his disciples, but they persist and come to him on Guru Purnima wanting to do *puja*. He may even let them do *puja* or whatever they want, but inside he knows that he is not their guru. It's just that he feels that at this time these people need his support, so he will give it." Several of Anand Mata's "well-wishers" did indeed come to visit her on Guru Purnima, the day when Hindus honor their guru. One performed a *puja* to her; Anand Mata allowed it but would claim, I suppose, that it meant nothing to her. All this suggests that the extent to which disciples create their gurus has been underestimated. There are contemporary examples of notorious gurus such as Rajneesh who became popular and attracted thousands of disciples, but then, toward the ends of their lives, withdrew into isolation within their own ashrams as if trying to escape what they had created or, depending on one's perspective, what created them. Is this so different from Baiji's retreating to Uttarkhand? A couple of sadhus did in fact criticize Baiji for "selling out" to her influential disciples. According to Anand Mata, it is crucial that a guru maintain an equilibrium. Some compromise too much for their disciples, she felt, and others refuse to bend at all. Refusing to bend is also a weakness. "It is like walking on a tightrope high in the air where if you fall one way or the other you will die," she said, invoking one of her favorite metaphors. "You must keep a balance." She emphasized the need to know when to bend and when not to, when to scold someone and when not to. "One should have the *vivek* to know when a disciple needs scolding. Sometimes even when they do something wrong they should be excused, and at other times they should be scolded for something small. It's like with children or employees . . . the parent must consider not what the child wants but what he needs. One must also do this with disciples—sometimes they may need only love and sometimes scolding or discipline." A guru who compromises too much for his or her disciples becomes controlled by them, while one who refuses to compromise becomes controlling of others.

When I asked Anand Mata if she would ever consider making a disciple, she shook her head vehemently. "No! If I have a choice, I'll never have a disciple. But I generally don't talk about the future because I have surrendered my existence to God, and if God wants me to have a disciple, I will. Personally, I don't want one. First of all, one cannot just *make a shishya*. If a person says, 'I will become a guru' then he is not fit to be a guru. The guru is only a 'catalytic agent.' If people come to him because they are impressed with his personality or his life, and if they want his guidance, and if they sit at his feet and say, 'Please show me the path. I want to be the way you are,' then this is how a guru is made. A guru is a guru only because someone has made him a guru. The guru does not change; he is not elevated in any way because someone has asked him for guidance. The guru also understands that it is only a matter of time before the disciple does become like him. Today he is only a bud, but tomorrow he will blossom into a flower. Thus, the *shishya* makes the guru a guru. So this guru-*shishya* relationship is very one-sided. It is the *shishya* who decides, 'I want to learn from you, and whatever you say I will follow.' The guru just accepts what the *shishya* wants. And the guru knows and accepts that a day will come when this *shishya* will no longer need his help. Being a guru is very otherworldly (*alaukik*) and requires a lot of understanding on the guru's part. So if someone tells me, 'I have so many *shishyas* and I am such a great guru,' I don't consider that a true guru-*shishya* relationship. I call it 'running a shop' (*dukandari*). If the guru considers it a business then it is a business."

Anand Mata once observed that for very rich Hindus having a guru or an ashram is a luxury like any other in that it enhances their prestige. "They can tell their friends, 'We have an ashram in such and such a place' or 'Our Guruji is so great and see how much special attention he gives us.' They have no thirst for spiritual knowledge. This is what I call mature exploitation. The prestige of one increases the prestige of the other." With her usual irreverence, she insisted that both parties see the hypocrisy in what they are doing. Thus, "mature exploitation" is when both guru and disciple use one another for their own purposes and both know that it is exploitation, but it continues because both benefit. "And mahatmas are jealous of each other's disciples. They guard their own and they try to steal other people's disciples by bad-mouthing the guru.

"The rich," she continued, "also need some place to put their black money because it is too much for them to spend on themselves.⁹ So they give it in *dan*, and it is used for some good purpose. It converts some of their black money into clean money, you see, so it eases their conscience." Local wisdom had it that much of the new growth of ashrams in the Haridwar area was a direct result of wealthy urbanites' need to spend their undeclared or "black" income. Although Anand Mata felt that it was the duty of sadhus to accept *dan* from householders, I knew that she herself was particular about taking money from people. She would accept money for personal expenses only from "those who give with feeling." The rest she would deposit into a separate box in her cupboard and give it away to the needy.¹⁰ R. K. Narayan's novel *The Guide* (1958) offers a humorous portrait of the making of a guru, but scholarly accounts have underestimated the role that devotees play in the making of gurus.

Hiddenness and Authenticity

While the validity of the distinction between *asli* and *nakli* sadhus is a matter of general consensus among Hindus (even among sadhus themselves), the two categories are not seen as dichotomous. Moreover, there are no objective criteria for making the distinction. I have highlighted two contradictory values that inform Hindus' approach to saints. Discrimination (*vivek*) is an attempt, usually made by nondisciples, to discern interior states by observing exterior signs. Faith (*shraddha*), by contrast, is favored by disciples and rests on the assumption that an interior state of detachment exists regardless of exterior signs. Faith assumes that there may or may not be a congruence between interior and exterior, that it does not matter what a saint is doing on the outside as long as the inside is genuine. The alternative values of discrimination and faith may be seen as an experiential process in the sense that people are expected to shop around carefully for a guru, but then, when they find one and become a disciple, their faith should become unshakable. This is not to say that disciples never approach their guru with discrimination or question their activities or words, but, when they do, they know they are not being good disciples. Moreover, while disciples may have faith in their own guru, they continue to evaluate the exterior behavior, words, and bodily signs of other saints. The problems for a Hindu layperson trying to ascertain the authenticity of particular saints are, first, that the relationship between interior and exterior is multiple and shifting and, second, that the interior may be deliberately hidden by the exterior. This, combined with the lack of institutional controls, as Hindu seekers readily recognize, creates fertile soil for deception.

When the faithful speak of their own guru, they describe him or her as somehow extraordinary, unlike ordinary sadhus (Narayan 1989:153). Praise for Anand Mata usually centered around the fact of her intense *tapasya* of silence and that fact that she had so much to renounce, unlike ordinary sadhus. Praise for Baiji usually revolved around her proclivity for serving others. Baiji's disciple Bhavna once declared, "Everything is backward (*ulta*) here in this ashram because you find the guru doing *seva* of the disciples all the time. In any other ashram, you'll find the guru sitting there relaxing in silk clothes while everyone else looks after him." A disciple's own guru is great specifically because he or she stands above the rest.

There are many varieties of renunciant deceit. Some false sadhus are simply insincere while others are actually dangerous. *Asli* sadhus do not constitute a homogenous category either. Some are sincerely, if imperfectly, performing spiritual practice with the aim of liberation while a rare few have already attained it. McDaniel contrasts Western myths of meeting the guru, described as love at first sight, to a more Hindu model based on hesitation and growing compatibility. "All seek someone they can believe in," she writes, "but nobody (except perhaps a *pagal* Westerner) would accept a guru without question, any more than one would buy a used car from a lot without question" (1989:242). If there is agreement about the difficulty in judging the authenticity of sadhus in general, there is rarely a consensus regarding the sincerity of any particular sadhu. While maintaining the belief that frauds exist, most laypeople I met nonetheless held that ordinary people cannot be certain because the divine appears in many disguises. This may be why the larger society is not very harsh in its treatment of fallen sadhus; such persons tend to be ignored rather than villified. I have further argued that there is an underlying assumption in Hindu attitudes toward holy people that the best saints are elusive and hidden. The ultimate goal of renunciation is also invisible to those who have not reached it. Only liberated persons can perceive the inner natures of other people and say anything certain about their sincerity.

To the extent that saintliness in the Hindu world has to do with the relationship between interior and exterior, it is a matter of what Westerners would call "sincerity." But to the extent that the Western concept, which Trilling (1972) has linked to the emergence of modern individualism, implies a *congruence* between interior and exterior, the use of our term "sincerity" may be misleading. The concept of authenticity has also been linked to individualism (Handler 1986; Trilling 1972). Authenticity has to do with the belief that ultimate reality is located in each person. Since, according to Moffatt (1989), friendship in American culture is about the true self, an inward entity, its ultimate proofs are invisible and cannot be constituted by external actions or rituals. Thus, two people are true friends only if both consider the other to be a true friend "in their hearts," and neither party can be completely sure of what the other person feels in their heart. The North American college students studied by Moffatt spent a great deal of time discussing the sincerity and authenticity of particular friendships (Moffatt 1989:43). The ontology of self and ultimate reality is obviously different for Hindus than it is for Anglo-Americans. Advaita Vedanta holds that there is an essence called *atma*, but what constitutes liberation is the realization that the individual *atma* is identical to and continuous with the other essence called God or Paramatma. The independence of the individual essence is denied. Thus, authenticity, like sincerity, may be a problematic word to use here.

Still, it is clear that Hindus are concerned with discerning who people "really are" underneath their deceptive exteriors, just as Anglo -Americans are. This point seems to have been lost in anthropological theories that insist that there is no Indian identity, except that which exists as the sum of social roles, à la Dumont, or the balance of continually transacting substances, à la Marriott, Daniel, and others (Ram 1992). I certainly don't want to argue that Hindus, even renouncers (as Dumont suggested), are replicas of Western individuals. Rather, I wish to stress that they are not exact opposites of Western individuals and, furthermore, that the latter have no monopoly over the concern with sincerity, authenticity, and deception. At the same time,

commentaries about sincerity among sadhus (especially *by* sadhus) are complicated by Hindu frames of reference that suggest sadhus speak in both worldly
and otherworldly voices about both worldly and otherworldly realities.

Chapter Six

Sannyasinis as Women

*H*ow are the gender identities and roles of women affected when they enter the world of renunciation? Does sannyasa look different when viewed through the lives of women? While most sadhus responded to my initial queries with a remark about how, when it comes to sannyasa, there is no male and female, much of what they said and did implied that gender differences are indeed relevant, even elaborated, in the world of renunciation. Such contradictory messages about the relevance of gender are not simply a case of rhetoric denying what occurs in practice, for both perspectives are ideologically situated. Here I highlight ambiguities in renunciant statements regarding first, the relevance and second, the content, of gender imagery as expressed in the comments of contemporary sannyasinis and in scripture and hagiography. Gender distinctions are important in structuring both the social organization and meaning of sannyasa. I argue here that sannyasinis reject the notion that women must become men, either metaphorically or literally through rebirth, in order to renounce worldly life; they identify as women. Although the sannyasinis I met distanced themselves from female householders and traditional femininity by renouncing marriage, sexuality, and fertility (and I do not underestimate the radical nature of this move), they had not renounced femininity per se. Rather, they saw themselves as maintaining, even perfecting, other qualities of female householders.[1] I also outline below two alternative models of *male* saintliness, the hypermasculine and the maternal.

Transcending Gender: Advaitic Perspectives on Body and Soul

It is conventional wisdom that renouncers seek to transcend the body. However, transcending the body (*sharir*) means more than simply ignoring physical needs, like eating or sleeping, and material distinctions, like that between the taste of kidney beans and the taste of feces. It means rising above social and moral distinctions as well, since the Hindu body (*sharir*) is not simply physical but simultaneously moral and social. The body as conceived by Advaita is a different entity from the body of Western philosophy in that it refuses to dichotomize body and mind, physicality and morality, emotion and thought. All are aspects of the body and all are to be transcended. Even pride is part of the body (remember, there is no body-mind split here) that needs to be stripped away. Emotions and thoughts, after all, are both ultimately transient and illusory.

Sharir is the locus of all personal attributes, including physical appearance, emotions, thoughts, desires, habits, likes and dislikes, attachments to particular persons, pride, and social characteristics such as caste and gender. It contains all those attributes, determined by the thoughts and deeds of previous lives, which define a person for a particular lifetime. In contrast to *sharir*, the inner *atma* is eternal and without attributes. Thus, in realizing the true nature of the *atma*, a renouncer seeks to transcend all the particulars of a single lifetime that are inscribed within the body. Julia Leslie has used the metaphor of a nut to describe this conception of the person. "The kernel hidden inside is the transmigrating soul or self, the essence or religious potential of the individual. The outer shell combines the circumstances of birth, personality, and all the existential trappings of a particular lifetime. Femaleness is evidently to do with 'existence' not 'essence'" (Leslie 1983:89).[2]

What Leslie refers to as "kernel" and "outer shell" actually consists of several layers. As Daniel (1984) outlines, the outermost layer is the gross body (*sthul sharir*) which requires food to sustain itself and can be perceived by sight and touch. It is created from past actions and disintegrates at the time of death. The gross body is, of course, immediately recognizable as male or female. The subtle body (*sukshma sharir*) is identical in form to the gross body, even down to the coloring of skin and hair, but it lacks weight and, therefore, cannot be touched. It is marked with karma, the deeds and thoughts of previous lives, and a spiritually advanced person is thought to have the ability to see the subtle bodies of other people, thereby gaining knowledge of their past lives. The subtle body also leaves the gross body temporarily to roam about during sleep or meditation and permanently at the time of death. While the gross body disintegrates at death, the subtle body, with its karmic markings, is preserved. Attached to the *atma* it is eventually reborn. It is the seat of emotions such as love and hate (Daniel 1984:278–81). It has subtle organs and body parts, including not only male and female genitals but also organs that control the ways of thinking, feeling, imagining, and acting that most Hindus would hold to be gendered. The inner subtle body, then, like the gross body, is either male or female. Thus, the *atma* itself is without attributes such as caste or gender, but it is encased by bodily layers on which physical and social characteristics are inscribed. The purpose of renunciation is to peel away the layers in which gender difference and all other attributes are embodied, to lose one's identity at least for "a fleeting moment" if not forever (Daniel 1984:286). When this happens the *atma* is free to merge with Paramatma and attain a state of liberation beyond all distinctions. Renouncers are expected to focus on the inner, eternal, ungendered *atma* rather than the outer body, with essence rather than existence, in their perceptions of themselves and others. One implication, of course, is that my highlighting of the category gender in this investigation satisfies my agenda, not theirs.

A renouncer who treats everyone equally is considered to be spiritually advanced, capable of perceiving others' *atma* and being undistracted by their outer physical and social characteristics. Dumont (1980) defined Hindu renunciation as a negation of the caste system's value on hierarchy and interdependence. However, to privilege the rejection of caste is to lose sight of the point that renunciation asks its initiates to transcend *all* social distinctions (Narayan 1989:75). Egotism is often identified as constituting the distinction between the individual soul and Brahman and as the final hurdle in the search for liberation. Most of us are so infatuated with the body that we cannot see beyond it to our inner soul. Since attachment to the body is what prevents us from realizing that *atma* and Paramatma are one and the same, renouncers begin their spiritual quest by breaking down their identification with *sharir*. The practice of austerities is intended to facilitate this process by shifting the renouncer's attention inward away from his or her body. Renouncers may choose, for example, to travel long distances on foot, eat little or nothing for extended periods, or endure the icy Himalayan winters wearing little or no clothing. Such activities are intended to cultivate detachment from the body, to gradually peel away the outer layers so that only the *atma* remains. This detachment (*vairagya*), it is said, allows a renouncer to overcome desires that arise from the body and to transcend dualities that only exist at the level of the external, transient body.

The abstract philosophy of Advaita is self-consciously expressed in the everyday behavior and speech of contemporary renouncers when, for example, they ignore distinctions between purity and pollution by taking food from a low-caste household, claim to feel the pain of others as if it is their own, or announce that in sannyasa there is no male and female. One day I was sitting with Anand Mata and three other female householders when Swami Visvanand joined us. Anand Mata joked, "Swamiji, there is nothing but goddesses before you," to which he offered a very serious reply—"No, before me is only me"—suggesting that he saw only *atma* within each of us and, by implication, that he was liberated. On another occasion, in response to my question about whether women are more oriented toward bhakti, Swamiji remarked that "Faith is not a feminine or masculine thing. . . . Sannyasa begins with meditation on *atma*, and for this, it is necessary that whatever nouns we have used to describe a person be abolished. I am a man. I am a woman. I am a child. I am an old man, and so forth." This perspective represents the highest ideal, shared by all the renouncers I met. Indeed, the most common evidence that disciples gave for the elevated spiritual status of their own guru was that he or she treated everyone the same.

Coming Back to Earth: Brahmanical Perspectives on the Relevance of Gender

At the same time as renunciation claims to be concerned with *atma* and Paramatma rather than external forms, the distinction between male and female is more tenacious than any other in renunciant ideology and practice. Thus, when people described particular renouncers as treating everyone equally, the evidence offered almost always had to do with categories of caste, wealth, education, and national location (that is, not favoring European or North American disciples for the money and prestige they confer upon their gurus) rather than gender. Gender distinctions seem to have a taken-for-granted relevance among sadhus despite explicit statements to the contrary. When male sadhus spoke of their female counterparts, whether to criticize or praise them, they often emphasized their femaleness. While this tendency may be explained in part as a response to my own research interests in *female* renunciation, it can be found in written works as well. For example, Anandamayi Ma is referred to positively as "the woman saint" by Yogananda (1985:447), and I often heard female renouncers referred to in this manner. As often, women are denigrated rather than glorified. Gender differences are institutionalized as well in the sense that many orders have separate residential and seating areas for women and men. For example, the Ramakrishna headquarters in Calcutta wanted an affiliated women's monastic institution in Kerala to abandon its conveniently located property for the sole reason that the building was directly across the street from the Ramakrishna Ashram for men; administrators did not want sannyasinis and sannyasis living in such close proximity in an isolated village (Sinclair-Brull 1997:77).

The dominant perspective on gender, certainly in textual and arguably in contemporary renunciant discourse as well, is the misogyny inherent in the brahmanical tradition. Women and gold, as renunciant symbols for the bondage of domestic life, are held to be the two things likely to bring a renouncer (assumed to be male) down. Hostility toward women is not limited to those explicitly institutionalist texts that prohibit women from being initiated, like the Dharmashastras, for in the *Siva-Purana*, the ascetic Shiva rejected the goddess Parvati. When she was brought before him, Shiva exclaimed, "This auspicious slender-bodied maiden of comely hips and moon-like face should not be brought near me. I forbid you again and again. A woman is a phase of illusion. As the scholars who have mastered the Vedas say particularly, a young damsel is a hindrance to ascetics" (XII:28–29, trans. A Board of Scholars 1970). In response, however, Parvati eventually obtained her mother's permission to go to the Himalayas to perform austerities (XXII:24–26) by exposing herself to the elements and meditating on Shiva (XXII:40–43). Wearing matted locks and clothes made from the bark of trees, she surpassed even the sages in her austerities (XXII:51) and ultimately triumphed in her desire to win Shiva.

Similar statements are found in the Upanishads. There exists in sannyasa a deeply rooted fear and contempt of women for the desire that they arouse in celibate men (Olivelle 1992). For example, the *Yajnavalkya Upanishad* (YU) expresses its gynophobia in the following passages:

> With stylish hair and painted eyes, hard to touch but pleasing to the eye, women are like the flame of sin and burn a man like straw.
>
> Burning even from afar, sweet and yet bitter, women indeed are the fuel of hellfire, both lovely and cruel (YU 315–16). (Olivelle 1992:77)

The danger of lust does not wane in old age, for even a very old man should not place his confidence in a very old woman (Ibid.: 77). Women are seen not merely as attractive creatures but as evil seductresses who actively tempt men, pulling them from a path of virtue. Many passages in renunciant literature are striking attempts to arouse a sense of revulsion toward the female body.[3]

> Examine her eyes after separating the skin, the flesh, the blood, the tears, and the fluid, and see if there is any charm. Why are you bewitched in vain?
>
> The same breast of a girl, on which we see the brilliant splendor of a pearl necklace . . . is in time eaten with relish by dogs in remote cemeteries as if it were a little morsel of food (YU 315). (Olivelle 1992:78)

Such uncharitable views of women expressed in a range of texts are evident in contemporary renunciant rhetoric as well. Sannyasa has not lived up to its own transcendent values in practice or ideology.

So, *Does* Gender Matter?

Even when sannyasinis do confront gynophobic attitudes from their male peers, the advaitic emphasis on nondistinction as the ultimate truth provides them with a moral platform from which to counter it. Uma Bharati began delivering religious lectures at age eight. When she was in her early thirties, she recalled in a magazine interview how some holy men refused to share the stage with her because she was female. Once, when she began a lecture by chanting the sacred sound "Om," a respected Shankaracarya (abbot of a Dashnami

monastery) objected, saying, "Hey, you girl, you have no right to say 'Om'!" She
says that at first she was stunned but that, after regaining her composure, she
retorted, "I am surprised that an eleven-year-old girl looks like a woman to you.
And a sadhu who discriminates between men and women himself has no right
to say 'Om'!" (Sinha 1991:17). Baiji recalled how depressed she became when,
in her youth, a forest-dwelling sannyasi responded to her question about
whether a woman could ever become a yogi with a simple and unambiguous
"Never." But at the same moment, another swami put his hand on her shoulder
and said, "I will teach you." Contemporary renouncers express both stances and
legitimate them with scripture. From the perspective of the *laukik* (worldly) and
the *jiva* (living person) gender is an obstacle to asceticism, but from the perspective of the *alaukik* and the *atma*, it is irrelevant.

One way to understand this ambivalence is to see the gynophobic tendencies within sannyasa as institutionalist and worldly and the indifference to
social distinctions as advaitic and otherworldly. Worldly values have to do with
the institutional and everyday life of sannyasa—the path itself—while otherworldly values inspired by Advaita are oriented toward the ultimate goal of
sannyasa. The one who "has arrived" at the state of liberation is said to rise
above distinctions of worldly life. Should "their soul depart from the body"
(that is, should they die), then they leave the realm of worldly existence, literally. Should they continue to inhabit their body as a *jivanmukt*, then they must
live in the world while simultaneously transcending it. Even those who have
not yet "arrived" must attempt to walk this fine line. Since the women whose
lives I shared have neither left their bodies literally through death nor left
society by living in a cave far removed from worldly life, both otherworldly and
worldly orientations are central to their lives. Their reflections distinguish
between the goal of a liberated state that transcends distinctions and the path
itself, the everyday challenges of trying to cultivate detachment while living in
the world.

While all distinctions must be transitory at one level, they are nonetheless
real at another level. Khare argues that the Hindu world displays a continual
making and dissolving of differences, for "self-evident reasoning" places
Paramatma or Brahman at one end and the contingencies related to karma,
birth, caste, and rebirth at the other. This reasoning concerns the lived social
world (Khare 1993:197). Gender identities are not eternal, but as long as we
remain embodied and unliberated, they will continue to color our thoughts, feelings, and actions in important ways. And, even if we are liberated, as long as we
continue to exist in the embodied world, gender will impinge on our lives.
Differences of gender are "real" without being "Really Real." From the perspective of contemporary female renouncers, gender is relevant in the world of sannyasa, not in the ultimate transcendent sense (person as *atma*) but in the
domain of social relationships and mundane activities (*atma* as person).

This ambivalence in the indigenous rhetoric of sannyasa as being beyond social distinctions on the one hand and a males-only club on the other seems to have shaped scholarly approaches to the study of renunciation. While a few have noted sannyasa's contradictory stances toward the observation of social distinctions,[4] most scholars have tended to represent sannyasa as either synonymous with masculinity or as outside society in a realm where social distinctions such as gender and caste are irrelevant.[5] Both analytical frames render the question of "female renunciation" moot, assuming either that women who renounce become symbolic men or, alternatively, that all renouncers transcend gender identities. Both positions assume that female renouncers give up their femininity in order to gain legitimacy in the world of sannyasa. The notion that a woman must be reborn a man before she can renounce worldly life finds its clearest expression in the Dharmashastras and is not limited to textual authorities or even to orthodox renunciant orders, for even the reform-minded saint Ramakrishna is reported to have said, "If a woman embraces Sannyasa, she is certainly not a woman, she is really a man" (King 1984:77). One way to make sense of sannyasinis is to turn them into men, but this does not reflect sannyasinis' own views or experiences. We cannot take what elite men have said about women in sacred texts to reflect the opinions of women themselves (Bynum 1987, 1991; Leslie 1989). I argue that women who renounce remain symbolically and socially female, but I also remain attentive to the ambiguities and ambivalences of gender issues in renunciant thought and practice.

Everyday Obstacles: Sannyasinis as Women

Sannyasinis see themselves as facing a myriad of problems in renunciant life specifically because of their femaleness. Gender is an everyday reality. The brahmanical notion that female bodies are in a constant state of pollution because of menstruation affects many sannyasinis of childbearing age. One young sannyasini of the Giri Dashnami Order told me that her order prohibited female renouncers from reciting the Gayatri Mantra. "Only men can recite the Gayatri Mantra," she said, "because there is a certain tone (*svar*) that only men have. Ladies do not possess this thing, so the mantra becomes impure." Independent sannyasinis appear to be less constrained by such brahmanical rules. Baiji, for example, dismissed the prohibition on women chanting the Gayatri Mantra as a rule made by men to keep women down. "But we don't need to take permission from men to chant," she said, "because Gayatri herself is a goddess."

Opposition and disapproval from family members is the first obstacle that most sannyasinis had to confront when they first decided to renounce marriage and family life, especially if they were young at the time. This opposition may have ranged from repeated attempts at persuasion to outright condemnation.

While family pressure to marry may also affect men, it is likely to be both more intense and more universal for women. This, of course, contradicts economic rationalism; middle-class families would be saved what can be a financially debilitating cost of marrying their daughters if those daughters chose to renounce rather than marry. While a few sannyasinis I met who were orphans or the youngest of many sisters, or who for some other reason lacked good marriage prospects, faced little opposition from their families, this was hardly typical. One sannyasini told me that in her adolescence she corresponded with a swami but kept it secret from her parents because if they found out they would have said, "Oh, this girl is going to become a sannyasini," and, according to her, would have locked her up in a room. Anand Mata, who left her husband to take sannyasa, described how difficult it was for her family to accept this decision, not only because of their political belief that social service was superior to renunciation, but also because she was a woman. "When I decided to follow this path there were many attempts to dissuade me," she elaborated. "In Hindu society a woman is always supposed to do what her father, husband, or son wants her to do, and she is never supposed to be independent. The very idea that she would do something other than what society expects of her is difficult for people to accept. Being free means 'I'll choose my own path and won't put up with any interference from you.' For a woman to declare this—and I was a *married* woman . . . it was a real shock to both my parents and of course to my in-laws. A woman's parents will try and understand, but her in-laws never will; they will take it as open revolt. . . . When they were convinced of my determination and courage, my relatives finally accepted it and blessed me." While family opposition was often assumed to be motivated by loving concern, a few sannyasinis described to me a different kind of disapproval from male peers. This is illustrated in the experiences of Baiji, described in chapter 4, who faced vocal opposition from male sadhus at the time of her initiation. Even after her initiation, hostile male peers threw stones onto the roof of her cottage in the hope that she would become frightened and run away. Her guru would stand guard while she meditated inside.

By far the most significant problem facing sannyasinis seems to be their general vulnerability to violence and sexual exploitation. This was expressed in the insistent warnings I received not to visit ashrams alone or converse with unfamiliar sadhus. One middle-aged sannyasini never sleeps with her bedroom doors open, even in the hottest weather when a breeze would be welcome, and she was cautioned not to walk along the Ganges alone, even in the morning. Another young ascetic I interviewed lived in a cottage with her spiritually inclined father rather than alone, and Uma Bharati has an older brother who remained unmarried so that he could act as her escort on lecture tours. She once said of him, "He protects me from the dangers in life and even from men" (Sinha 1991). Sannyasinis do enjoy greater autonomy regarding life decisions and may also have more freedom of movement relative to female householders. Still, it is difficult to separate the effect of age from the effect of ascetic status on their mobility, and when they do travel it is more often with companions than alone. Denton's observation that sannyasinis travel freely in the world (1991:231) needs to be tempered, for most prefer the security of an ashram to the perils of life on the move. Sinclair-Brull also observed that for the women of Sarada Math, sannyasa has not meant the freedom to wander; instead, it has meant that they must set an example by being especially circumspect in their behavior (1997:179).

Local wisdom has it that women must protect themselves not only from violence perpetrated by strangers but also from the sexual advances of their own gurus and peers. The theme of lecherous men in sannyasinis' conversations resonates with the theme of false ascetics found in popular Hindu culture, but diverges from orthodox opinions which tend to portray *women* as creatures of lust. Manu says this explicitly, after warning that wandering freely is one thing that corrupts women, "Good looks do not matter to them, nor do they care about youth; 'A man!' they say, and enjoy sex with him, whether he is good-looking or ugly" (IX.13–14, trans. Doniger 1991). Women's essential sexuality renders them unsuited for renunciation. However, all the sannyasinis I met spoke as if women are generally the *objects* of male sexual attraction rather than the pursuers of men. I have never heard a sannyasini describe women as essentially sexual or as more sexual than men. On the contrary, they see the portrayal of women as lustful as nothing more than a projection of male fears about their own lack of self-control.

While most female renouncers seem to prefer the safety of an ashram to the prescribed life of constant wandering, I did meet an exceptional older sannyasini who spent most of her time wandering alone. She traveled by train, bus, or even on foot, but was always careful to find a safe place to sleep at night. She began our interview by emphasizing that if people have a firm desire for sannyasa, nothing can stop them. "But for a woman it is harder because there are more obstacles," she continued. "I managed because I had Gurudev who looked after me. It will be very difficult for a woman if she is fearful or young. A woman must always be careful about traveling or living alone or going out at night; she must always find a safe place to sleep. . . . She must not wander or live alone; it is difficult and dangerous. She must be careful of men in robes, whether guru, fellow disciples, or whoever. She must keep a distance because if she gets too close she will always find lust in them. Few women are strong enough to go alone in the world. It is better to go to a senior *sadhvi* (holy woman) for guidance. I went alone from age sixteen, but I had a good guru. At one point I wanted to go north alone, but he said to stay at the ashram and do my *sadhana* until I was older. I am now fifty-eight and when I reflect I sometimes marvel at the risks I took in my youth. I would not advise any youngster to go this path."

It is clear that ochre robes do not provide an escape from the everyday perils of being a woman in North India. In recognition of this, sannyasinis live cautiously and many seek the protection of a man or an older female sadhu.

While the obstacles faced by sannyasinis are an everpresent subtext in their remarks, they are mentioned matter-of-factly and given little spiritual importance. The limitation they impose on, say, mobility or dress, are accepted simply as pragmatic accommodations to imperfect social institutions. Scholars too often assume continuity between convention and experience, particularly when it comes to women. However, women may veil themselves, for example, before certain men not because they feel inferior to those men, but because the convention is required to maintain the honor of the family—they may veil more for reasons of respect than personal conviction (Raheja and Gold 1994:xxii). While these obstacles make renunciation difficult for women, they do not *determine* the lives of sannyasinis.

Allowing for exceptions, such as the occasional sannyasini who takes on a masculine name or dress (I met a "He-She Swami" and two called "Babaji"), I claim that these women take on neither the social roles nor identities of men. When they do act like male peers by wandering alone, living alone, or exposing their bodies, they are likely to raise suspicions about their character and put their safety at risk. In any case, when sannyasinis behave in accordance with conventional femininity or take on male attributes, we must ask whether they imbue these actions with spiritual importance rather than assume that they do. Bynum has pointed out that, while male biographers of medieval women saints in Europe were fascinated by female cross-dressing, the male dress adopted by female saints was, for the women themselves, less a religious symbol than a social mechanism used to escape marriage or travel safely (1991:38). Women wore male dress in the world in order to accomplish certain goals (occasionally even religious goals), but in the safety of a cloister they did not use "acquiring maleness" as a spiritual symbol (Ibid.: 171).

Spiritual Advantage and Motherhood: Women as Sannyasinis

If the sannyasinis I met noted the disadvantages of being female, they also deliberately and self-consciously pointed to the maternal qualities that make renunciation easy for women, emphasizing the moral and spiritual strengths of being a woman and, more specifically, a mother. "When a woman is recognized as a Guru, the devaluation of single women is overshadowed by the cultural idealization of motherhood. As holy mother—Mataji, Amma, Gurumai—she is likely to gain a large following" (Narayan 1989:66). Though few have actually had children of their own, sannyasinis tend to identify themselves as mothers. Anand Mata, for example, recalled the ecstasy (*anand*) she felt when, during her initiation ceremony, the word *ma* (mother) was included in her new name because it showed that, even though she was not literally a mother and was still quite young at the time, her guru perceived the quality of motherhood in her. Terms of address are one of the most obvious indications that female renouncers are symbolic if not literal mothers. "*Mataji*" (Respected Mother) is an almost universal term of address for sannyasinis and may be replaced with the more intimate form "*Ma*." In contrast, the most common terms of address for male renouncers have meanings such as "master" (*swami*) and "great king" (*maharaj*). Images of the male renouncer as king or lion are ubiquitous in Hindu imagery and emphasize the qualities of dominance and authority.[6]

The asymmetry in terms of address for male and female renouncers seems to mirror the differences in their relationships with female disciples. Rules of social distance between the genders are sometimes relaxed but not ignored by sadhus, so female disciples often maintain a respectful distance from male gurus. Admittedly, religious discipleship does allow for unusual, physical intimacies (such as massaging the feet) between female disciples and male gurus,[7] and the potential sexual threat posed by such intimacies is somewhat diffused if the guru is elderly or infirm. In general, though, while physical contact between male gurus and female devotees does occur it is often viewed with suspicion, and the mere mention that a particular guru "surrounds himself with female devotees" or "allows them to massage his body" is an unambiguous criticism. In contrast, relationships between a sannyasini and her female followers have no constraints on physical expressions of devotion. Women are also likely to speak more openly to a female guru than to a male guru, either because there is less embarrassment in speaking intimately with another woman, especially in matters of sexuality, or because they presume that she will understand the problems women face at home (see White 1980:31). Moreover, women might prefer to confide in a sannyasini rather than turning to other female family members simply because women's problems are often imbedded in those same household relationships. Thus, as renouncers, sannyasinis are relative outsiders to the webs of family relationships in which women's problems tend to be imbedded. It is this unusual combination of being women and renouncers that makes sannyasinis so valued as providers of advice.

One implication of this dual status is that householder women come to sannyasinis for advice specifically because they are *like* mothers rather than actual mothers. A real mother or mother-in-law may have family interests that conflict with those of her daughter or daughter-in-law. Although sannyasinis may behave as mothers, their lack of *actual* kin association to a female disciple may be part of the reason that the relationship is so valued. So, at least with respect to their roles as advisors to female householders, sannyasinis are at the same time motherly and better than real mothers. Although Anand Mata refused to take on disciples of her own, women of all ages sought her help in dealing with various problems, from unwanted sexual attention at work to marital discontent. The following story, as told to me by Anand Mata, poignantly illustrates the kind of situation that might lead a young woman to take her problems to a sannyasini rather than to a male guru or her own mother.

A local girl named Sushila was married at age seventeen. When she arrived at her marital home and realized that her new in-laws intended to put her to work as a prostitute, she ran away and arrived back at her natal home in tears. She told her father, but no one else, what happened and threatened to commit suicide if he sent her back there. He promised not to. She began working in the family's shop, which was fairly unusual in those days. One day, Anand Mata walked by and, seeing this girl sitting in the shop, smiled at her. Sushila went home that day and told her parents that she had seen some Mataji on the street whom she really liked. Her mother told her to invite the Mataji over next time she saw her. This is how Anand Mata came to know the family. After a couple of years the father died. The mother wanted Sushila to return to her in-law's place, but she refused and eventually obtained a divorce. Anand Mata used to tell Sushila to marry again, but her mother opposed this idea. Anand Mata knew a boy whom she thought was perfect for Sushila, and the girl also knew him. Anand Mata advised her to get to know the boy better, even offering suggestions as to how to go about doing this. She also stressed the importance of hiding the affair from her family, since her younger sister was still unmarried. Eventually Sushila and the boy did get married and are now very happy. Sushila found support in Anand Mata regarding a problem that she could not take to her own mother. As Vimla Auntie once said of Baiji, "She is a mother to me—*more* than a mother." Householder women visit female renouncers in search of solutions to mundane problems, guidance in religious matters, and meaning in times of crisis. I suggest that it is the dual position of sannyasinis, as both women (like mothers) and as renouncers (unlike mothers), that makes them so intimately involved in the lives of other women and, further, that this intimacy increases their legitimacy as gurus. Emotional intimacy is conventionally opposed to renunciation (whether it is in fact is another issue). It is also viewed as more maternal than paternal. Thus, the intimate relationships that sannyasinis have with householder women is one aspect of their maternal ethos.[8]

In addition to the emotional closeness and accessibility expressed by terms of address, food is another area in which sannyasinis seem to behave as mothers. In her study of temple dancers, Marglin (1985a) points to procreative sexuality and feeding as realms that define Hindu femininity. If sannyasinis renounce procreative sexuality by taking sannyasa, many embrace the role of food provider so central to motherhood. Baiji would not only plan and help prepare the meals served in her ashram but generally saw to it that everyone else was fed before she took her own food. This habit of eating last, which inverted standard relationships between gurus and disciples, was interpreted by Baiji's followers as an expression of maternal love and saintly authenticity. A first-time visitor once likened Baiji's ashram to a home and Baiji herself to the lady of the house because of her enormous key ring and because she was always busy supervising the cooking and distribution of food. As we saw in chapter 3, she also did much of the actual work herself and joked about the irony of sadhus doing the work of householders. While renouncers are ideally the takers (in the form of alms) rather than the givers of food, many female renouncers display a marked concern for feeding people. One such example is Swami Yogananda's description of the non-eating female saint who loves to cook and feed people (1985:460)! The women I met would invite me over for meals that they prepared and insist that I eat with enjoyment until satiated. The male renouncers I met displayed no such tendencies; they also seemed more comfortable in the position of eating food (usually prepared by someone else) before an audience of visitors. For example, when Anand Mata took Mehraji and me to meet Swami Visvanand for the first time, he was in the midst of a meal, so we sat down silently and respectfully in front of him to wait. He nodded to acknowledge our presence without even breaking momentum and, after a while, instructed the young man serving him to offer us the grapes that had been placed beside his plate. Each of us, viewing the fruit as *prasad* rather than ordinary food, took a single grape and popped it into our mouths. Swamiji noted sullenly that we had each taken only one grape but did not insist that we have more. All holy people distribute food in the form of *prasad*. Those with their own ashrams may also orchestrate the large-scale, ritualized feeding of sadhus as a form of charity, service, or virtuous activity. But for women such as Baiji the food itself—its nutritional value, quantity, and taste— was a matter of such concern that feeding people was more than simply the distribution of *prasad*. Women, even women renouncers, are more personally *involved* with food. For male sadhus the role of being fed is consistent with their identities as both male and renouncer, while women, especially those who choose a settled lifestyle, seem to be very comfortable in the quintessentially female role of feeding people. But because they are sadhus the food they offer is never ordinary; it conveys both the nourishment and pleasure of ordinary food and the spiritual power of *prasad*. Sannyasinis, I might add, do not hesitate to hijack the term *prasad* for their own motherly purposes. For example, while Baiji would usually pay attention to individual likes and dislikes, it would occasionally happen that a particular food suddenly became "*prasad*" when she wanted to force an otherwise reluctant person to eat it!

In combination with this emphasis on providing food, sannyasinis see it as their prerogative and even their duty to scold people when necessary. While all gurus scold their disciples, female gurus self-consciously interpret these scoldings as expressions of intimacy and motherly love. Anand Mata, as discussed in chapter 2, would offer frequent criticism and advice to Swamiji, and she would always preface her remarks by saying, "Since I am your mother, I can also scold you." A sannyasini might reprimand a servant for being lazy, a devotee for failing to discipline her own children, a foreign anthropologist for some social blunder, or even a male priest for neglecting his ritual duties. One evening the resident priests at Baiji's ashram completed their devotional rituals and then assembled at her feet. Several of them had been chosen by her to visit someone's home in Delhi to perform a ritual, and they awaited instructions regarding their trip. Baiji took the opportunity to lecture the young men on the cleanliness of their clothes: "Even the Goddess herself said that there are six types of faith, and if the outer purity (*shuddhata*) is not there then how will the inner purity ever come? Soap is always available for you and if you do not know how to wash clothes properly then just ask me and I can teach you." She ridiculed them for being meticulously concerned with their street or "*fashionvala*" clothes when going off to college but then wearing unlaundered *dhotis* in the temple, when that is exactly the time to wear clean clothes. "You are going to the home of a respectable man in Delhi," she said. "What will they think if they see such dirty clothes? You must wash your *dhoti* daily when you are there." Baiji saw such scoldings as necessary both to educate the young men and to protect the integrity of the ashram. Although I cannot say how the priests interpreted these scoldings, Baiji's disciples viewed her occasional displays of anger as a confirmation rather than a betrayal of her wisdom and love.

If sannyasinis consider it necessary to scold those who are straying from a path of virtue, they also, as renouncers, emphasize that the anger expressed at such moments should never be felt inside. Sannyasinis, insisted Anand Mata, are like *ideal* mothers because they are motivated by love (*prem*) rather than attachment (*moh*). With respect to scolding then, sannyasinis are not merely *like* mothers but are *ideal models* of motherhood. Sannyasinis clearly emphasize maternal qualities in their actual behavior as well as in their understanding of what it means to be a renouncer. Social intimacy and accessibility, feeding and scolding are related to an attitude of love that all women are thought to embody. It is in the higher forms of love (*prem, karuna*) that the ideals of renunciation and motherhood come together. Female householders can attain ideal motherhood if they forsake attachment for compassionate love.

Anand Mata spoke explicitly about the essential principle (*tattva*) of motherhood that all women possess. She described an incident when the young man who kept the accounts for the ashram where she lived came unexpectedly to see her one day. After some hesitation, he asked her for a loan of three thousand rupees. He knew the ashram had a policy not to loan money or even give advances to anyone; Anand Mata herself had insisted on that rule. He was a contractor by trade and had to pick up some materials that same day, but the banks were closed. She reasoned that since he knew her rules about loaning money and still came to request a loan, he must have already exhausted all other avenues. She offered him one thousand rupees from her personal fund, but he declined apologetically because he could only purchase the materials if he had the full amount. After thinking about it for a moment, she told him that she could not take money from the ashram but that she knew there was some cash in the temple account and would loan him the amount from there. He was very grateful and offered a check in exchange for the cash, but she did not want it because she was not planning to tell anyone. While she would not give even two rupees of the ashram's money to someone else, she said to me later, she gave that boy three thousand. And, in doing so, she broke her own rule. Why did she do it? "I knew that if I didn't help this boy, then whatever trust he had in the *tattva* of motherhood would be lost. At this point I stopped being the administrator and became the mother." She emphasized that women's flexibility is their strength and contrasted this with the inflexibility of men who make a rule and feel they must stick to it. "This is why a man is called 'swami' (master); when a woman takes sannyasa she is called 'mother.'" The essence of both motherhood and sannyasa is a spiritual and moral love, an encompassing love unbounded by rules.[9]

One implication of the notion that women are the embodiment of love is that they have less ego or pride, a point which elicited an unusual level of consensus among female sadhus. According to Anand Mata, when Mahavir made a rule that an older sannyasini must bow down before even a younger male initiate, ignorant people thought that the reason behind this was that women are inferior. Mahavir, she insisted, knew that when a sannyasini bows to even a younger male, the man's ego will be boosted and he will feel that he must protect her rather than exploit her. "You see," she said, "since women are icons of surrender it is easy for them to prostrate to a younger man; but a young male will be reluctant to bow down to even an elderly sannyasini because his ego will come in the way." The ability to surrender, the lack of ego, and the predominance of love over other emotions, are all interrelated goals of renunciation. "If a mother saw anything less than Bhagwan in her own child," explained Anand Mata, "then she could strangle the child in a moment of anger. And, for her, the husband becomes Bhagwan. To see one's husband as God seems absurd, but it is not. Even if a husband is a drunkard and his wife surrenders to him totally with full feeling (*bhava*), then she need not go to a temple. With her emotion she will invoke God in her drunkard husband, just as a devotee invokes God in a piece of stone. Sannyasinis can surrender because their intellect is under the control of emotion. These subtle truths about the nature of women in the field of religion were not understood by men. Only shallow thinkers who did not know the difference between the inherent natures of men and women raised these questions about whether women were qualified for sannyasa. Their aggressive thinking was accepted by society and became a tradition in India. This is all a system of society. All the scriptures have been laid down by men and the debates are also held by men. It is not that debating the texts is wrong, but it's necessary in the beginning of the career, like teaching children the ABC's. Eventually the men must also surrender like women do."

Egotism is often held up as the most tenacious obstacle in the pursuit of liberation, so having less of it to begin with is a tremendous advantage. The sannyasinis I met seem to retain many female, specifically motherly, values, and these relate primarily to intimacy, food, scolding, and compassionate love. Moreover, maternal values are viewed by these women not only as entirely consistent with the goals of renunciation but as actually facilitating their fulfillment. For example, it is essential motherhood that allows women's love to prevail over ego and lust, thereby making sannyasa relatively easy for them. Female renouncers do not see themselves as renouncing femininity in any simple or complete way.

Masters and Mothers: Will the Real Sannyasi Please Stand Up?

Even a brief examination of available sources indicates that the gender identities of male renouncers are more complex than often acknowledged. In the context of a renunciant discourse about polluting and sexually aggressive women, it is not surprising to find renouncers imagined as hypermasculine. A few examples are images of the spear-wielding warrior-ascetic, the "swami" or master, and the fearsome lion. Moreover, the association between the practice of ascetic celibacy and male virility has been well-documented (O'Flaherty 1981; Bennett 1983; Marglin 1985a; Alter 1997). However, images of male renouncers are not always so unambiguously masculine as cultural statements about male virility and female pollution would have us believe. It was a remark made to me by a sannyasini about her male guru that first led me to question the representation of sannyasa as hypermasculine. This elderly sannyasini had been a disciple of Swami Shivananda since childhood and spoke glowingly of her guru as having great love and compassion. "When he sat in *satsang*," she reminisced, "every person present would feel that he is giving them some partiality or special attention. He used to be so loving." When I added that people often attributed this quality to Matajis, her eyes lit up. "Yes, you know once Gurudev told me to call him Father, and I said, 'No, I will call you Mother instead.' It was a mother's love he had. He was very happy to be called Mother and considered it the greatest compliment." The praising of male renouncers for their motherly qualities suggests an alternative image to that of the fearsome and detached male renouncer.[10]

Hagiography indicates that male renouncers may become not only lions and masters but mothers as well. In *Bapu—My Mother*, Mahatma Gandhi's niece describes how "Bapu" (Papa) was father and guru to innumerable men and women, but a mother to her. "Generally," she writes, "it is not possible for a man to become a mother to any one because he has not been endowed by God with a mother's loving heart. But Bapu appropriated for himself a share of even this divine gift" (Gandhi 1955:3). One Western devotee writes about Ramana Maharishi, "Those whose hearts were open would find him more solicitous than a mother" (Osborne 1970:88). He also describes an incident when a mother brought a little child in and Ramana Maharishi smiled to it "more beautifully than a mother" (Ibid.:129). A female devotee is said to have described him thus: "I don't understand the philosophy but when he smiles at me I feel safe, just like a child in its mother's arms" (Ibid.:126). The metaphor of feeding, the quintessential motherly activity, also appears in descriptions of male saints. Thus Vivekananda admits to being dismayed when his guru Ramakrishna brought sweets and fed him with his own hands, like a mother feeding a little child (Anna no date:81). Ramana Maharishi likened the guru's giving of *satsang* to a mother feeding her child during its sleep at night, so that the next day the child thinks it took no food, although she knows it did and in fact the food sustains it (Osborne 1970:149). If Kakar's claim that maternal and "feminine" powers of nurturance, warmth, concern, intuitive understanding, and relatedness are necessary for the healing encounter is correct, then we should find that male saints who heal must also be motherly (1982:59).

Whatever misogynistic comments renouncers and their texts have made about women as creatures of pleasure who bring men down, many well-known sannyasis have exalted women as mothers, including their own mothers. Paramhansa Yogananda describes a conversation that his guru had with his own mother: The guru was trying to convince his mother of something, when the mother shook her head vigorously and said, "Nay, nay, my son, go away now! Your wise words are not for me! I am not your disciple!" The author then describes how his guru backed away without further argument, like a scolded child, and indicates how touched he was by his guru's great respect for his mother "even in her unreasonable moods" (Yogananda 1985:126). A famous verse in the *Saundaryalahari*, traditionally attributed to Shankara and reproduced in vernacular expressions, is "A son may be a bad son, but a mother can never be a bad mother" (Erndl 1989:249 n. 5). Shankara is said to have broken his own renunciant rules by going to his mother at her death and performing her funeral rites (Menon 1976:118). Vivekananda and Sri Yukteswar are reported to have done the same (Anna no date:95; Yogananda 1985:127). These examples suggest that maternal identities and actual mothers may be highly esteemed by men who renounce, although this is consistent with the brahmanical split between exalted mothers and dangerous wives. Several scholars have written about Ramakrishna's feminine identification (Kakar 1991; Kripal 1995; Roy 1998). Parama Roy contrasts Ramakrishna's femininity with the masculine identification of his disciple Vivekananda, who felt that Indian men under colonialism were too weak and effeminate. Ramakrishna exhorted his unmarried male disciples to avoid all contact with women, and he himself also avoided women, except maternal figures (Roy 1998:96). "The only way to shun woman (as seductive figure) was to become woman (of another kind)," writes Roy, stressing that this feminine identification was compatible with gynophobic attitudes (1998:97). Thus, just because sannyasa is sometimes gendered feminine does not mean that it is not misogynistic.

Can We Speak of a "Female Voice" in Sannyasa?

My challenge in writing about sannyasinis is to identify what is specific to women without rendering the distinction between male and female more foundational and rigid than it actually is. While the previous chapters have emphasized some of the differences among sannyasinis, here I present what is one of the few generalizations supported by my data: Sannyasinis are women, and they identify at least as much with their female counterparts in the home as they do with their male peers who have renounced householder life.

I believe it is possible to talk about the specificity of a renunciant female voice. In addition to remarks about motherly gurus and motherly behavior on the part of female renouncers, the insistence that women don't *need* sannyasa because they can achieve all of its goals within the home indicates that sannyasinis stress the similarities between renunciation and the domestic roles of most women. They distinguish themselves from literal mothers by becoming more universal models of motherhood and by emphasizing compassion over attachment and celibacy over sexuality and fertility. While sannyasinis admit to facing certain hardships that do not concern their male peers, there seems to be a consensus that being a woman actually facilitates the pursuit of liberation. Because the obstacles are especially severe for younger sannyasinis, they are more likely to seek the protection of an ashram or older guru. That age brings greater freedom supports the comparison I have tried to draw between the lives of sannyasinis and those of householder women.[11] Scholars have tended to liken the inauspicious upper-caste widow to a renouncer because she is expected to maintain a celibate, austere, and pure lifestyle even while living at home. However, when the sannyasinis I met likened themselves to female householders, it was usually with reference to mothers, sometimes wives, but never widows. Since it is the role of mother that offers them power and respect in Hindu society, desexualizes them, and is least threatening to their male peers, it is not so surprising that they emphasize maternal identities.

More generally, I have argued that renunciant discourse and practice are not only highly gendered, but they are sometimes gendered feminine. Sannyasa imagines itself alternatively as ungendered, as hypermasculine, and as maternally feminine. Ultimately, gender is ephemeral and meaningless, a mere attribute of the body. At the same time, the gender categories of standard brahmanical ideology are reproduced and even elaborated, from the demonization of feminine sexuality to the idealization of motherhood. These gender stereotypes are part of a dominant, male-authored discourse and are shared only partially by female renouncers who may glorify motherhood but de-emphasize female sexuality. They view women not as sexual predators but as victims of male lust. Further evidence that sannyasinis have not "internalized" a patriarchal discourse is provided by the explicitly political and sociological explanations of why women have been excluded from sannyasa, namely, society's interest in women's domestic labor and male fears of competing with women.

In spite of the advaitic rhetoric of transcending differences, gender differences play a more important role in the lives of male and female renouncers than any other social distinction. To the question of the *meaning* of gender, however, there is no simple answer. Sometimes, women are denigrated and masculinity valorized. Other times, culturally constructed feminine qualities (such as feeding, nurture, and compassion) are held up as renunciant qualities par excellence. Either way, those gender categories found in mainstream Hindu society are for the most part highly elaborated and affirmed. Acknowledging the importance of gender distinctions in the domain of sannyasa is a necessary first step toward better understanding both the nature of renunciation and the place of sannyasinis in a world composed primarily of men. Contrary to orthodox perspectives which view femininity as the antithesis of sannyasa, sannyasinis indicate that feminine qualities and experiences lead to greater success in renunciation. To say that there exists a "female voice" in renunciation is not to say that sannyasinis are always women first and renouncers second. On the contrary, previous chapters have emphasized the diversities that exist *among* women renouncers.

The dominant (male) rhetoric of sannyasa reproduces the familiar gender categories of classical Hinduism, for it simultaneously demonizes female sexuality and exalts motherhood. This split meaning of femininity is one version of the familiar brahmanical separation of mother and whore, fertility and sexuality, that has been discussed by various authors (O'Flaherty 1980; Bennett 1983; Kakar 1989; Raheja and Gold 1994). This renunciant discourse differs from the conventional brahmanical model only in that the mother imagined by renouncers embodies the qualities of selflessness, love, and nurturing rather than fertility.

Does this mean that when female renouncers imagine themselves as mothers, they have "internalized" brahmanical discourses about split female identity? Even those who emphasize the spiritual advantages women have in pursuing renunciation are still left with the undeniable fact that the vast majority of renouncers are men and that, throughout history, relatively few women have been initiated. No sannyasini I met suggested that the underrepresentation of women in sannyasa has to do with women's spiritual inferiority. Anand Mata spoke of society being disrupted if women were to start taking sannyasa and of men's fear of being outshone by women. She noted that renunciant orders, like all religions, were started by men and that men have always felt threatened by women. She also, however, explained that not only were women deliberately excluded, but they themselves did not seek initiation into sannyasa; women were not interested in investigating "external" things because they are "self-contained." "Though women are now pursuing different fields of work, it is not because of any lack that they feel," said Anand Mata. "Because men feel incomplete they go out in search of something: a profession, sannyasa, and so forth. Women need not go out seeking Bhagwan in the forest or on the banks of a river. Since a woman is the personification of love, she can realize Bhagwan within herself while performing her household duties. In the Vedas and the Puranas, giving sannyasa to women is not prohibited as such, but they felt that women don't *need* sannyasa and therefore they did not *provide* for women to take sannyasa. . . . So to say that women have no right to sannyasa is wrong. It is an aggressive practice and is appropriate for a man's aggressive nature. Since a woman can surrender, she has no need for sannyasa."

A young *brahmacharini* (female celibate student) who proclaimed the prohibition against women taking sannyasa to be valid and has not herself donned the ochre robes nevertheless rejected the male notion that this prohibition has any relevance to women's worthiness. "The good and learned gurus say it is not written in any scripture for women to get initiated into sannyasa. And the scriptures never lie." She emphasized that a woman can do yoga, meditation, and everything, and that if she wears white, no one will expect her to attend family weddings or funerals. In other words, if she wears the white clothing of brahmacharya she can live like a renouncer even without taking sannyasa. She noted that only those who wear a topknot and sacred thread are eligible for sannyasa, and that women do not wear them. Her words suggested an acceptance of orthodox values—until she elaborated. "What *use* does a woman have for a little topknot?" she grinned. "She can keep a whole, big ponytail back there if she wants to! She has her certificate from Bhagwan and doesn't have to do anything, while men have to wear a thread and all that to show their qualifications. The *rishis* and *munis* used to consider the monthly periods of women to be unholy, so the sacred thread was not given to them. And if they aren't given the sacred thread then they are not considered men, and if they are not men then they are not qualified. Maybe they thought women didn't need sannyasa. There must be some reason. Maybe they didn't want women to surpass them. [She laughs.] Another reason could be that if both men and women were to take sannyasa then who would look after the home? If women had written the scriptures, then they would have said that sannyasa should not be given to men. What does it mean to be a renouncer? You can become a renouncer in the literal sense, or you can be one without wearing the outward symbols."

Thinking about Celibacy *and* Sexuality

The discourses about saintly authenticity are also gendered and draw from ideologies and practices of sexuality in the larger society. This should not surprise us since, in Hindu India at least, sexuality and celibacy, or sensuality and asceticism more generally, have always been in conversation with each other. Thus, they must be considered as part of the same analytic framework (Alter 1994, 1997; Doniger and Kakar 2002:13–14). While sannyasinis can, like their male counterparts, succumb to greed and egotism, the aspect of their character that is most readily questioned is their celibacy. They must be even more circumspect in their behavior than men in order to maintain respectability in the eyes of householders and other sadhus. Thus, the sannyasinis I met were modest in behavior and dress. Anand Mata always had her head covered in public (though female householders in the area did not) and wore many layers of clothing, even in the summer. Over ochre-colored underpants and bra, she layered a pair of loose pants and undershirt, and then, finally, a full-length robe. One of her female peers lamented that Anand Mata had to wear so many clothes because she lived in an ashram among men and had to be careful of her reputation. Bodily exposure in male renouncers implies austerities rather than sexuality and is associated with the most otherworldly sorts of sadhus. Baiji's own guru Avadhutji did not wear clothes, but rarely do women take this route. A few legendary women saints are known to have shed their clothes. Ramaswamy maintains, however, that Mahadeviakka's nudity was met with a negative reaction from other Virashaivite saints, both male and female; most refused to acknowledge the transcendence of her act (1997:174–75). Rare (and controversial) exceptions aside, male nudity and female nudity mean different things for renouncers.

This gender asymmetry can be seen in other contexts as well. For example, male renouncers are criticized for being sexually attracted to women while only female sadhus can ever be suspect simply for being sexually attractive. Comments made about Uma Bharati offer an example. Because of her loose hair, her black-lined eyes (incongruous for a sannyasini), her "hour-glass figure swathed in saffron silk," her "fetching ways" and husky voice, the *Illustrated Weekly of India* (June 3, 1990) felt justified in labeling her "the sexy sannyasin." A male renouncer in her position is unlikely to be described as "sexy" and, even if he were, it would hardly have a detrimental affect on his saintly reputation. Indeed, celibacy is thought to make a man virile and sexually attractive (Bennett 1983), with positive connotations. Even the smallest immodesty on the part of a female celibate, however, can raise immediate and persistent suspicions about her legitimacy.

Brahmanical discourse attributes women with a dangerous, lustful sexuality. Sudhir Kakar describes a core fantasy of Indian culture as the "horrific vision of an overpowering feminine sexuality" (1982:28). Sannyasinis renounce their own sexuality and flatly deny the essential sexuality of women in general. They describe the rhetoric of lustful women as nothing more than a projection of male fears about their own self-control and maintain that women's exclusion from sannyasa has more to do with the weakness of men than of women. By denying the essential sexuality of women, sannyasinis take a critical stance toward elite patriarchal representations. Anthropologists have tended to uncritically accept what are in fact ideological statements that, "according to Hinduism," women are seen as less able to control their sexuality. While it is clear that in Hindu society female modesty is accepted as normative and the double standard treats women's sexual impropriety more harshly than men's, this does not imply a widespread belief that women are less able to control their sexual urges than men. The sannyasinis I interviewed agree that celibacy is much easier for women than for men and describe a world in which women, even celibate women, are the victims of male lust rather than the temptresses who lead male celibates to fall from their path. If there is such a gap between brahmanical claims about uncontrolled female sexuality on the one hand, and everyday (female?) discourse about uncontrolled male sexuality on the other, then should we represent the former as representative of Hindu culture? Is the discourse on uncontrolled and dangerous female sexuality really the dominant one just because it is a textual one? Several studies have addressed the gendered aspects of celibacy, sexuality, and anxieties about the loss of sexual fluids from both textual and ethnographic perspectives (Babb 1970; Edwards 1983; Marglin 1985b; Alter 1994, 1997; Doniger and Kakar 2002; Osella and Osella 2002). "Reading between the lines" of some ethnographic sources suggests that there is a widespread belief in women's ability to successfully control their sexual urges and their vulnerability to uncontrolled male desire. For example, Lamb notes that women in the Bengali village Mangaldihi spoke in general terms about women's greater sexual urges, yet when speaking of their *own* experience, almost all described the men in their lives as pursuing sex more fervently than they (2000:189). Puri writes that "[o]ne aspect of growing up that uniformly stirs anxiety and anger in middle-class women is sexual aggression" and that, by adolescence, they internalize the burden of protecting their bodies against male sexual aggression (Puri 1999:75-77). Uma Bharati has said that her outrage about rape and the exploitation of women's bodies in the media played a role in politicizing her (Basu 1995:166). The Brahma Kumaris similarly, if less directly, point to a central hypocrisy: men are full of vices, but, to the degree that man has fallen, woman is seen as the temptress who pulls him down (Babb 1984:408). If ideas about dangerous female sexuality are indeed pervasive in popular culture, how are they gendered? Do they represent a male point of view? If so, as Yanagisako and Collier have warned, we must not assume that a male perspective is more encompassing of the larger cultural system (1987:27). I suggest that everyday discourse among women, sannyasinis and householders alike, is that men, sannyasis and householders alike, are associated with an uncontrolled and dangerous male sexuality.

Female Agency and Indeterminacy of Sannyasa

Investigating female renunciation has made me aware of entrenched representations of religion in general, and sannyasa in particular, as a locus of brahmanical orthodoxy and conservatism, as a place unlikely to produce examples of female agency. Uma Narayan considers the appeal to religion as the cause of gender inequality to be a ritual of Western scholarship on third world women (1997:46–54). *Is the Hindu Goddess a Feminist?* (Hiltebeitel and Erndl 2001) tackles this issue head on, but in most work written from a Marxist or liberal perspective, religion, much like the family, is seen as a "traditional" institution that condemns women to a subordinate position. If religion in general is seen to play a conservative force, sannyasa represents the very center of brahmanical patriarchy, Hinduism's "heart of darkness." In (a male view of) sannyasa, women serve primarily as a sign for sexuality, the comforts of domestic life, and all that is threatening to male renouncers. Moreover, men abandon their wives and families, which creates hardship for the women left behind. Women are usually the ones renounced.[12]

The rise of Hindu nationalism has complicated this view of religion as disempowering for women. This movement has mobilized sadhus, glorified Sati, and criticized its (Indian) feminist opponents as "Westernized." However, two young female ascetics, Uma Bharati and Sadhvi Rithambara, emerged as militant leaders of the nationalist cause. The visibility of women in this movement, both in grassroots activism and in roles of political leadership, have seemed incongruous. "Paradoxically," observes Amrita Basu, "while Hindu nationalism is a deeply patriarchal project, it has created possibilities for women's expression of their subjectivities" (1996:76).[13] If these events have prompted feminist scholars to seriously consider the possibilities for female agency in right-wing movements, it has not prompted us to consider such possibilities within sannyasa. Sangari (1993), in her otherwise astute analysis of Sadhvi Rithambara's claim that saints want only Ram—not political power in Delhi—makes the following statement: "Through the very energy of her [Rithambara's] disavowal sadhus emerge *as they are*: heads of decayed priestly groups, locked in internecine battles, seeking new sources of political, electoral, and institutional power, and being sought as subsidiary allies by those emergent classes and class factions investing in the ideology of Hindutva" (Sangari 1993:878) [italics mine]. This statement is a persuasive commentary on Rithambara and the VHP role in nationalist politics, but it is remarkable as a general statement on sadhus. I hope this book has shown that this is a partial view of sannyasa, for sannyasa also exists as a dynamic contemporary practice outside of the monastic centers and the VHP. Uma Bharati and Rithambara are important political figures, but they should not be allowed to define female renunciation.

Equating sannyasa with brahmanical orthodoxy makes it difficult to see the general "undetermined" potential of sannyasa, the potential for protest and eccentricity. More importantly, it makes it hard to recognize that a woman taking sannyasa is a transgressive act that highlights women's agency.[14] I would like to argue that female renunciation *is* what Sangari refers to as a "site of undetermination" and, as such, it is a place where agencies slip through the structures (1993:872). Sannyasa's privileging of Advaita philosophy, its anti-institutional tendencies, and its lack of authoritative hierarchy combine to render it a powerful potential site for women's individual agency.

I am not suggesting that sannyasa is the only, or even the best, example of a site of undetermination in Indian culture. Nor do I wish to simply reproduce the

Dumontian view of sannyasa as an expression of extreme individualism, not unlike its Western counterpart. The notion of becoming involved in social relationships and activities with detachment, as if "playing a role," bears striking resemblance to what has been described as the individualism of modern Western culture (Dumont 1986; Trilling 1972). While renunciation's emphasis on equality and independence resonates with behavioral norms of Western individualism, the intent and underlying ontology of sannyasa is quite different from that of Western individualism. The latter places ultimate meaning in a kind of essentialized inner self, while Advaita philosophy finds ultimate meaning in the breaking down of all differences, including the distinction between the individual *atma* and the transcendent Paramatma. In other words, the essence implied in the two types of individual are quite different, the Hindu essence or *atma* being without attributes of any sort. Both the Western individual and the Hindu renouncer may set out to discover their "true identity," but for the renouncer this identity is a loss of all social attributes, likes, and dislikes—the very qualities that are at the heart of Western identities, especially in a consumer society.

Most importantly, a woman's act of taking sannyasa transgresses family values and expectations. Puri argues that middle-class urban Indian women take for granted the social mandate of marriage and motherhood (1999:153–54), and Dickey goes even further to say that "heterosexual marriage is virtually universal" for Indian women (2000:468). If heterosexual marriage is indeed a mandate for contemporary Indian women, then we might expect that a woman's refusal to marry would mean trouble. My informants told stories of family battles at the moment of renunciation. Many sannyasinis, particularly if young, confronted family disapproval when they first decided to renounce marriage and family life. Vidya Mata describes herself as a middle-class village girl. An Arya Samaji, she was working as a physical education instructor and pursuing an M.A. in Sanskrit. "I desired to sit in *samadhi* and forget the world and to go into the line of spiritualism," she says. "As soon as I took sannyasa, it was natural for my folks at home to be angry, but later they all got used to it." We need more ethnographic research to really conclude anything about why some women faced more family opposition than others and whether the opposition faced by women is, in fact, greater than that faced by men. Are, for example, class or caste status implicated in the marriage requirement or in the autonomy of daughters? Are certain circumstances of unmarriageability factors in how a family responds to a daughter's renunciation?

Sannyasinis transgress not only by rejecting domesticity but also by entering the male world of renunciation. However, the sort of overt hostility that Baiji faced from male peers was not a typical experience; most women renouncers did not speak to me about overt gender discrimination from male peers. The most potent of their transgressions has to do with renouncing family, not entering the male world of sannyasa. The primary obstacles that constrain women's agency once they enter sannyasa are more subtle forms of structural inequality, to which I now turn.

Subversion and Complicity—What Do We Make of Sannyasinis' Acts of Agency?

When women act with agency and transgress boundaries, their actions can either subvert or perpetuate power structures. Sangari (1993) cautions us to avoid valorizing either the subversive or complicit elements in women's social agency. Furthermore, she argues, in analyzing a particular act of women's agency for its potential subversion and complicity, we must consider both social practices and discursive modes, or, more importantly, look at the relationship between the two. I think this is a useful way to try and understand the agency of sannyasinis, given that they are entering a world that is, on the one hand, a tradition by and for elite men and, on the other, proposes the possibility of transcending gender. What, then, might we make of their assertions of social agency in rejecting marriage and sexuality?

If sannyasinis recall battles with family members who wanted them to marry, they also, through strategies of stubborn persistence, persuasive argumentation, and compromise, managed to successfully evade marriage. That they rejected marriage altogether is a triumph of autonomy, at least in the realm of social practice. However, there seems to be a disjuncture between their social practice (the rejection of marriage) and their discursive statements about the importance of marriage for ordinary women. The sannyasinis I met neither proclaimed marriage to be generally oppressive for women nor encouraged other young women to leave their families.[15] I suggest that the tendency to discourage other women from taking sannyasa should be seen, in part, as a pragmatic response to everyday experiences of life in a patriarchal society. Furthermore, from an emic perspective, this is likely to be taken as a sign of their authenticity, since it is considered improper for any sadhu—male or female—to recruit disciples. From an etic perspective, however, one must also acknowledge that sannyasinis' tendency to discourage other women from renouncing also serves patriarchal interests by limiting the threat that female renunciation poses to society. In the context of interviews and casual conversation, many sannyasinis did acknowledge that if women were to begin renouncing in large numbers it would pose a threat to both the household (which depends on women's unpaid labor) and male sadhus (who would have to compete with women for saintly achievements and resources). However, women did not articulate such ideas in more formal contexts; instead, they constructed themselves as exceptions. This supports Ojha's insight that women ascetics are rebels but not revolutionaries (1981:280). Similarly, even though they do not themselves "buy into" sannyasa's patriarchal rhetoric (about women's unfitness for renunciation), neither do they flagrantly and loudly critique it. For the most part, they quietly do their own thing. Narayanan alludes to this in her discussion of "women who questioned the logic of patriarchal society, or who, without as much as questioning it, simply went on to do what they wanted to" (1999:34). I am reminded of the grand-mother in the classic ethnographic film "Dadi's Family" who, in reminiscing about her days as a young married woman, passionately declares, "I said yes to everyone. . . . I piled on the yes's but I did what I wanted to do." If sannyasinis' social practices can be described as more subversive than their discursive forms, this may be read as a compromise for being able to live without family. However, following Sangari, I want to avoid privileging discursive forms of resistance, which I see as an ethnocentric incorporation of the American T-shirt slogan "Question Authority" into analytical frames for looking at agency in other places. To focus exclusively on sannyasinis' discursive compliance and ignore their transgressive act of rejecting marriage would be to miss what I think is a particularly Indian mode of resistance—piling on the yes's but doing what one wants to do.[16] It also contributes to their being perceived as traditional and orthodox. Sannyasinis may not be creating feminist movements, but they do manage to live the relatively autonomous lives that they want to live.

By vowing celibacy, sannyasinis are transgressing cultural expectations not only of marriage but also of female sexuality. Hinduism's positive evaluation of celibacy in the context of purposeful ascetic lifestyle highlights the cultural specificity of Freudian assumptions that abstinence can never be anything but pathological.[17] Chastity must be distinguished from celibacy because the latter rejects entirely the normatively expressed heterosexuality that is assumed for chaste women. Marglin noted the threatening aspects of female celibacy when she argued that it is female *celibacy* rather than female sexuality that is powerful and dangerous in the context of independent Hindu goddesses (Marglin 1985b). In spite of this rejection of conjugal heterosexuality, all of the "respectable" sannyasinis I observed regulated their behavior according to con-ventions of female modesty.

While sannyasinis may be motivated to regulate their behavior to maintain a good reputation, it is important to acknowledge that female modesty (even for sannyasinis) is also ultimately enforced by the threat of male violence. Female celibacy, like female chastity, can be violated by male sexual aggression, and most sannyasinis, like householder women, assume the responsibility for protect-ing their virtue. This responsibility appears to be so taken-for-granted that it is not experienced as oppressive. Sherry Ortner, in accounting for the culturally widespread "complex" of female modesty, argues that women internalize its values and enforce its practices because it is rewarded with social mobility (1996:57). Sheffield, in identifying what she calls "sexual terrorism" in the United States, focuses instead on how women's lives are bounded by both the reality of pervasive sexual danger and the fear that reality engenders (1995:2). Informal conversation among sannyasinis includes references to the kinds of dangers that face women who choose to live independently among men. Since I have no way to ascertain the statistical occurrence of sexual aggression against sannyasinis in the world of ashrams, I take these stories and warnings as a kind of folklore that circulates informally among sannyasinis. Of course, the threat of violence is as effective as actual violence in constraining women's behavior. When I was presented with the exciting opportunity to travel to Ayodhya by train with an itinerant sannyasini (at the peak of the Ramjanambhoomi agitation), the concern for my safety created a family crisis. The key issue was not "What will people think?" but rather "What could happen to you?" The threat of male sexual aggression coerces sannyasinis, and ordinary women like me, to consent to restrictions on dress, demeanor, and mobility. Compared to middle-class female householders, sannyasinis are both more protected due to their spiritual status (at least for the "respectable" sannyasinis I have written about) and more vulnerable due to their autonomy.[18] Although I have argued that sannyasa is a site of undetermination that allows women to "slip through the structures" of society, the demands of sexual modesty (in its coercive *and* complicit aspects) may constitute the primary limits to their agency. I am aware that warnings about sexual threats may have been especially prominent in my conversations with sannyasinis because of a message they were trying to convey to someone they thought vulnerable and naive, but I do not think my presence can completely account for the prevalence of this theme. It is ironic that, in the world of celibates, sexuality provides the primary constraint on women's agency in a space that is, in so many other ways, undetermined.

For women, the act of renouncing transgresses social norms. In looking more closely at sannyasinis' relationship to marriage and sexuality, however, it becomes clear that there is both subversion and complicity in their transgressions. Sannyasinis subvert the marriage requirement by rejecting marriage and family, but they do not (publicly) articulate a critique of these institutions for ordinary women. By taking vows of celibacy, sannyasinis subvert the mandate of normative heterosexuality, but they conform to, and perhaps internalize, the demands of female modesty. Even sannyasinis want to be respectable, and their respectability is tied up with the regulation of their sexuality, if not by family then by themselves.

Given the paucity of literature on contemporary women ascetics in India, it is not clear how far my specific findings can be generalized beyond the few cases presented here. I hope that my general interpretations and observations will hold up to further research: that sannyasinis do not renounce their femininity; that they identify as mothers; that they transgress social norms but construct themselves as exceptions; that they are thoughtful and determined people who exert agency in specific ways; that sannyasa itself is eclectic in both ideology and practice; that sannyasa offers women (and men) the possibility of leading unscripted and eccentric lives; that the dialogue between worldly and other-worldly occurs within sannyasa; that sannyasa is conceived as a journey; that Hindu laypersons are concerned with, and have strategies for, evaluating the sincerity of renouncers. Even if sannyasinis remain women in everyday life, they also insist on transcendence of gender as the final goal and the final Reality.

Notes

Introduction: *Sannyasinis* as Persons

1. For a description of the initiation ceremony (*diksha*), see Miller and Wertz (1976:84–87).

2. *Maths*, *akharas*, and ashrams are different types of Hindu ascetic institutions. *Maths* are monasteries where the scholarly monks of a particular order live and meditate. *Akharas* house the militant members of a particular sect. For historical background on the "fighting" ascetic orders, see Ghurye (1964:98–113) and Lorenzen (1978), and see Dazey (1990:303–5) for information on their current organization. Although I do not have first-hand information on women in the *akharas*, Ghurye reports that Juna Akhara included women (1964:103–4) and Hartsuiker (1993:33) includes a photograph of one young female initiate in the Juna Akhara. Ashrams, which provide the setting for my study, are similar to *maths* in terms of lifestyle but are more or less independent religious establishments. They may be associated with an order but are usually run by a single charismatic guru who manages the ashram separately from any overarching monastic system. Ashrams, unlike *maths* or *akharas*, may have householder residents who are disciples of the guru in addition to ascetic residents (Gross 1992:139).

3. See Obeyesekere's *Medusa's Hair* (1981) for a psychoanalytic analysis of ascetics' matted locks.

4. For information on the significance of *rudraksha* berries for Shaivites, see Briggs (1973:13–15). For an outline of the various forehead markings associated with particular orders, see Tripathi (1978).

5. As an alternative to leather footwear, plastic sandals have become more popular than the traditional wooden variety. Many ascetics go barefoot.

6. I am grateful to Ravindra Khare for helping me see the interrelatedness of these distinctions and the degree to which they underlie the reasoning sannyasinis use in different contexts.

7. Because sannyasa is defined negatively as the giving up of householder life, "renunciation" rather than "asceticism" (which implies the taking up of particular activities) is a

203

more accurate translation. "Renouncer" is an ungendered English gloss for the gendered Hindi terms "sannyasi" (male renouncer) and "sannyasini" (female renouncer). I use the English "renouncer" to include both male and female initiates and the Hindi terms when I wish to distinguish renouncers along gender lines.

8. Caplan (1973) published an early essay based on interviews with Dashnami sannyasinis in Nepal. Ojha (1981, 1985, 1988) and Denton (1991) published pathbreaking essays based on the first systematic studies of contemporary female ascetics in Benaras (note also Denton forthcoming). Babb's essay (1984) on the Brahma Kumari order of female celibates is also important. Ramaswamy's *Walking Naked* (1997) provides an overview of South Indian women ascetics from ancient through colonial times and includes material from hagiography, poetry, and contemporary interviews. Sinclair-Brull's *Female Ascetics* (1997) examines Sarada Mandiram, a women's branch of the Ramakrishna Mission in Kerala. Her analysis demonstrates that Sarada Mandiram is modeled after the local (but now largely defunct) Nayar institution of the matrilineage. This is a fascinating study of a particular monastic institution in an idiosyncratic regional context that has a modern and rather unique interpretation of sannyasa. Hallstrom's *Mother of Bliss* (1999) provides a detailed analysis of Anandamayi Ma's life and community of believers based on hagiography and interviews with contemporary devotees. An essay by White (1980) focuses on a Dashnami sannyasini in Madras and her role as guru, and another by McDaniel (1995) offers a portrait of a Bengali sannyasini of the Ramakrishna Order. Llewellyn (1995) has translated the autobiography of an Arya Samaj sannyasini. See the list of works cited for additional sources on female asceticism in ancient and medieval periods.

9. Both indigenous elites and scholars of India have assumed, until the last two decades, that Indian culture is constituted of codes of behavior established by both Brahmin and colonial elites and that these are internalized by Indians, especially women. That scholarly models have often reproduced the ideology of indigenous elites has become evident by research focusing on women and Dalits, including the work of subaltern studies historians.

10. Since the late 1980s, *sadhvi* seems to have taken on more clearly ascetic connotations with the rise of a sannyasini and nationalist leader who calls herself Sadhvi Rithambara.

11. Although reverberations of this opposition between male renouncer and housewife can be found in many studies of gender and/or asceticism in India, its most explicit formulation is found in Marglin's *Wives of the God-King* (1985). She argues that the temple dancers of Jagannatha temple in Orissa symbolize the auspiciousness of married women. As such, the dancer is opposed to the renouncer (assumed to be male) who has removed himself from the concerns of auspiciousness.

12. For a comparison of sadhus and hippies, see Neill (1970).

13. There are a few exceptions. Miller and Wertz's *Hindu Monastic Life* (1976) offers several portraits of colorful ascetics. Narayan's *Storytellers, Saints, and Scoundrels* (1989) focuses on the everyday use of narrative traditions by one male renouncer. Sinclair-Brull (1997) offers insight into the everyday lives of women living in a monastic setting.

14. Dumont (1980) argued from the perspective of structuralism that true individualism did not exist in caste-bound Indian society, except in the figure of the renouncer. Marriott and Inden (1977) argued from the perspective of ethnosociology that Indian society had "dividualism" rather than individualism. Ram (1992) and Mines (1994) have explicitly questioned the premise shared by Dumont and Marriott that Indians lack individualism, and, by implication, agency. Also relevant here is Madan's (1990) overview and evaluation of American anthropological representations of India; it offers an insightful discussion of Marriott's work in relation to other scholarship on India. Dirks' (2001) specifically historical critique is that the common anthropological discourse underlying the divergent theoretical claims of both Dumont and Marriott render India's colonial history insignificant. Dirks argues that "caste itself as we now know it is not a residual survival of ancient India but a specifically colonial form of (that is, substitute for) civil society that both justified and maintained an Orientalist vision" (2001:60).

15. Early on Papanek (1964) discussed various methodological strategies, and their respective advantages, for foreign women working in societies characterized by strict gender segregation. Later volumes (Golde 1986; Whitehead and Conaway 1986; Panini 1991) address the question of how the anthropologist's gender identity influences both the experience and products of research. Mascia-Lees, Sharpe, and Cohen (1989) point out that, while anthropologists are in a position of power vis-à-vis the subjects of ethnographic inquiry, men are in a position of power vis-à-vis women, including female researchers. Pat Caplan has noted, in her introduction to *Gendered Fields* (1993), that many ethnographers are extremely self-conscious about the issue of equality between informants and researchers. She points out a contradiction: while most of the volume's (female) contributors are painfully aware of their own privileged position based on race, class, education, etc., a common theme in their essays is the vulnerability of being a researcher (1993:24).

16. I thank John Cort for pointing this out to me (personal communication).

17. Dominguez has argued that we must pay attention to the presence or absence of love in our scholarship, and, if it is there, to show it to our readers so that they can evaluate its role in our work (2000:388).

18. Visweswaran (1994) addresses the dilemmas of being accountable to multiple audiences.

19. New research by other ethnographers working in this area promises to address some of these issues. For example, Sondra Hausner (2001) has written about a female ascetic in Haridwar who lives in a tent next to the Ganges and is known for her unruly behavior and fierce temper.

Chapter One. Gendering Hindu Renunciation

1. I thank Ravindra Khare for pointing out to me the connections between the various types of "message-making" that sannyasinis engage in and how central this theme is to the material presented here.

2. After his or her civil death upon initiation, a renouncer may acquire private property, which will devolve to disciples rather than to natural relatives (Narayanan 1993:288).

3. Government census information is not very helpful for understanding the demographics of renunciation, as in the 2001 census itinerant sadhus and sadhus not engaged in any economically productive activity were categorized along with beggars as "non-workers," and those who provide social or religious services enumerated simply as "workers." I thank C. Chakravorty of the Office of the Registrar General for clarifying this (personal communication). While scholars have estimated the number of female ascetics (not sannyasinis specifically) to be 10 to 15 percent of the entire ascetic population (Denton 1991; Ojha 1981; Gross 1992), more research is needed in this area.

4. Olivelle (1977) writes that the *Yatidharmaprakasa*, a medieval treatise on renunciation, provides what may be the only explicit and formal definition of renunciation in the literature. Sannyasa, according to this text, is essentially a negative state.

5. Hirst warns against inferring that devotionalism is peripheral to Advaita Vedanta. Shankara did not disparage temple worship, but rather insisted that it does not imply an ultimate difference between the Supreme Lord and the self, since focused bhakti can lead to knowledge of the ultimate reality as nondifferent (Hirst 1993:140). Dazey has explained the apparent contradiction between the professed philosophy of Advaita and the frequency with which renouncers practice devotional worship: "Possibly the Dasanamis have maintained both Vaishnava and Shaiva worship not only out of a sense of their own diverse origins, but in a conscious effort to legitimize the Order's claims for universal authority" (Dazey 1993:158). Still, philosophical study and reflection is the practice best known and most characteristic of Dashnami ascetics. The reciting of Om and ritual worship may be prescribed for renouncers in the monastic textbooks, but they are clearly presented as secondary (Ibid.: 161–62).

6. See Hacker (1965), Dazey (1993), and Hirst (1993) for further discussion of the relationship between the early followers of Advaita and Vaishnavism.

7. For further discussion of Shiva and of his paradoxical nature as both ascetic and erotic, see Dimmitt and van Buitenen (1978) and O'Flaherty (1981).

8. Embree outlines two alternatives to Shankara's monistic interpretation of Vedanta. Ramanuja proposed an opposing philosophy of qualified monism (*Vishishtadvaita*) that has shaped Vaishnava asceticism. Since Vaishnava asceticism was more deeply influenced by the bhakti movement, it tended to emphasize devotion rather than knowledge as the means to salvation. The philosophical systems of Shankara (c. A.D. 850) and Ramanuja (c. A.D. 1137) share a belief in the existence of an Impersonal Absolute called Brahman, but Shankara insisted on the ultimate oneness of Brahman and *atma*, while Ramanuja maintained a distinction between them (Embree 1988:297–98). Although sectarian differences are not always very clear, in general, the religious beliefs of Hindu ascetics roughly conform to the teachings of either Shankara or Ramanuja (Gross 1992:211). Madhava (1199–1278) espoused a third, theistic version of Vedanta philosophy. Philosophically, Madhava is closer to Ramanuja than to Shankara, but he moves closer to an uncompromising dualism (*Dvaita*) that posits a difference between the Supreme God who is Vishnu and the individual soul (Embree 1988:298).

9. For a description of Nath traditions, see Briggs (1973) and Gold (1992).

10. For a discussion of the origins of Virashaivism, see Michael (1992). For an analysis of women Virashaiva saints, see Ramaswamy (1996, 1997).

11. For an outline of the various types of female ascetics, see Denton (1991, forthcoming).

12. See Sir John Marshall's *Mohenjo-daro and the Indus Civilization* cited in Gross (1992:9) and Thapar (1984:67). For a more recent analysis, see Kenoyer (1998:112).

13. According to Thapar, the middle of the first millennium B.C.E. was a period of intellectual and religious turmoil on the subcontinent, due in part to a political shift from tribal organization to kingdoms and republics. With the growth of towns, artisans' guilds, and commerce, tribal loyalty gave way to caste identification. During the fifth and sixth centuries B.C.E., North India saw a proliferation of ascetic groups that quickly gained influence in society. Thapar explains this rise in asceticism as a response to rapid social change and the breakdown of tribal society (1984:69–70). Among the new religious orders were Buddhist and Jain sects, which rejected Vedic authority and eventually became independent religions. Upanishadic sages reinterpreted rather than rejected the Vedas, criticizing only their ritualistic emphasis.

14. Van der Veer (1987) describes a similar process of sedentarization for Ramanandi ascetics.

15. Brahmanical perspectives have received much scholarly attention. Although brahmanical orthodoxy has been viewed as worldly in orientation, Heesterman (1985) and Sanderson (1985) have shown that orthodox brahmanical thought encompasses both worldly and transcendent elements. Sanderson has described these two philosophical schools, exemplified by the *mimamsaka* ritualists and the *vedantins* as two extremes *within* orthodox brahmanical thought. The orthodox Brahmins oriented toward *mimamsaka* ritual criticized sannyasa as a shunning of the three debts (to the gods, the sages, and the ancestors). The vedantic element glorified the itinerancy and contemplation of sannyasa (Sanderson 1985:193–97). Giving renunciant thought the same amount of scholarly attention that brahmanical thought has received, from an ethnographic as well as textual point of view, will make its diversity more evident.

16. Findly writes that "the Vedic period (c.1200–600 B.C.E.) in many ways represents an era of unsurpassed advantage and opportunity for women" (1985:38). Olivelle also notes the evidence that women were initiated into Vedic study during the second half of the first millennium B.C.E. but prohibited from Vedic study during the classical and medieval periods (1993:184).

17. Members of the higher castes are called "twice-born" because they undergo an initiation into Vedic study.

18. See Young (1987:64–67) for an explanation of the origin and significance of the correlation between women and Shudras.

19. There is no consensus among scholars about the origins of the *ashrama* system. Some (Thapar 1984; Dumont 1980) have accepted the theory that renunciation began as a radical dissent from Vedic ritualism but that it was gradually co-opted by the brahmanical structure through a theory of life-stages that restricted sannyasa to the final stage of a

man's life. Olivelle (1993) argues that the original formulation offered the four *ashramas* as alternative and permanent modes of life unrelated to adolescence or old age. They simply represented four equally legitimate modes of life from which a young man could freely choose (Olivelle 1993:74). Gradually, according to Olivelle, renunciation began to be associated with old age and the stages were reformulated to constitute a sequence. Women were excluded from all but the stage of married householder, though the fact that the system was intended for men does not mean that women did not participate in the system's institutions, like Vedic initiation and renunciation (Ibid.: 188).

20. According to Olivelle, once the rules of customary law were codified in the texts, they were imbued with transcendent authority and became the model of proper conduct in society. Moreover, much of what was in the Dharmashastras did become law and, therefore, could be enforced by judicial and executive authorities (the king and heads of castes). In this respect, renouncers existed outside of society in that they do not appear to have been subject to any judicial authority until much later, when the Dashnami Order was established. It is possible that the lay population on which renouncers depended for alms exerted some influence on their conduct, but the Dharmashastric rules concerning renunciation, without a central authority to enforce them, could only have functioned as guidelines (Olivelle 1984:108–9). As indicated elsewhere in this book, recent scholarship in postcolonial and feminist theory attributes the institutionalization of Dharmashatric rules to colonialism.

21. Recent research warns against assuming that women's schooling is necessarily empowering. Kishwar 1986, Chatterjee (1997), and Kumar (1994) have demonstrated the ideological foundation of girls' educational curriculum during the colonial period, and a book edited by Jeffery and Basu (1996) questions the assumption that schooling leads to greater autonomy for women.

22. Here I summarize at length from a translation by Swami Venkatesananda (1984:288–334). Because the system of citation in this abridged edition is confusing, I simply cite by page number rather than by verse.

23. In contrast to these saints who rejected worldly marriage, there were others, such as the seventeenth century Marathi saint Bahina Bai, who managed to reconcile wifely duties with devotion to god (Feldhaus 1982:593). For an analysis of contemporary women religious virtuosi who also try to reconcile their devotionalism and domestic lives, see Hancock (1995).

24. My argument here supports Van der Veer's description of Ramanandi asceticism as an "open social category" (1987:686).

25. Both Anand Mata and Baiji came from Brahmin families, which is not surprising given sannyasa's elite origins and its continued focus on learning. However, since this may be a function of the "respectability" of the women I met, I caution against assuming a Brahmin background for independent renouncers. More research will determine whether most sannyasinis do in fact come from high-caste backgrounds.

Chapter Two. Walking a Tightrope: Renunciation as Love

1. Sadhus gather from all over India at this religious festival that rotates between Allahabad, Haridwar, Nasik, and Ujjain. Ascetics and lay pilgrims come to bathe at the

confluence of the Ganges River, the Yamuna River, and the mythical Saraswati. Media reports of the numbers of pilgrims visiting the 2001 Kumbh during a period of forty-four days range from twenty million reported by the *New York Times* (Bearak 2001) to seventy million reported by *India Today* (Prasannarajan 2001). Although the Kumbh Mela is reputed to be ancient, James Lochtefeld argues that historical evidence suggests that it is not more than 150 years old ("History of *Kumbhamela*" paper presented at University of Iowa, February 2003).

2. For a discussion of harshness and cruelty as aspects of the ideology of love in South Indian family life, see Trawick (1990:100–04).

3. In bhakti, surrender results in divine energy and power (Narayanan 1999:67–68).

Chapter Three. Real Saints Don't Need Sleep: Renunciation as Service

1. While this may resonate with the Western notion of intuition as a female way of knowing, Baiji never suggested that she considered intuition to be feminine (though Anand Mata did).

2. The term *"avadhut"* (literally, "one who has dispelled all imperfections") is used for any ascetic believed to be above all rules, although it is most appropriately used to refer to advanced Dashnami Nagas (Ghurye 1964:77).

3. Dazey (1990:296) discusses the difference between a guru's relationship with a monastic disciple (*shishya*) and householder devotee (*chela*).

4. Similarly, Sinclair-Brull observes that the Ramakrishna centers and monastery are often landscaped with lawns, just like the homes of wealthy and Westernized families (1997:42).

5. The part of my family people in Haridwar knew consisted of those relatives on my mother's side who have property in Haridwar. While they are indeed wealthy and Brahmin, my father's side is neither. My name revealed that I was born of a Brahmin mother and Baniya father and that I did not take the name of my husband. No one seemed to find these facts problematic.

6. Baiji said that, because feeding one person costs the ashram about four hundred rupees per month, the salary is only two hundred rupees. At the time, the exchange rate was about eight rupees per U.S. dollar.

7. A renouncer's "birthday" (*janamdin*) refers to the anniversary of their initiation.

8. Ramakrishna was a nineteenth century charismatic saint who was barely literate in his mother tongue of Bengali. His states of rapturous devotion to the goddess Kali interfered with his abilities to perform his ritual duties, and for this reason he lost his job as a temple priest (Sinclair-Brull 1997:14). Although he was reportedly initiated by a Dashnami sannyasi, he continued to live with his wife and family and to wear ordinary clothes (Ibid.: 18). Eventually, he began to attract disciples, especially young men from the educated

Bengali middle classes who found his message about the limits of science and rational knowledge appealing (Chatterjee 1992:51). After Ramakrishna's death in 1886, eleven of his disciples donned the ochre robes of sannyasa, although the legitimacy of their sannyasa is suspect in the eyes of many orthodox renouncers and lay persons (Sinclair-Brull 1997:24).

9. Baiji's emphasis on *seva* illustrates the difficulty in identifying renouncers as "traditional" or "orthodox." While Baiji has a local reputation for being orthodox because of the presence of *pandits* in her ashram, her scholasticism, her attention to rules of purity and pollution, and her attitudes toward manual labor and social service are hardly "traditional." Classical sannyasa required much more distance from worldly activities like cooking and accounting, and from householders themselves. While Anand Mata was reputed to be unorthodox because of her views on social issues, her inattention to rules of purity and pollution, her lack of scholasticism, and her guru (who had foreign disciples), it is evident that her approach to sannyasa as solitude and contemplation is closer to the classical renunciant ideal. The categories of "traditional" and "orthodox" require further specification to be meaningful.

Chapter Four. (Ir?)reconcilable Tensions: Individual Existence as Spiritual Journey

1. For analyses of the tensions between forest monks and established temples in Buddhism, see Carrithers (1983) and Tambiah (1984). Jaffrelot (1996), McKean (1996), and Bhatt (2001) offer recent studies of Hindu renouncers' role in nationalist politics. For more on renouncers' role as guru, see Cenkner (1983), Miller and Wertz (1976), and Narayan (1989).

2. Since Dumont, the nature of the Indian "person" or "individual" or "dividual" vis-à-vis its Western counterpart has remained a central problematic in South Asian studies (Mariott and Inden 1977; Collins 1985; Dumont 1980, 1986; Daniel 1984; Ram 1992; Mines 1994). Although the material and concepts I present here contribute centrally to these debates, limitations of space do not allow me to develop this thread more fully.

3. *Lingam* is a phallic symbol, usually carved from stone, used to represent Shiva.

4. For more on the connections between Hinduism, sacred spaces, and contemporary environmentalism, see *Hinduism and Ecology* (2000) edited by Chapple and Tucker.

Chaper Five. The Genuine and the Fake: What's Attitude Got to Do with It?

1. Although I use the term "saint" here to translate *sant*, the two terms are not etymologically related. As Hawley has explined, the term *sant* is derived from the Sanskrit participle of a verb meaning both "to be good" and "to be real" but has several meanings in

vernacular North Indian usage (1987:57 n.11). In fifteenth and sixteenth century usage, it means "the good" in the specific sense of those who are worshiping and singing of God. Since then, it has come to refer to holy men whose lineage extends back to the Nath Yogis. In current Panjabi usage, the term "sant" has come to refer to any holy man who lives apart from ordinary society (Ibid.: 57). In Hardiwar, I noted that the term "sant," as in "sant log," was often used in a very general sense to refer to sadhus, with implications of authenticity. Hallstrom has noted that the Christian category "saint" has slipped into common usage in Bengal, especially among the English-speaking classes (1999:90). I too found that in Hardiwar the English "saint" was often used to refer to respected religious figures.

2. Ramanujan (1989b) discusses various Indian traditions reflecting one another.

3. In the Siva-Purana, Parvati performs austerities in order to win Shiva as her husband.

4. For example, tantric practice prescribes the ritual consumption of five substances and activities that classical sannyasa prohibits: meat, fish, parched grains, liquor, and sexual intercourse. The "left-handed" path of Tantrism inverts, certainly in its language and allegedly in its ritual, such "right-handed" practices as the ingestion of pure substances. Specifically, brahmanic orthopraxy includes the ingestion of the five bodily secretions of cows and of gods, while the tantric practice substitutes five illicit substances, conceived as secretions of the human body (White 1995:6).

5. The body of texts called the Tantras, seen as the direct revelation of Shiva and Parvati, deal with esoteric and erotic elements of Shakta worship. These works are concerned with yoga and its goal of awakening the kundalini, the coiled or sleeping goddess lying dormant at the base of the spine. For men, awakening of the kundalini shakti is sometimes hastened by sexual practices, since shakti is personified not only in the goddess but in every woman. The practitioner meditates on the goddess sitting in the lap of Shiva, worships a picture of the female organ or a living, beautiful woman, or engages in ritualized sexual intercourse without regard to distinctions of caste (Briggs 1973:164–72). As the kundalini rises, the practitioner is said to acquire miraculous powers (siddhis) which may include the ability to remember past lives, know another's thoughts, become invisible, fly, or walk on water.

6. For a fascinating discussion of the relationship between supernatural Yoginis and human "witches," see White (2003:267–72).

7. Baiji's criticisms take on a different light when applied to a foreigner. I heard of three instances of North American or European women who came to Haridwar as spiritual seekers and then ended up living in a conjugal state with their (supposedly) previously celibate guru. One such couple had even started a family. Such stories attract attention because of their notoriety and construct a stereotype of foreign women who come to India in search of a guru.

8. Ghurye (1964:77) notes that an avadhut may eat meat or drink liquor.

9. The term "gupt dan" means "secret" or "quiet" donation and commonly refers to a donation for which no receipt is given and no record kept.

10. See Raheja (1988) on the inauspiciousness transferred with *dan* and Parry (1994) on the way funeral priests digest sin in accepting *dan*.

Chapter Six. *Sannyasinis* as Women

1. My conclusion resonates with those of Ramanujan and Hawley regarding Hindu holy women in history and myth. Ramanujan has shown how the lives of women saints differ from those of their male counterparts, who must undergo a conversion or change in gender identity. "The woman saint may fight the male husband, priest, and elder; she may love a male god. But she remains feminine, and in her love poetry she rejoices intensely in this identity" (Ramanujan 1982:324). Similarly, Hawley argues that Hindu women do not need to renounce their identities to the same extent that men do. "They are perceived in Hindu tradition as already close to the intimacy and naturalness of spirit that it is the purpose of *bhakti* (loving devotion) to cultivate" (Hawley 1986:238). Because the female figures described by both authors are firmly positioned in the bhakti tradition, which is seen as a feminized form of worship, we might expect them to rejoice in their femininity. The sannyasinis who are the focus of this book, however, have been initiated into a more androcentric, Vedanta-inspired tradition. It is, therefore, more surprising to find that they too emphasize their femininity.

2. This ontology of the body suggests the inapplicability and irrelevance of Euro-American feminist theories that are based on an opposition between essentialist explanations grounded in the body and constructivist explanations that are not. For sadhus, "essentializing" gender identities in the body does not render them universal, unchangeable, inevitable, or ultimately real (Khandelwal, unpublished manuscript).

3. Liz Wilson (1996), in her study of early Buddhist hagiographic literature, argues that representations of decaying women's bodies play a crucial role in inspiring a commitment to chastity and detachment among male monastics.

4. See Masson (1976:611 n.4) for mention of contradictory attitudes toward caste and Olivelle (1977:31–33) for a discussion of different ideas about prerequisites for initiation, whether relating to an internal disposition of detachment or an external attribute of social class. Gold (1992:319) makes similar observations about gender.

5. The tendency to represent sannyasa as unambiguously masculine is especially evident in scholarly works that do not focus on renunciation, but, rather, refer to it as an abstract point of contrast to whatever phenomenon is being studied, whether female auspiciousness (Marglin 1985a:19), female courtesans (Oldenburg 1990), or male wrestlers (Alter 1992). Others have represented sannyasa as outside of society (see Dumont 1980:273; Wadley 1977:129; Kumar 1994:229).

6. A male renouncer may also be called by a paternal term of address such as "*Baba*." Even so, the relationship with a paternal figure is not symmetrical to that with an intimate and nurturing mother. Madan's (1987) observation that a debt to the mother is the only one that cannot be repaid resonates with the remarks of one of my informants:

"Male renouncers are called 'Swami' but even a swami has a mother. Swami means one who controls but even those who have control in society have their own mothers. No religion has called its female renouncers swamis because women by nature are not controllers. They are called 'Ma' or mothers or Mother Superior."

7. I thank Lise McKean for pointing this out to me.

8. Kakar suggests an association between fatherliness and distance and further notes the importance of "feminine" powers of nurturance, warmth, concern, intuitive understanding, and relatedness for the healing encounter (1982:59). The question of whether female renouncers are more likely than their male counterparts to practice healing is an interesting question for further ethnographic research.

9. See Samanta (1992) and Trawick (1990:104-06) for further discussion of love overriding social rules. Gross (1992:297) indicates that most sadhus, but especially Vaishnavas, adhere to brahmanical orthopraxy in minute detail. He says that while sadhus are more concerned with spiritual purity than with ritual purity, the two are closely associated. It is possible that the emphasis on love is stronger among female than among male renouncers.

10. Gold contrasts the male gurus in two different Rajasthani tales: Gorakh Nath, the guru of the disciple's father, is hard and strict. Jalindar, the guru of the disciple's mother, is a soft, forgiving, "motherly" guru who nourishes, encourages, and supports his disciple in every way (Gold 1992:184). Kakar, in describing one female guru as a "possessive mother" and a male guru as a "loving but detached patriarch," calls for a model of Indian parental styles (1982:212–13).

11. For a nuanced analysis of gender and aging in Indian culture, see Lamb (2000).

12. Narayanan (1993) has addressed the issue of what happens to the social and legal status of a woman renounced by her husband.

13. Also see the essays in Sarkar and Butalia's *Women and Right-Wing Movements* (1995) and Jeffery and Basu's *Appropriating Gender* (1998) on the complex ways in which Hindu nationalism is gendered. Bacchetta (2002) analyzes the agency of Hindu nationalist women.

14. Amrita Basu, in "Feminism Inverted" (1995), points out that the three women nationalist leaders, Vijayraje Scindia, Uma Bharati, and Sadhvi Rithambara are all celibate, even if only the latter two are actually considered sannyasinis, and elaborates on the manner in which all three have transgressed gender roles. Denton (1991) does not directly address the issue of any opposition women may have faced for their decision to renounce worldly life, but her material does suggest other ways in which female asceticism transgresses gender roles. She points to the conceptual identification between womanhood, motherhood, and householdership (1991:213). Babb (1984) describes the hostility that the Brahma Kumaris faced from family and the larger society in their efforts to promote celibacy for young women.

15. The observation that women do not encourage other women to follow their example is supported by other work on women ascetics (Denton 1991; Ojha 1988).

16. Rayaprol describes egalitarian practices combined with traditional ideologies among Indians in the United States (1997:108–12). Similarly, Leonard argues that second-generation Indian women in the United States engage in secret marriages and avoid confrontational resistance to family expectations and notes that sexuality is a crucial area of resistance even though it is not openly expressed (1999:107–09). In her historical analysis of girls' schooling in India, Kumar suggests that women are more radical in what they do than in what they say (1994:229).

17. For a general approach to the anthropology of abstinence, see *Celibacy, Culture, and Society* (2001) edited by Sobo and Bell. Caplan (1987) has written on Mahatma Gandhi's celibacy, Alter (1997) on medical understandings of male celibacy in contemporary India, and Phillimore (2001) on celibate Hindu women who take on a quasi-ascetic role without becoming symbolic males. See Kishwar (1999) for discussions of the power of celibacy for Hindu wives and Khandelwal (2001) for a gendered analysis of ascetic ideologies of celibacy and sexual fluids.

18. Interestingly, Doniger and Kakar note that the author of the third century text *Kamasutra* "describes men in power who can take whatever women they want: 'the man in charge of threads may take widows, women who have no man to protect them, and wandering women ascetics; the city police-chief may take the women who roam about begging, for he knows where they are vulnerable, because of his own night-roamings' [5.5.7–9]" (2002: xxxi).

Glossary

I have chosen not to employ the full range of diacritical marks used in the transliteration of Hindi words. However, in order to aid the unfamiliar reader with pronunciation, I use the macron to indicate the difference between long and short vowels and the subdot to indicate retroflex consonants.

adrishṭa	the unseen
Advaita Vedānta	philosophy of absolute nondualism or absolute monism
ahamkār	egotism; pride
alaukik	otherworldly; transcendent; celestial
ānand	happines; bliss; ecstasy
āratī	offering of light made to a deity using a circular gesture
āshram	hermitage
āshrama	classical system of four life-stages prescribed for a caste Hindu male
aslī	genuine; true; pure
ātmā	soul; essence
avadhūt (f. *avadhūtinī*)	ascetic believed to be above all rules
Bhagwān	God; the Lord
bhakti	devotion
bhaṇḍārā	feast, especially a feast honoring ascetics
Brahman	Impersonal Absolute; Ultimate Reality
brahmacharya	celibate studentship or first stage of *ashrama* system; celibacy
chelā (f. *chelī*)	follower or disciple, especially a lay or householder disciple

dān	contribution; donation
darshan	auspicious viewing; glimpse of a deity or holy person
Dashnāmī	orthodox renuciant orders founded in the eighth century
dharma	moral duty; virtuous behavior; cosmic order; religion
dīkshā	initiation; ceremonial introduction into a religious order
drishṭa	the seen
ghāṭ	riverbank, sometimes lined with paved steps to facilitate bathing
grihastha	household life or second stage of ashrama system
guru	spiritual teacher
havan	sacrificial fire
jādū	magic; witchcraft
jap	quiet repetition of a deity's name or a mantra
jīva	living being; creature; life
jīvanmukt	liberated from worldly bonds while still living
jnāna	knowledge; wisdom
jūṭhā	an object or food rendered polluted by contact with saliva
karma	act; action
kathā	a mythological story; an event in which such a story is read aloud to an audience
laukik	worldly
mahārāj	great king; term of address for (male) saints
mahātmā	great soul; term of address for (male) saints
mārg	path
mast	(n. *masti*) carefree; radiant with joy; intoxicated
mātā	mother; term of address for (female) saints
maun	silence, as in a vow of silence (*maun vrat*)
moksha	liberation; enlightenment
muni	religious scholar
mūrti	icon in which a deity resides
mūrti pūjā	devotional worship of icons

naklī	false; spurious
nirākār	without form
nirguna	without attributes or qualities
pāgal	crazy
pandit	Brahmin scholar or priest
Paramātmā	Universal Soul (another name for Brahman)
pāṭh	lesson; reading; recitation of a sacred text
pranām	respectful greeting; salutation; bow
prārthnā	prayer; request
prasād	gift from a deity or holy person
pūjā	devotional worship; veneration; adoration
pūjā-pāth	bhakti religiosity
rishi	sage
roṭī	unleavened flatbread made from wheat
sādhana	spiritual discipline; religious method
sādhu (f. *sādhvī*)	ascetic; masculine form may also refer to female ascetics
saguna	with attributes or qualities
sākār	with form
samādhi	meditative trance; tomb of a holy person
samsāra	"the world"; that from which renouncers seek liberation
samskāra	mental impressions forming on the mind
sannyāsa	renunciation or fourth stage of *ashrama* system
sannyāsī (f. *sannyāsinī*)	renouncer
satsang	religious assembly
sevā	service or worship to the guru; social service
shakti	energy or power, conceptualized as feminine
Shankara	eighth-century saint usually credited with founding the Dashnami Order
sharīr	body
shishya	disciple, especially an ascetic or monastic disciple

shraddhā	faith; veneration
shuddha	pure; unadulterated; sacred
siddhi	supernatural power acquired through yogic practice
sthūl	gross
sūkshma	subtle
swāmī	lord or master; term of address for male sadhus
tapas (Skt. *tapasyā*)	austerities
vairāgya	detatchment; desirelessness
vānprastha	forest-dwelling life or third stage of *ashrama* system
vedānta	"the end of the Vedas"; one of the six systems of Hindu philosophy
vivek	discrimination; intellectual analysis
vrat	religious vow or fast
yajnashālā	the enclosure or altar within which a fire sacrifice (*havan*) is performed
yogī (f. *yoginī*)	practitioner of yoga; tantric ascetic

Works Cited

Abu-Lughod, Lila. "Writing Against Culture." In *Recapturing Anthropology*, edited by Richard G. Fox, 137–62. Santa Fe: School of American Research Press, 1991.

———. *Writing Women's Worlds*. Berkeley: University of California Press, 1993.

Alter, Joseph S. "The Sannyasi and the Indian Wrestler: The Anatomy of a Relationship." *American Ethnologist* 19, no. 2 (1992): 317–36.

———. "Celibacy, Sexuality and the Transformation of Gender into Nationalism in North India." *Journal of Asian Studies* 53 (1994): 45–66.

———. "Seminal Truth: A Modern Science of Male Celibacy in North India." *Medical Anthropological Quarterly* 11, no. 3 (1997): 275–98.

Anna. *Saints of India*. Madras: Sri Ramakrishna Math, n.d.

Appadurai, Arjun. "Is Homo Hierarchicus?" *American Ethnologist* 13, no. 4 (1986): 745–61.

———. "Global Ethnoscapes." In *Recapturing Anthropology*, edited by Richard G. Fox, 191–210. Santa Fe: School of American Research Press, 1991.

Asad, Talal. *Anthropology and the Colonial Encounter*. London: Ithaca Press, 1973.

Babb, Lawrence A. "Marriage and Malevolence." *Ethnology* 9 (1970): 137–48.

———. "Indigenous Feminism in a Modern Hindu Sect." *Signs* 9, no. 3 (spring 1984): 399–416.

Bacchetta, Paola. "Hindu Nationalist Women: On the Use of the Feminine Symbolic to (Temporarily) Displace Male Authority." In *Jewels of Authority: Women and Textual Tradition in Hindu India*, edited by Laurie L. Patton, 157–76. New York: Oxford University Press, 2002.

Basu, Amrita. "Feminism Inverted: The Gendered Imagery of Read Women in Hindu Nationalism." In *Women and Right-Wing Movements*, edited by Tanika Sarkar and Urvashi Butalia, 158–80. London: Zed Books, 1995.

———. "Mass Movement or Elite Conspiracy?" In *Contesting the Nation*, edited by David Ludden. Philadelphia: University of Pennsylvania Press, 1996.

Bearak, Barry. "When Hindus Brave a Big Crush for a Little Dip." *New York Times*. January 25, 2001.

Behar, Ruth. *The Vulnerable Observer*. Boston: Beacon Press, 1996.

Bennett, Lynn. *Dangerous Wives and Sacred Sisters*. New York: Columbia University Press, 1983.

Bhatt, Chetan. *Hindu Nationalism*. New York: Berg, 2001.

Bloomfield, Maurice. "On False Ascetics and Nuns in Hindu Fiction." *Journal of the American Oriental Society* 44 (1924): 202–42.

Briggs, George Winston. *Gorakhnath and the Kanphata Yogis*. Delhi: Motilal Banarsidass, 1973.

Brown, Karen McCarthy. *Mama Lola: A Vodou Priestess in Brooklyn*. Berkeley: University of California Press, 1991.

Burghart, Richard. "Wandering Ascetics of the Ramanandi Sect." *History of Religions* 22, no. 4 (May 1983b): 361–80.

———. "Renunciation in the Religious Traditions of South Asia." *Man* 18, no. 4 (1983a): 635–53.

Bynum, Caroline W. *Holy Feast and Holy Fast*. Berkeley: University of California Press, 1987.

———. *Fragmentation and Redemption*. New York: Zone Books, 1991.

Bynum, Caroline W., S. Harrel, and P. Richman. *Gender and Religion*. Boston: Beacon Press, 1986.

Caplan, Pat. Introduction to *Gendered Fields*. New York: Routledge, 1993.

———. "Ascetics in Western Nepal." *The Eastern Anthropologist* 26, no. 2 (1973): 173–82.

———. "Celibacy as a Solution? Mahatma Gandhi and *Brahmacharya*." In *The Cultural Construction of Sexuality*, edited by Pat Caplan, 271–95. New York: Tavistock Publications, 1987.

Carrithers, Michael. *The Forest Monks of Sri Lanka*. Delhi: Oxford University Press, 1983.

Carrithers, Michael, Steven Collins, and Steven Lukes, eds. *The Category of the Person*. New York: Cambridge University Press, 1985.

Cenkner, William. *A Tradition of Teachers: Sankara and the Jagadgurus Today*. Delhi: Motilal Banarsidass, 1983.

Chakraborti, Haripada. *Asceticism in Ancient India in Brahmanical, Buddhist, Jaina, and Ajivika Societies*. Calcutta: Punthi Pustak, 1973.

Chapple, Christopher Key and Mary Evelyn Tucker, eds. *Hinduism and Ecology*. Cambridge, Mass.: Center for the Study of World Religions, Harvard Divinity School, 2000.

Chatterjee, Partha. "A Religion of Urban Domesticity: Sri Ramakrishna and the Calcutta Middle Class." In *Subaltern Studies VII*, edited by Partha Chatterjee and Gyanendra Pandey, 40–68. Delhi: Oxford University Press, 1992.

———. "The Nationalist Resolution of the Women's Question." In *Recasting Women*, 3rd ed., edited by Kumkum Sangari and Sudesh Vaid, 233–53. New Brunswick, N.J.: Rutgers University Press, 1997.

Clifford, James, and George E. Marcus, eds. *Writing Culture*. Berkeley: University of California Press, 1986.

Daniel, E. Valentine. *Fluid Signs*. Berkeley: University of California Press, 1984.

Das, Veena. "Subaltern as Perspective." In *Subaltern Studies VI*, edited by Ranajit Guha, 310–24. Delhi: Oxford University Press, 1989.

Dazey, Wade H. "The Role of Bhakti in the Dasanami Order." In *Love Divine: Studies in Bhakti and Devotional Mysticism*, edited by Karel Werner, 147–72. Surrey: Curzon Press, 1993.

———. "Tradition and Modernization in the Organization of the Dasanami Samnyasins." In *Monastic Life in the Christian and Hindu Traditions: A Comparative Study*, edited by Austin B. Creel and Vasudha Narayanan, 281–321. Lewiston, N.Y.: The Edwin Mellen Press, 1990.

Denton, Lynn Tesky. "Varieties of Hindu Female Asceticism." In *Roles and Rituals for Hindu Women*, edited by J. Leslie Cranbury, 211–31. N.J.: Associated University Presses, 1991.

———. *Female Ascetics in Hinduism*. Forthcoming. Albany: State University of New York Press.

Dickey, Sara. "Permeable Homes: Domestic Service, Household Space, and the Vulnerability of Class Boundaries in Urban India." *American Ethnologist* 27 (2000): 462–89.

Dimmitt, C., and J. A. B. van Buitenen., ed. and trans. *Classical Hindu Mythology*. Philadelphia: Temple University Press, 1978.

Dirks, Nicholas B. *Castes of Mind*. Princeton: Princeton University Press, 2001.

Dominguez, Virginia R. "For a Politics of Love and Rescue." *Cultural Anthropology* 15, no. 3 (2000): 361–93.

Doniger, Wendy, with Brian K. Smith, trans. *Laws of Manu*. New York: Penguin Books, 1991.

Doniger, Wendy and Sudhir Kakar, trans. *Kamasutra*. New York: Oxford University Press, 2002.

See also O'Flaherty, Wendy Doniger.

Dumont, Louis. *Homo Hierarchicus: The Caste System and Its Implications*. Chicago: University of Chicago Press, 1980.

———. *Essays on Individualism*. Chicago: University of Chicago Press, 1986.

Eck, Diana L. "India's Tirthas: 'Crossings' in Sacred Geography." *History of Religions* 20, no. 4 (May 1981): 323–44.

Edwards, James W. "Semen Anxiety in South Asian Cultures." *Medical Anthropology* 7, no. 3 (1983): 51–67.

Embree, Ainslie T. *Sources of Indian Tradition. Vol. 1: From the Beginning to 1800* (Rev. ed.). New York: Columbia University Press, 1988.

Erndl, Kathleen M. "Rapist or Bodyguard, Demon or Devotee? Images of Bhairo in the Mythology and Cult of Vaisno Devi." In *Criminal Gods and Demon Devotees*, edited by Alf Hiltebeitel, 239–50. Albany: State University of New York Press, 1989.

Falk, Nancy E. "*Shakti* Ascending: Hindu Women, Politics, and Religious Leadership During the Nineteenth and Twentieth Centuries. In *Religion in Modern India*, edited by Robert D. Baird, 298–334. New Delhi: Manohar, 1995.

Feldhaus, Anne. "Bahina Bai: Wife and Saint." *Journal of the American Academy of Religion* L, no. 4 (1982): 591–604.

Findly, Ellison Banks. "Gargi at the King's Court: Women and Philosophical Innovation in Ancient India." In *Women, Religion, and Social Change,* edited by Yvonne Yazbeck Haddad and Ellison Banks Findly, 37–58. Albany: State University of New York Press, 1985.

Gandhi, Manubehn. *Bapu—My Mother*. Ahmedabad: Navajivan Publishing House, 1955.

Ghurye, G. S. *Indian Sadhus*. Bombay: Popular Prakashan, 1964.

Giovannini, Maureen. "Female Anthropologist and Male Informant: Gender Conflict in a Sicilian Town." In *Self, Sex, and Gender in Cross-Cultural Fieldwork*, edited by Tony Larry Whitehead and Mary Ellen Conaway, 103–16. Chicago: University of Illinois Press, 1986.

Gold, Ann. "The Once and Future Yogi: Sentiments and Signs in the Tale of a Renouncer-King." *Journal of Asian Studies* 48, no. 4 (1989a): 770–86.

————. *A Carnival of Parting*. Berkeley: University of California Press, 1992.

————. *Fruitful Journeys*. Delhi: Oxford University Press, 1989b.

Gold, Daniel. *Comprehending the Guru*. Atlanta: Scholars Press, 1988.

Golde, Peggy. *Women in the Field: Anthropological Experiences*. Berkeley: University of California Press, 1986.

Gross, Robert L. *The Sadhus of India*. Jaipur: Rawat Publications, 1992.

Haberman, David L. "River of Love in an Age of Pollution." In *Hinduism and Ecology*, edited by Christopher Key Chapple and Mary Evelyn Tucker, 339–54. Cambridge, Mass.: Center for the Study of World Religions, Harvard Divinity School, 2000.

Hacker, Paul. "Relations of Early Advaitins to Vaisnavism."(1965) reprinted in Wilhelm Halbfass (ed.), *Philology and Confrontation: Paul Hacker on Traditional and Modern Vedanta*, 33–39. Albany: State University of New York Press, 1995.

————. "On Sankara and Advaitism." (1964) reprinted in Wilhelm Halbfass (ed.), *Philology and Confrontation: Paul Hacker on Traditional and Modern Vedanta*, 27–32. Albany: State University of New York Press, 1995.

Hallstrom, Lisa Lassell. *Mother of Bliss: Anandamayi Ma, 1896–1982*. New York: Oxford University Press, 1999.

Hancock, Mary E. "The Dilemmas of Domesticity." In *From the Margins of Hindu Marriage* edited by Harlan Lindsay and Paul B. Courtright, 60–91. New York: Oxford University Press, 1995.

Handler, Richard. "Authenticity." *Anthropology Today* 2, no. 1 (February 1986): 2–4.

Hansen, Kathryn. "The Virangana in North Indian History." *Economic and Political Weekly.* April 30, 1988: WS-25–WS-33.

Haraway, Donna. "Situated Knowledges: The Science Question in Feminism and the Privilege of Partial Perspective." *Feminist Studies* 14 (fall 1988): 575–99.

Hartsuiker, Dolf. *Sadhus: Holy Men of India.* London: Thames and Hudson, 1993.

Hatley, Shaman and Sohail Inayatullah. "Karma Samnyasa: Sarkar's Reconceptualization of Indian Asceticism." *Journal of Asian and African Studies* 34, no.1 (1999): 139–51.

Hausner, Sondra. "Staying in Place: Contemporary Women Renouncers and Community Involvement." Presented at the American Anthropological Association Annual Meeting in Washington, D.C. November 30, 2001.

Hawley, John Stratton. "Images of Gender in the Poetry of Krishna." In *Gender and Religion*, edited by C. W. Bynum, S. Harrel, and P. Richman. Boston: Beacon Press, 1986.

———. "Morality Beyond Morality in the Lives of Three Hindu Saints." In *Saints and Virtues*, edited by John Stratton Hawley, 52–72. Berkeley: University of California Press, 1987.

Heesterman, J. C. *The Inner Conflict of Tradition.* Chicago: University of Chicago Press, 1985.

Hiltebeitel, Alf, and Kathleen M. Erndl, eds. *Is the Hindu Goddess a Feminist? The Politics of South Asian Goddesses.* New York: New York University Press, 2000.

Hirst, Jacqueline. "The Place of Bhakti in Sankara's Vedanta." In *Love Divine: Studies in Bhakti and Devotional Mysticism*, edited by Karel Werner, 117–45. Surrey: Curzon Press, 1993.

Hsuing, Ping-Chun. "Between Bosses and Workers." In *Feminist Dilemmas in Fieldwork*, edited by Diane L. Wolf, 122–37. Colorado: Westview Press, 1996.

The Illustrated Weekly of India. June 3, 1990.

Jackson, Carl T. *Vedanta for the West.* Bloomington: Indiana University Press, 1994.

Jaffrelot, Christophe. *The Hindu Nationalist Movement in India.* New York: Columbia University Press, 1996.

Jeffery, Patricia and Amrita Basu, eds. *Appropriating Gender.* New York: Routledge, 1998.

Jeffery, Roger and Alaka Basu, eds. *Girls' Schooling, Women's Autonomy and Fertility Change in South Asia.* New Delhi: Sage Publications India, Pvt. Ltd., 1996.

Kakar, Sudhir. *Shamans, Mystics, and Doctors.* Boston: Beacon Press, 1982.

———. "Ramakrishna and the Mystical Experience." In *The Analyst and the Mystic,* 1–40. New Delhi: Viking 1991.

———. *Intimate Relations.* New Delhi: Penguin Books, 1989.

Kenoyer, Jonathan M. *Ancient Cities of the Indus Valley Civilization.* Karachi, New York: Oxford University Press, 1998.

Khandelwal, Meena. "Walking a Tightrope: Saintliness, Gender, and Power in an Ethnocentric Encounter." *Anthropology and Humanism* 21, no. 2 (1996): 111–34.

———. "Sexual Fluids, Emotions, Morality: Notes on the Gendering of Brahmacharya." In *Celibacy, Culture, and Society: The Anthropology of Sexual Abstinence,* edited by Elisa J. Sobo and Sandra Bell, 157–79. Madison: University of Wisconsin Press, 2001.

———. "The Ungendered Atma, Masculine Virility and Feminine Compassion: Ambiguities in Renunciant Discourses on Gender." *Contributions to Indian Sociology* 31, no. 1 (1997): 79–107.

———. "Essentialism and Cross-Cultural Research: A Hindu View of Sexual Difference." Unpublished manuscript.

Khare, R. S. *The Untouchable as Himself.* Cambridge: Cambridge University Press, 1984.

———. "The Seen and the Unseen: Hindu Distinctions, Experiences and Cultural Reasoning." *Contributions to Indian Sociology* 27, no. 2 (1993): 191–212.

King, Richard. *Orientalism and Religion.* New York: Routledge, 1999.

King, Ursula. "Who Is the Ideal Karmayogin?" *Religion* 10 (spring 1980): 41–59.

———. "The Effect of Social Change on Religious Self-Understanding: Women Ascetics in Modern Hinduism." In *Changing South Asia,* edited by K. Ballhatchet and D. Taylor, 69–83. London: School of Oriental and African Studies, 1984.

Kishwar, Madhu. "Arya Samajand Women's Education: Kanya Mahavidyalaya, Jalandhar." *Economic and Political Weekly* 21, no. 17 (April 26, 1986): WS-9–WS-24.

———. "Women, Sex and Marriage." In *Off the Beaten Track*, 209–33. New Delhi: Oxford University Press, 1999.

Kripal, Jeffery. *Kali's Child*. Chicago: University of Chicago Press, 1995.

Kumar, Nita. "Oranges for the Girls, or, the Half-Known Story of the Education of Girls in Twentieth-Century Banaras." In *Women as Subjects*, edited by Nita Kumar, 211-29. Charlottesville: University of Virginia Press, 1994.

Lamb, Sarah. *White Saris and Sweet Mangoes: Aging, Gender, and Body in North India*. Berkeley: University of California Press, 2000.

Leonard, Karen. "The Management of Desire: Sexuality and Marriage for Young South Asian Women in America." In *Emerging Voices*, edited by Sangeeta R. Gupta, 107–19. Walnut Creek, Calif.: Alta Mira Press, 1999.

Leslie, I. Julia. "Essence and Existence: Women and Religion in Ancient Indian Texts." In *Women's Religious Experience*, edited by Pat Holden, 89–112. New Jersey: Barnes and Noble, 1983.

———. *The Perfect Wife*. Delhi: Oxford University Press, 1989.

Lewin, Ellen. "Writing Lesbian Ethnography." In *Women Writing Culture*, edited by Ruth Behar and Deborah A. Gordon, 322–35. Berkeley: University of California Press, 1995.

Lingat, Robert. *The Classical Law of India*. Berkeley: University of California Press, 1973.

Llewellyn, J. E. "The Autobiography of a Female Renouncer." In *Religions of India in Practice*, edited by Donald Lopez, Jr., 462–72. Princeton, N.J.: Princeton University Press, 1995.

Lochtefeld, James G. "History of Kumbhamela." Paper presented at the University of Iowa, February 2003.

Lorenzen, David. "Warrior Ascetics in Indian History." In *Journal of the American Oriental Society* 98, no.1 (1978): 61–75.

Lutgendorf, Philip. "City, Forest, and Cosmos: Ecological Perspectives from the Sanskrit Epics." In *Hinduism and Ecology*, edited by Christopher Key

Chapple and Mary Evelyn Tucker, 269–89. Cambridge, Mass.: Center for the Study of World Religions, Harvard Divinity School, 2000.

Madan, T .N. *Non-Renunciation*. Delhi: Oxford University Press, 1987.

———. "India in American Anthropology." In *Conflicting Images*, edited by Sulochana Raghavan Glazer and Nathan Glazer. 179–202. Glendale, MD.: Riverdale, 1990.

Madhavananda, Swami, and Ramesh Chandra Majumdar. *Great Women of India*. Mayavati, Almora, Himalayas: Advaita Ashrama, 1982.

Mani, Lata. "Contentious Traditions: The Debate on *Sati* in Colonial India." In *Recasting Women*, edited by Kumkum Sangari and Sudesh Vaid, 88-126. New Brunswick, N.J.: Rutgers University Press, 1990.

Mankekar, Purnima. *Screening Culture, Viewing Politics*. Durham, N.C.: Duke University Press, 1999.

Manu. 1886. *The Laws of Manu*. Translated by Wendy Doniger, with Brian K. Smith. New York: Penguin, 1991.

Marcus, George E., and Michael M. J. Fischer. *Anthropology as Cultural Critique*. Chicago: University of Chicago Press, 1986.

Marglin, Frederique A. *Wives of the God-King*. Oxford: Oxford University Press, 1985a.

———. "Female Sexuality in the Hindu World." In *Immaculate and Powerful: The Female in Sacred Image and Social Reality*, edited by C. W. Atkinson, C. H. Buchanan, and M. R. Miles, 39–59. Boston: Beacon Press, 1985b.

Marriott, McKim, and R. Inden. "Toward an Ethnosociology of South Asian Caste Systems." In *The New Wind*, edited by K. David, 227–38. The Hague: Mouton, 1977.

Mascia-Lees, Frances E., Patricia Sharpe, and Colleen Ballerino Cohen. "The Postmodernist Turn in Anthropology: Cautions from a Feminist Perspective." *Signs* 15, no. 1 (1989): 7–33.

Masson, J. Moussaieff. "The Psychology of the Ascetic." *Journal of Asian Studies* 35, no. 4 (1976): 611–25.

McDaniel, June. *The Madness of the Saints*. Chicago: University of Chicago Press, 1989.

———. "A Holy Woman of Calcutta." In *Religions of India in Practice*, edited by Donald Lopez, Jr., 418–25. Princeton, N.J.: Princeton University Press, 1995.

McGee, Mary. "Desired Fruits: Motive and Intention in the Votive Rites of Hindu Women." In *Roles and Rituals for Hindu Women*, edited by J. Leslie, 71–88. Cranbury, N.J.: Associated University Presses, 1991.

———. "Ritual Rights: The Gender Implications of *Adhikāva*." In *Jewels of Authority: Women and Textual Tradition in Hindu India*, edited by Laurie L. Patton, 32-50. New York: Oxford University Press, 2002.

McKean, Lise. *Divine Enterprise: Gurus and the Hindu Nationalist Movement.* Chicago: University of Chicago Press, 1996.

Menon, Y. Keshava. *The Mind of Adi Shankara.* Bombay: Jaico Publishing House, 1976.

Michael, R. Blake. *The Origins of Virasaiva Sects.* Delhi: Motilal Banarsidass, 1992.

Miller, David M. and Dorothy C. Wertz. *Hindu Monastic Life: The Monks and Monasteries of Bhubaneswar.* Montreal: McGill-Queen's University Press, 1976.

Mines, Mattison. *Public Faces, Private Voices: Community and Individuality in South India.* Berkeley: University of California Press, 1994.

Moffatt, Michael. *Coming of Age in New Jersey.* Brunswick, N.J.: Rutgers University Press, 1989.

Mohanty, Chandra Talpade. "Under Western Eyes: Feminist Scholarship and Colonial Discourses." *Boundary* 2 12, no. 3 (1984): 333–58.

Moore, Henrietta. *Feminism and Anthropology.* Minneapolis: University of Minnesota Press, 1988.

Mukta, Parita. *Upholding the Common Life: The Community of Mirabai.* Delhi: Oxford University Press, 1994.

Narayan, Kirin. *Storytellers, Saints, and Scoundrels.* Philadelphia: University of Pennsylvania Press, 1989.

———. "How Native Is a 'Native' Anthropologist?" *American Anthropologist* 95 (1993a): 671–86.

———. "Refractions of the Field at Home: American Representations of Hindu Holy Men in the 19th and 20th Centuries." *Cultural Anthropology* 8, no. 4 (1993b): 476–509.

Narayan, R. K. *The Guide.* New York: Viking Press, 1958.

Narayan, Uma. *Dislocating Cultures.* New York: Routledge, 1997.

Narayanan, Vasudha. "Renunciation and Law in India." In *Religion and Law in Independent India*, edited by Robert D. Baird, 279–91. New Delhi: Manohar, 1993.

———. "Brimming with *Bhakti*, Embodiments of *Shakti*: Devotees, Deities, Performers, Reformers, and Other Women of Power in the Hindu Tradition." In *Feminism and World Religions*, edited by Arvind Sharma and Katherine K. Young, 25–77. Albany: State University of New York Press, 1999.

Naveed-I-Rahat, "'Participation Observation' and Identity Crisis." In *From the Female Eye*, edited by M. N. Panini, 41–51. Delhi: Hindustan Publishing Corporation, 1991.

Neill, Roderick. "Sadhus and Hippies." *Quest* 65 (1970): 20–27.

Obeyesekere, Gannanath. *Medusa's Hair*. Chicago: University of Chicago Press, 1981.

O'Flaherty, Wendy Doniger. "The Origin of Heresy in Hindu Mythology." *History of Religions* 10, no. 4 (1971): 271–333.

———. *Siva*. 2nd ed. New York: Oxford University Press, 1981.

———. *Women, Androgynes, and Other Mythical Beasts*. Chicago: University of Chicago Press, 1980.

See also Doniger, Wendy

Ojha, Catherine. "Feminine Asceticism in Hinduism: Its Tradition and Present Condition." *Man in India* 61, no. 3 (September 1981): 254–85.

———. "The Tradition of Female Gurus." *Manushi* 31, no. 1 (November-December 1985): 2–8.

———. "Outside the Norms: Women Ascetics in Hindu Society." *Economic and Political Weekly*. April 30, 1988: WS-34–WS-36.

Oldenburg, Veena. "Lifestyle as Resistance: The Case of the Courtesans of Lucknow, India." *Feminist Studies* 16, no.2 (summer 1990): 259–87.

Olivelle, Patrick. *Vasudevasrama Yatidharmaprakasa*. Part 2: Translation. Vienna: The De Nobili Research Library, 1977.

———. "Renouncer and Renunciation in the Dharmasastras." In *Studies in Dharmasastra*, edited by R. W. Lariviere, 81–152. Calcutta: Firma KLM Private Ltd., 1984.

———. *Samnyasa Upanishads*. New York: Oxford University Press, 1992.

———. *The Asrama System*. New York: Oxford University Press, 1993.

———. "Ascetic Withdrawal or Social Engagement." In *Religions of India in Practice*, edited by Donald Lopez, Jr., 533–46. Princeton, N.J.: Princeton University Press, 1995.

———. *The Early Upanishads*. Annotated text and translation. New York: Oxford University Press, 1998.

Ong, Aihwa. "Women Out of China." In *Women Writing Culture*, edited by Ruth Behar and Deborah A. Gordon, 350–72. Berkeley: University of California Press, 1995.

Ortner, Sherry. *Making Gender*. Boston: Beacon Press, 1996.

Osborne, Arthur. *Ramana Maharishi and the Path of Self-Knowledge*. Bombay: Jaico, 1970.

Osella, Caroline and F. Osella. "Contextualizing Sexuality: Young Men in Kerala, South India." In *Coming of Age in South and Southeast Asia*, edited by Lenore Manderson and Pranee Liamputtong, 113–31. Surrey: Curzon, 2002.

Panini, M. N. *From the Female Eye*. Delhi: Hindustan Publishing Corporation, 1991.

Papanek, Hanna. "The Woman Field Worker in a Purdah Society." *Human Organization* 23 (1964): 160–63.

Parry, Jonathan. *Death in Benaras*. New York: Cambridge University Press, 1994.

Patai, Daphne. "U.S. Academics and Third World Women: Is Ethical Research Possible?" In *Women's Words: The Feminist Practice of Oral History*, edited by Sherna Berger Gluck and Daphne Patai, 137–53. New York: Routledge, 1991.

Pearson, Anne Mackenzie. *Because It Gives Me Peace of Mind*. Albany: State University of New York Press, 1996.

Phillimore, Peter. "Private Lives and Public Identities: An Example of Female Celibacy in Northwest India." In *Celibacy, Culture, and Society*, edited by Elisa J. Sobo and Sandra Bell, 29–46. Madison, Wis.: The University of Wisconsin Press, 2001.

Potter, Karl H. *Presuppositions of India's Philosophies*. Delhi: Motilal Banarsidass, 1991.

Prasannarajan, S. "Kumbha Karma." *India Today*. January 22, 2001.

Puri, Jyoti. *Woman, Body, Desire in Post-colonial India.* New York: Routledge, 1999.

Radhakrishnan, S., trans., *The Bhagavadgita.* New York: Harper and Row, 1973.

Raheja, Gloria Goodwin and Ann Grodzins Gold. *Listen to the Heron's Words.* Berkeley: University of California Press, 1994.

Raheja, Gloria Goodwin. *The Poison in the Gift.* Chicago: University of Chicago Press, 1988.

Ram, Kalpana. "Modernist Anthropology and the Construction of Indian Identity." *Meanjin* 51, no. 3 (1992): 589–614.

Ramanujan, A. K. "On Women Saints." In *The Divine Consort,* edited by J. S. Hawley and D. M. Wulff, 316–24. Boston: Beacon Press, 1982.

———. "Is there an Indian way of thinking? An informal essay." *Contributions to Indian Sociology* 23, no. 1 (1989a): 41–58.

———. "Where Mirrors Are Windows: Toward an Anthology of Reflections." *History of Religions* 28, no. 3 (February 1989b): 187–216.

———. *Speaking of Siva.* Baltimore, Md.: Penguin Books, 1973.

Ramaswamy, Vijaya. "Rebels-Conformists? Women Saints in Medieval South India." *Anthropos* 87 (1992): 133–46.

———. *Walking Naked.* Shimla: Indian Institute of Advanced Study, 1997.

———. *Divinity and Deviance: Women in Virasaivism.* Delhi: Oxford University Press, 1996.

Rayaprol, Aparna. *Negotiating Identities.* Delhi: Oxford University Press, 1997.

Reader, Ian and George J. Tanabe, Jr. *Practically Religious.* Honolulu: University of Hawaii Press, 1998.

Robinson, Catherine A. *Tradition and Liberation: The Hindu Tradition in the Indian Women's Movement.* Surrey: Curzon, 1999.

Roy, Parama. *Indian Traffic.* Berkeley: University of California Press, 1998.

Rukmani, T. S. "Foreword." In *Jewels of Authority: Women and Textual Tradition in Hindu India,* edited by Laurie L. Patton, vii–xi. New York: Oxford University Press, 2002.

Samanta, Suchitra. "*Mangalmayima, sumangali, mangal:* Bengali Perceptions of the Divine Feminine, Motherhoood and 'Auspiciousness'." *Contributions to Indian Sociology* 26, no. 1 (1992): 51–75.

Sanderson, Alexis. "Purity and Power among the Brahmans of Kashmir." In *The Category of the Person*, edited by Michael Carrithers, Steven Collins, and Steven Lukes, 190-216. Cambridge: Cambridge University Press, 1985.

Sangari, Kumkum. "Consent, Agency and Rhetorics of Incitement." *Economic and Political Weekly*. May 1, 1993: 867–82.

Sarkar, Tanika and Urvashi Butalia. *Women and Right-Wing Movements*. New Jersey: Zed Books, 1995.

Scott, James. *Domination and the Arts of Resistance: Hidden Transcripts*. New Haven: Yale University Press, 1990.

Sheffield, Carole. "Sexual Terrorism." In *Women: A Feminist Perspective*, 5th ed., edited by Jo Freeman, 1–21. London: Mayfield Publishing Company, 1995.

Shinde, Tarabai. "Stri Purush Tulana." trans. by Maya Pandit. In *Women Writing in India*, Volume I, edited by Susie Tharu and K. Lalitha, 223–35. New York: The Feminist Press, 1991.

Siegel, Lee. *Laughing Matters*. Chicago: University of Chicago Press, 1987.

Sinclair-Brull, Wendy. *Female Ascetics*. Surrey: Curzon Press, 1997.

Sinha, Raka. "Savvy Woman of the Month." *Savvy*. May 1991.

Sinha, S., and B. Saraswati. *Ascetics of Kashi*. Varanasi: N. K. Bose Memorial Foundation, 1978.

Siva-Purana. Trans. by A Board of Scholars and ed. by J. L. Shastri. *Ancient Indian Tradition and Mythology*. Volume II. Delhi: Motilal Banarsidass, 1970.

Slocum, Karla. "Negotiating Identity and Black Feminist Politics in Caribbean Research." In *Black Feminist Anthropology*, edited by Irma McClaurin, 126–49. Brunswick, N.J.: Rutgers University Press, 2001.

Srinivas, M. N. *Remembered Village*. Berkeley: University of California Press, 1976.

Stacey, Judith. "Can There Be a Feminist Ethnography?" *Women's Studies International Forum* 11 (1988): 21–27.

Sobo, Elisa J. and Sandra Bell, eds. *Celibacy, Culture, and Society*. Madison, Wis.: University of Wisconsin Press, 2001.

Sunder Rajan, Rajeswari. "Is the Hindu Goddess a Feminist?" *Economic and Political Weekly* 33, no. 44 (October 31, 1998): WS-34–WS-38.

————. "The Story of Draupadi's Disrobing: Meanings for Our Times." In *Signposts: Gender Issues in Post-Independence India*, 331–58. New Delhi, India: Kali for Women Press, 1999.

Tambiah, Stanley J. *The Buddhist Saints of the Forest and the Cult of Amulets*. New York: Cambridge University Press, 1984.

Tedlock, Barbara. "Works and Wives: On the Sexual Division of Textual Labor." In *Women Writing Culture*, edited by Ruth Behar and Deborah A. Gordon, 267–86. Berkeley: University of California Press, 1995.

Thapar, Romila. *Ancient Indian Social History*. 2nd ed. Hyderabad: Orient Longman, 1984.

Tharu, Susie, and K. Lalitha. *Women Writing in India*. Vol I. New York: The Feminist Press, 1991.

Traube, Elizabeth G. *Cosmology and Social Life*. Chicago: University of Chicago Press, 1986.

Trawick, Margaret. "Ambiguity in the Oral Exegesis of a Sacred Text." *Cultural Anthropology* 3, no. 3 (August 1988): 316–51.

————. *Notes on Love in a Tamil Family*. Berkeley: University of California Press, 1990.

Trilling, Lionel. *Sincerity and Authenticity*. London: Oxford University Press, 1972.

Tripathi, B. D. *Sadhus of India: The Sociological View*. Bombay: Bombay Popular Prakashan, 1978.

Tsing, Anna. "Review of *Self, Sex, and Gender in Cross-Cultural Fieldwork*." American Anthropologist 89 (1987): 763–64.

Van der Veer, Peter. "The Power of Detachment: Disciplines of Body and Mind in the Ramanandi Order." *American Ethnologist* 16, no. 3 (1989): 458–70.

————. "Taming of the Ascetic: Devotionalism in a Hindu Monastic Order." *Man* 2, no. 2 (1987): 680–95.

Venkatesananda, Swami, trans. *Yoga Vasistha* (abridged edition). South Fremantle, Australia: The Chiltern Yoga Trust, 1984.

Visweswaran, Kamala. *Fictions of Feminist Ethnography*. Minneapolis: University of Minnesota Press, 1994.

Wadley, Susan, and D. Jacobson. *Women in India*. New Delhi: Manohar Book Service, 1977.

White, Charles J. "Mother Guru: Jnanananda of Madras, India." In *Unspoken Worlds*, edited by Nancy Auer Falk and Rita M. Gross, 22–37. San Francisco: Harper and Row, 1980.

White, David G. "Playing with Food, Playing with Words: Hostile Takeovers of Orthodox Food Categories by Indian Tantrics." Unpublished manuscript.

———. *Kiss of the Yogini: "Tantric Sex" in its South Asian Contexts*. Chicago: University of Chicago Press, 2003.

Whitehead, Tony Larry and Mary Ellen Conaway. *Self, Sex, and Gender in Cross-Cultural Fieldwork*. Chicago: University of Illinois Press, 1986.

Williams, Brackette. "Skinfolk, Not Kinfolk: Comparative Reflections on the Identity of Participant-Observation in Two Field Situations." In *Feminist Dilemmas in Fieldwork*, edited by Diane L. Wolf, 72–94. Colorado: Westview Press, 1996.

Wilson, Liz. *Charming Cadavers*. Chicago: University of Chicago Press, 1996.

Yanagisako, Sylvia Junko and Jane Collier. "Toward a Unified Analysis of Gender and Kinship." In *Gender and Kinship*, edited by Jane Collier and Sylvia Yanagisako, 14-50. Stanford, Calif.: Stanford University Press, 1987.

Yogananda, Paramahansa. *Autobiography of a Yogi*. 6th ed. Bombay: Jaico Publishing House, 1985.

Young, Katherine. "Hinduism." In *Women in World Religions*, edited by Arvind Sharma, 59–103. Albany: State University of New York Press, 1987.

———. "*Om*, The Vedas, and the Status of Women With Special Reference to Śrīvaiṣṇavism." In *Jewels of Authority: Women and Textual Tradition in Hindu India*, edited by Laurie L. Patton, 84–121. New York: Oxford University Press, 2002.

Young, Serenity. "Gendered Politics in Ancient Indian Asceticism." *Union Seminary Quarterly Review* 48, nos. 3–4 (1994): 73–92.

Index